Covent Garden & Soho
The Illustrated A-Z
historical guide

First published 2009
by Historical Publications Ltd
32 Ellington Street, London N7 8PL
(Tel: 020 7607 1628; www.historicalpublications.co.uk)

ISBN 978-1-905286-31-7
British Library Cataloguing-in-Publication Data
A catalogue record for this book is available from the British Library

Typeset by Historical Publications Ltd
Reproduction by Tintern Graphics
Printed in Zaragoza, Spain by Edelvives

Acknowledgements

We would like to thank Gaby Williams of Waterstone's, Covent Garden and Andrew Steed and Tim Cleary of Stanford's, Long Acre for their help and encouragement in publishing this book.

The Illustrations

We are grateful to the following for permission to reproduce illustrations:

Robert Bard: *32*
British Library, Crace Collection: *67*
Moss Brothers: *170 (L, bottom)*
National Portrait Gallery: *55*
Rule's Restaurant: *156 (L)*
St Patrick's church presbytery, Soho Square: *36 (top)*
W. Sitch & Co: *169 (bottom)*
Richard Tames: *title page, 7, 10 (R), 13, 18 (top R), 25 (R), 29 (bottom), 37 (R), 38 (both), 40, 41, 45, 47 (L), 49 (top R), 54, 57, 60, 70 (both), 72 (R), 76, 79, 91 (both), 96 (L), 102 (both), 103, 106, 108 (R), 128, 130, 132 (L), 135, 137 (top), 140, 144 (both), 154, 158, 179 (R), 182, 185 (L)*
City of Westminster Archives Centre: *46, 116 (R), 169 (top R)*
All other text illustrations were supplied by the Publisher.

The front cover: all illustrations are by permission of Ivor Kamlish.
The back cover is an 1874 oil painting by James Tissot (1836-1902) entitled London Visitors. *It is reproduced by permission of Toledo Museum of Art, Ohio. It was purchased with funds from the Libbey Endowment, Gift of Edward Drummond Libbey, 1951.409. The photograph was by Photography Incorporated (Ray Sess and Carl Schultz), Toledo.*

The cover design is by Ivor Kamlish

Covent Garden & Soho
The Illustrated A-Z historical guide

Richard and Sheila Tames

With two walks on pp 187-188

HISTORICAL PUBLICATIONS

Bohemian Rhapsody in bygone Soho – the Café Royal. A 1912 painting by Sir William Orpen (1878-1931), now in the Musée d'Orsay, Paris. The artist Augustus John is seated to the right.

Introduction

Covent Garden

In his Introduction to *London: A Social History,* the late Professor Roy Porter chose Covent Garden to epitomise the history of London as a whole, observing how the collision of "nature, communities and artefacts ... shapes ... a future more unintended than planned." Charles Dickens, who knew the area from childhood and, as a busy magazine editor, had his office there, catalogued its many facets in *Little Dorritt*, conjuring up "Courtly ideas of Covent Garden ... where gentlemen wearing gold-laced coats and swords had ... fought duels; costly ideas ... as a place where there were flowers in winter at guineas apiece; picturesque ideas ... as a place where there was a mighty theatre, showing wonderful and beautiful sights; desolate ideas ... where the miserable children in rags ... slunk and hid, fed on offal, huddled together for warmth; teeming ideas ... as a place of past and present mystery, romance, abundance, want, beauty, ugliness, fair country gardens and foul street-gutters, all confused together ....".

No. 43 King Street can stand as an epitome within the epitome. The site was originally occupied by the home of the Restoration courtier and dramatist Sir Thomas Killigrew. His residence was rebuilt in 1717 by Thomas Archer, the architect of St John's, Smith Square, for his relative Admiral Edward Russell, who had played a significant part in bringing William III to the throne and had been created Earl of Orford as a reward. After Orford's death the house was acquired by Archer for himself. The building then became one of Covent Garden's many coffee-houses and, in 1774, one of London's earliest family hotels, known from its first proprietor as Hudson's. Coleridge stayed there in 1801 and again in 1810. In the 1840s W C Evans converted a large dining-room in the basement into a song-and-supper saloon, known, in deference to the immediately previous proprietor, as Evans', Late Joy's. While performers sang on stage customers at Evans's regaled themselves with hearty fare and copious quantities of drink into the early hours of the morning. Thus was born one of Victorian London's first music halls. Sam Collins, founder of the celebrated Collins' Music Hall in Islington, made his stage debut at Evans's. Another entertainer, Paddy Green, took over management in 1844. Between 1853 and 1857 the Royal Institute of British Architects rented rooms in the building. In 1855 a music hall was constructed to the rear of the hotel. In 1857 the Savage Club was established at No. 43 by the gourmand and journalist George Sala, the actor George Grossmith and the librettist W S Gilbert, who had been born a few hundred yards away in Southampton Street. Evans's was eventually overtaken by the proliferation of more lavish music halls and closed in 1880. From 1892 to 1929 the building housed the National Sporting Club, whose dinner-jacketed members gathered to dine, drink and watch young lads knock each other about in the boxing-ring. Market trader

43 King Street in the 1970s, derelict after years as a fruit and veg warehouse. It was reincarnated as a smart office address in the 1980s.

Restored to glory – Thomas Archer House, 43 King Street today, now a fashion store.

George Monro then took over the vacated premises to use as a warehouse for produce and in 1932 drove a passageway right through the middle of the ground floor to enable lorries to reach the old music hall, now a warehouse, at the rear. In all this the grand staircase from the hallway was removed. In 1934 the Player's Theatre took over part of the premises upstairs and in 1937 launched a revival of Victorian music hall. Since the war the building has served more prosaically as the offices of a public relations company and an advertising agency and is, at the time of writing, an up-market retail fashion outlet, very much a representative of Covent Garden's current incarnation as a showcase of cutting-edge style.

The historical development of the Covent Garden area has been neatly summarised as an evolution from pasture to piazza to pizza. Originally grazing ground, it became the vegetable garden of the monks of Westminster Abbey (hence convent into covent). Seized by the Crown at the dissolution of the monasteries in the 16th century, it was bestowed on John Russell, Earl of Bedford. One of his successors built a London residence, Bedford House, on the north side of the Strand. In the 1630s the fourth Earl of Bedford commissioned royal architect Inigo Jones to lay out London's first square at the rear of Bedford House and to build houses "fit for the habitacions of Gentlemen and men of ability'. For perhaps half a century the Piazza was a prestigious residential enclave, then shaded into becoming an artists' quarter and then underwent a raffish transformation into an entertainment district where varied appetites could be satisfied. Local magistrate Sir John Fielding observed of the Piazza that "one would imagine that all the prostitutes in the kingdom had picked upon the rendezvous". By the nineteenth century, dominated by its reconstructed market and Opera House, Covent Garden was synonymous with vegetables and Verdi. The departure of the market in 1974 brought the threat of 'comprehensive redevelopment' which was vigorously and successfully resisted.

Nowhere has Covent Garden's renaissance been more marked than in the formerly notorious slum district of Seven Dials. Now promoted as 'Covent Garden's Hidden Village', it promises "the antithesis to impersonal high street shopping". As "a seven day shopping destination" it boasts twenty-six outlets devoted to women's fashion, twenty-five to men's and twenty-seven serving both, plus twenty-five 'health and beauty' specialists, and twenty-five specialist specialists, including two devoted to beads and another two to astrology.

Preserved and pedestrianized, Covent Garden has, in Roy Porter's words, become "a centre for strolling and diversion" and "has unexpectedly recaptured some of the spirit of the eighteenth century".

Soho

"Soho – magic syllables! For when the respectable Londoner wants to feel devilish he goes to Soho, where every street is a song. He walks through Old Compton St. and instinctively he swaggers; he is abroad; he is a dog." Thomas Burke

That sense of Soho's separateness was reiterated more than half a century later by Christopher Petit in *Robinson* (1994), in which he identified the archway from Manette Street to Greek Street as "a border-post, the crossing-point where obligations could be left behind". Equally one could call it a gateway to the world – where else in so small a compass can one meet the ghosts of Hogarth and Reynolds, Marx and Mozart, Boswell, Burke and Blake, Casanova, Canaletto and Constable, Newton and Darwin, Wagner, Whistler and Wilde?

Soho probably takes its name from a traditional hunting call, indicating sight of the prey. Certainly the Lord Mayor of London and his retinue are known to have hunted and feasted there in 1562, after inspecting the conduits which brought water to the City. Combining business with pleasure has, therefore, been the Soho style for centuries. A plan drawn in 1585 shows the area still virtually undeveloped, apart from a dozen or so scattered houses of a very humble character. By 1650 there was a cluster of some sixty buildings – 'Cottages ... Shedds or meane habitacons' – along what is now Wardour Street. But, just over twenty years later, a Secretary of State was living only a few hundred yards away. What had happened? In brief, the Great Fire of 1666. Rendering 100,000 Londoners homeless, the fire led many of the dispossessed to move west and build anew. Golden Square was begun in 1674, Rupert Street in 1676, (Old) Compton Street a year later, Berwick Street in 1688 and Poland Street in 1689. St Anne's, Soho was consecrated in 1686.

Soho's equivalent of 43 King Street stands at 12-13 Greek Street. Originally a single building, the largest house in the street, it was first known as Portland House. In 1684 the occupant was Elizabeth Price, probably the actress and courtesan of that name. A Huguenot refugee, Abraham Meure, converted the premises into an academy for young gentlemen. The building then reverted to residential use as the home, first of the Sicilian ambassador, then of Viscount Chetwynd, former British ambassador to Savoy and, after him, of Peter Legh, a Cheshire gentleman. In 1766 upholsterer James Cullen, a partner of the colourful Mrs Cornelys of Carlisle House in Soho Square, spent £1,500 extending the back of the property to hold entertainments. In

Academy, embassy, workshop, showroom, hotel – and home: Portland House, 12-13 Greek Street.

1774 the royal potter Josiah Wedgwood took over the premises for use as his London showroom. After his departure in 1797 the building was sub-divided into apartments whose short-term occupants included a dramatist, a sculptor and three painters. In 1846 a passageway was driven through the centre of the ground floor to give access to the yard at the rear. By 1886 the building had become Wedde's, a German hotel.

Soho, like Covent Garden, an aristocratic *quartier* in origin and then an artistic one, was still described in favourable, if slightly patronising terms, by Dickens in *A Tale of Two Cities* – "The quiet lodgings of Dr Manette were in a quiet street-corner not far from Soho Square ... A quainter corner than the corner where the doctor lived was not to be found in London". But the district had plunged much further down-market by the mid-Victorian period. Karl Marx, having escaped his dismal Dean Street lodgings, recalled that "the region round Soho Square still sends a shiver down my spine if I happen to be anywhere near there". In R L Stevenson's *Dr Jekyll and Mr Hyde* (1886) Hyde's home was in "the dismal quarter of Soho ... with its muddy ways and slatternly passengers". It was not a salubrious abode "... a dingy street, a gin palace, a low French eating-house, a shop for the retail of penny numbers and two-penny salads, many ragged children huddled in the doorways and many women of different nationalities passing out, key in hand, to have a morning glass."

In Patrick Hamilton's *Twenty Thousand Streets Under the Sky* (1935) pub waiter Bob is fascinated by Wardour Street "because it was the principal resort of the women of the town ... they lurked solitary in shop doorways, or aimlessly crossed the road, or came down the street in couples, absorbed by that frantic garrulity and backbiting which rend their kind". In Gerald Kersh's *Night and the City* (1946) the pimp Harry Fabian lives off the Rupert Street prostitute Zoe and supplements his income by blackmailing her clients. Harry "... saw London as a kind of Inferno ... a series of concentric areas with Piccadilly Circus as the ultimate centre".

Synonymous with sin and strip-clubs by the Sixties, Soho has reinvented itself as a redoubt of gastronomy, with some two hundred and fifty eating-places to choose from. To be fair, though, this was more a matter of reassertion than reinvention. In 1937 William Kent, author of *An Encyclopaedia of London*, had counselled his readers that "those with an appetite for Chinese dishes can get them in ... Soho. In the latter district can be found French, Italian and Greek restaurants and the citizen of the world who wants gastronomically to proclaim the fact cannot do better than dine there regularly".

In the 1960s Carnaby Street became the epicentre of the fashion revolution which was turning young Englishmen into – or back into? – dandies, peacocks and fops. Now this iconic thoroughfare has rebranded itself and corralled surrounding streets into adopting a new shared identity as 'Carnaby', a 'style village' with 165 shops, bars, clubs and restaurants where one can peruse and purchase whatever is 'cult',' preppy', 'edgy', 'retro','hand-crafted' or 'ethnic-inspired', from 'heritage trainers' to 'kitsch gadgets'. Having worked through these, the visitor may then select from a cosmopolitan range of cuisines – Indian, Chinese, Spanish, Japanese, Korean, American, 'Royal Thai' and 'Southern Hemisphere' or else choose one of six establishments styling themselves 'traditional English' pubs or the one which defines itself as 'traditional London', leaving yet one more to proclaim itself defiantly as 'traditional Scottish'.

Like Covent Garden, Soho was threatened with devastation, only more so. Planners proposed wholesale demolition of the entire district to make way for a dystopian wasteland of fast-flowing traffic lanes, aerial walkways and tower-blocks. This spectre galvanised local residents to found the Soho Society in 1972. The Society not only stymied the scheme but rolled back the sex trade to tolerable proportions, freeing commercial premises to cater for other appetites. Surviving purveyors of lager, leather and lingerie ensure that some aura of raffishness remains.

Text names in bold indicate separate entries

Academy of St Martin in the Fields

The chamber orchestra known as the Academy of St Martin-in-the-Fields was founded at the church of **St Martin-in-the-Fields** in 1959 by (Sir) Neville Marriner (b. 1924).

It has since become the most recorded chamber orchestra in the world, having completed more than five hundred sessions as well as supplying the soundtrack for numerous films including *Amadeus* (1984), based on the life of **Mozart**, *The English Patient* (1996) and *Titanic* (1997). The orchestra has since acquired an independent existence. The church retains a strong musical tradition, including a programme of free concerts and some candlelit evening occasions. (www.asmf.org)

Friedrich Accum

German-born pharmacist Friedrich Accum (1769-1838) studied at **William Hunter's** anatomy school before settling at 11 **Old Compton Street** as a self-employed science teacher and author of popular texts like the best selling *Chemical Amusements*. As a technical adviser Accum was instrumental in the introduction of gas-lighting in London's streets. His pioneering exposé of food adulteration, however, made him powerful enemies and in 1821 he fled back to Germany rather than face (almost certainly false) charges of stealing and selling expensive colour plates from books in the library of the Royal Institution.

Adelaide Street

The street was named for Adelaide (1792-1849), William IV's queen. A complaisant German princess, she married William in 1818 after it became apparent that he might succeed the childless George IV. Both the daughters born to Adelaide died in infancy and this led, eventually, to Victoria, daughter of William's brother, the Duke of Kent, becoming queen.

Maverick architectural critic Ian Nairn regarded the St Martin's National Schools, designed by George Ledwell Taylor, architect of **Morley's Hotel**, in 1827-30, as "one of London's loveliest buildings ... as important to London as the Tower". The street's other interesting feature is its monument to **Oscar Wilde**.

Oscar Wilde hails passers-by in Adelaide Street.

Adelphi Theatre, Strand

Built on the Strand in 1806, by local tradesman John Scott to launch his daughter's projected stage career, this theatre opened with *Miss Scott's Entertainment*, a potpourri of songs, recitations, magic lantern shows and fireworks. Initially known as the Sans Pareil, the Adelphi was re-named in 1818 and achieved notoriety in 1821 with *Tom and Jerry; or, Life in London*, which ran for over a hundred performances and inspired a craze embracing tacky souvenirs, novelty items and memorabilia. The Adelphi then built on this breakthrough by presenting stage adaptations of the novels of Sir Walter Scott. In 1834, by then self-styled as the 'Theatre Royal, New Adelphi', it installed England's first sinking stage. In 1838 Edward Stirling (1809-94) adapted **Dickens'** *Nicholas Nickleby* for the Adelphi, where it ran into the following season. Dickens himself gave a cautious approval. Rebuilt in 1858, the theatre enjoyed another success with Dion Boucicault's *The Colleen Bawn* (1860), which, half a century later, would become one of the earliest films ever made in Ireland. In 1897 **William Terriss**, leading man in a series of highly successful 'Adelphi melodramas', was sensationally murdered at the Adelphi's stage door. From 1908 George Edwardes, also manager of **Daly's**, made the Adelphi a home of musical comedy. A fourth, yet again rebuilt, Adelphi was opened in 1930. **Ivor Novello's** *The Dancing Years* opened in March 1942 and ran for 969 performances. The revue *London Laughs*

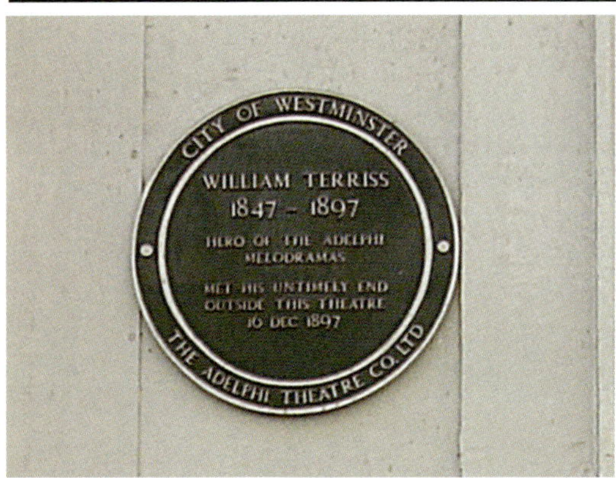

A plaque near the Stage Door of the Adelphi Theatre in Maiden Lane diplomatically records the murder of actor William Terriss.

(1952) became the first Adelphi production to pass a thousand performances, a record surpassed by *Charlie Girl*, which opened to bad notices but ran for 2,200 shows between 1965 and 1971. (www.adelphitheatre.co.uk)

Admiral Duncan pub, 54 Old Compton Street

Admiral Duncan (1731-1804), a Scot, won a bloody naval victory over the Dutch at the battle of Camperdown in 1797, reasserting the loyalty and commitment of the Royal Navy after an outbreak of mutinies. Duncan was rewarded with a Viscountcy and a pension of £3,000 a year for himself and his next two heirs.

Named for this hero, the early 18th-century building became Soho's leading gay pub but was the target of a bomb attack in 1999 which left three dead and over a hundred injured. The bomber, David Copeland, a neo-Nazi loner, had previously bombed Brixton market and Brick Lane. The bombing of the Admiral Duncan was his last outrage before being caught.

Aldwych

First mentioned in 1211, Aldwych means 'old trading settlement', presumably a reference to *Lundenwic*, the early Saxon community which lived west of the City and north of the Strand after the withdrawal of the City's Roman garrison ca. 410. Later medieval documents use it to denote the length of **Drury Lane** as the 'Via de Aldwych'. The present Aldwych is a result of a comprehensive redevelopment of 1900-35, associated with the creation of Kingsway (1907) as a major north-south thoroughfare.

The Admiral Duncan pub in Old Compton Street, 2009, at the heart of the capital's gay village.

Aldwych Theatre, Aldwych

The Aldwych, designed by the prolific theatre architect, W G R Sprague, was built (1905) for the actor-manager (Sir) Seymour Hicks (1871-1941), husband of the actress Ellaline Terriss, daughter of the murdered **William Terriss**. The first English production of Tchekov's *The Cherry Orchard* was staged here in 1911. Between 1925 and 1933 the theatre enjoyed consistent success with a series of 'Aldwych farces' from the facile pen of Ben Travers (1886-1980). In 1949 Vivien Leigh excelled as Blanche du Bois in Tennessee Williams' *A Streetcar Named Desire.* In 1960 the Aldwych became the London base of the Royal Shakespeare Company, whose outstanding productions during a tenure of twenty years included Bertolt Brecht's *Caucasian Chalk Circle* (1962), Peter Weiss's *Marat/Sade* (1964), Harold Pinter's *The Homecoming* (1965), Tom Stoppard's *Travesties* (1974) and an eight-hour adaptation of **Dickens**' *Nicholas Nickleby.* (www.aldwych-theatre.com)

Minarets, Minton tiles and Moorish arches – the Royal Panopticon, later the Alhambra, in 1853. It was on the east side of Leicester Square on the site of today's Odeon.

The Alhambra, Leicester Square

During the course of its existence (1854-1936) the Alhambra was built and rebuilt seven times and known under eight different names. What became one of London's most celebrated music halls originated as "an Institution for Scientific Exhibitions and for Promoting Discoveries in Arts and Manufactures". Chartered in 1850 as the Royal Panopticon of Science and Art, the brainchild of an Irish scientific instrument maker, Edward Marmaduke Clarke (?1806-59). He envisaged a permanent, albeit much reduced, version of the Great Exhibition which was to open shortly in Hyde Park. The Panopticon, built for a stupendous £80,000, dominated the east side of **Leicester Square,** incorporating a vast hall, the largest organ in England, lecture-rooms, offices and residential quarters. The interior fittings included a hydraulic lift, a fountain supplied from an artesian well beneath the premises, copies of famous sculptures, and walls embellished with alabaster, slate, glass and mosaic. Designed in a supposedly 'Saracenic' style, it sported twin towers like minarets, its façade covered with Minton tiles. Within a month of its opening in 1854 a thousand visitors a day were passing through the cast-iron portcullis which served as the main entrance, paying a shilling a time to witness an array of scientific wonders demonstrating the properties of steel, acids, gas, electricity etc. Regrettably the management proved to be as incompetent as the building was flamboyant. A cholera epidemic also kept many people away from the capital. By 1856 Clarke was bankrupt and the venture closed down.

In 1857 the Panopticon was acquired by showman Edward Tyrrel Smith (1804-77) for just £9,000. He sold off the contents, (the organ went to St. Paul's Cathedral), installed a circus ring and reopened as the Alhambra Palace, with Howes and Cushing's American circus. In 1861 French gymnast

Jules Leotard (inventor of the garment named after him) made his London debut, inspiring tribute in song as *The Daring Young Man on the Flying Trapeze*.

Caterer Frederick Strange took over in 1864, spent £25,000 on refurbishment and introduced ballet. In 1870 London's first presentation of the French 'Can-Can' cost Strange his dancing licence and he switched to concerts and comic opera.

The Alhambra was largely destroyed by fire in 1882, but the reconstruction preserved the original frontage, while enlarging the total capacity of the house to a massive 4,000, although only 1,800 of those could be seated. Ballet and music hall henceforth became the staple fare. The greatest successes of the revived establishment were *The Bing Boys are Here* (1916), in which artful droll George Robey added *If You Were the only Girl in the World* to the repertoire of 'standard' ballads, and the Diaghilev Ballet season of 1919. In 1923 Lancashire ingénue Gracie Fields attained early stardom in *Mr. Tower of London*. Like many of its rivals the Alhambra then succumbed to the challenge of the cinema and was demolished in 1936 to make way for the present **Odeon cinema**. A plaque on **Charing Cross Road** marks the Alhambra's former location. (www.arthurlloyd.co.uk/Alhambra.htm)

Apollo Theatre, Shaftesbury Avenue

Built (1901) for musicals and enjoying considerable success with forgettable comedies, the Apollo also staged Sean O'Casey's *The Silver Tassie* (1929) and Terence Rattigan's *Flare Path* (1942). Based on the tensions surrounding a bomber crew, *Flare Path* differed from much escapist wartime fare in actually being about the war. Long runs were achieved with the sentimental portrayal of service life, *Seagulls over Sorrento* (1950), the formulaic farce *Boeing-Boeing* (1962), Alan Bennett's satirical essay in pseudo-nostalgia *Forty Years On* (1968), Alan Ayckbourn's trilogy of petit-bourgeois marital frictions *The Norman Conquests* (1975) and Keith Waterhouse's *Jeffrey Bernard is Unwell* (1989). (www.apollo-theatre.co.uk)

Archer Street

Originally known as Arch Street, this was first mentioned in 1675. As home to the headquarters of the Musicians' Union Archer Street was long noted for the crowd of instrumentalists which gathered daily in search of casual employment in the theatres, restaurants and recording-studios of the West End. Nos. 13-14 were built (1912) as clubrooms for the Orchestral Association, with a carved reclining draped nude figure of Euterpe, the muse of lyric poetry.

Architecture

The architecture of this area is more remarkable for quality than quantity. The **French Protestant Church** on the north side of **Soho Square** is notable for its tiled façade, **Notre Dame de France** for its 1950s interior and **St Anne's** for its eccentric steeple. The **House of St Barnabas** has superb plasterwork. **Meard Street** is a gem of a speculative street developed 1722-32. Outstanding commercial buildings include **Stanford's** bookshop in Arts and Crafts style in Long Acre, **Liberty's**, one of a number of local **mock-Tudor** confections, **Willy Clarkson's** premises, the **Palace Theatre**, the **Odeon**, Leicester Square, Palladium House in **Argyll Street** and Quinlan Terry's office-block in **Dufour's Place**. The Red Lion in **Great Windmill Street** and **Dog and Duck** in Frith Street have flamboyant Victorian interiors.

Apart from **St Paul's** church and **St Martin-in-the-Fields**, Covent Garden's most significant architecture is similarly commercial – the **Royal**

The building at 41-43 Wardour Street which housed Willie Clarkson's wig-making business.

Zimbabwe House seen from the Strand, an innovative building by Charles Holden.

Opera House, the **Theatre Royal** and the Market Buildings of the **Piazza**. No. 43 **King Street** (Thomas Archer House) has had a complex history (see pp 5-6). Architectural peculiarities of greatly varying scale include the **Freemasons' Hall**, the **Seven Dials' Monument** and **Zimbabwe House**. (Simon Bradley and Nikolaus Pevsner *The Buildings of England London 6 Westminster* Yale University Press 2005)

Argyll Rooms

Standing at the junction of today's **Regent Street** and **Great Marlborough Street**, the Argyll Rooms were originally the creation of Henry Francis Greville (1760-1816), a charming, handsome former army officer with a passion for the stage. Feather-brained but well-connected, Greville borrowed heavily to buy out the lease of a house in Little Argyll Street, then borrowed even more to refurbish it as a place of fashionable assembly. Greville's establishment opened in 1807 but the entertainments he provided were amateurish and he was viciously lampooned by Lord Byron. Hounded by creditors, deserted by friends and broken in health, Greville, "an elegant ruin", fled England to die in Mauritius. In 1813 the Argyll Rooms became a concert venue for the newly-established Philharmonic Society. In the same year the celebrated dandy, George 'Beau' Brummell (1778-1840) put on a ball there to celebrate recent successes at the gaming table. It was on this occasion that Brummell, having fallen out with his former intimate, the future **George IV**, studiously ignored him, turning instead to address his companion with the immortal line, "I say, Alvanley, who's your fat friend?".

During the construction of Regent Street in 1819 severe weaknesses were revealed in the building and the royal protégé **John Nash** was obliged to undertake a complete rebuilding. Reopened in 1820, the Argyll Rooms witnessed memorable concert performances by child prodigy Franz Liszt (aged 12), Weber and Mendelssohn.

The Argyll Rooms burned down in 1830 and was replaced by shops, which in 1919 were themselves replaced by Dickins and Jones department store.

Argyll Street

Argyll Street was not built up until 1735-45, on land belonging to the Dukes of Argyll, whose own residence, Argyll House, was erected (1737-42) where the **London Palladium** now stands and was demolished in 1864. No. 8 dates from ca. 1740. Major-General William Roy (1726-90) an expert on Roman antiquities and founder of the Ordnance Survey lived at No. 10 from 1779 until his death. The American diplomat Washington Irving, author of *Rip Van Winkle*, lived at No. 8. In 1813-14 the French bluestocking Germaine Necker, better known as Madame de Stael (1766-1817) lived on the site later covered by Dickins and Jones. Once spoken of as a possible bride for the younger William Pitt, she established her intellectual reputation with her critiques of Rousseau and her exposition of German culture which popularised the notion of 'Romanticism'. Other residents included, from 1850 to 1861, Anthony Salvin (1799-1881), a pupil of **Nash**, who specialised in the restoration of castles and, from 1864 to 1877 the architect Richard Norman Shaw (1831-1912). The Argyll Arms pub (1868) is famed for its exuberant interior (ca.1895) of mahogany and mirrors; George Orwell drank here.

Thomas Arne

Composer Thomas Arne (1710-78) was born and brought up at 31 **King Street** where the site of his upholsterer father's shop is marked by a plaque. Best remembed for *Rule, Britannia* (1740), Arne worked as a musical arranger for the Theatre Royal Drury Lane, where he produced settings of such Shakespeare songs as *Under the Greenwood Tree* and *Blow, Blow thou Winter Wind*. Arne composed several operas, of which the most famous was *Artaxerxes* (1762), which **Jane Austen** saw on her visit to London in 1814. (www.chesternovello.com)

Thomas Arne, musician and composer of 'Rule Britannia'. Note the sword hilt, denoting his gentlemanly status.

Dr George Armstrong

Neither the date of birth nor of death are known for pioneering paediatrician George Armstrong, whose *Essay on the Diseases most fatal to Infants* (1767) was being republished more than forty years after its first appearance. After the death of Alderman **Beckford,** his house at 22 **Soho Square** was taken by Armstrong in 1769 for a dispensary for the sick children of London's poor. Armstrong was strongly opposed to parting ailing children from their parents and putting them into hospitals where there was a high risk of secondary infection. Supported by charitable contributions, Armstrong gave treatment and medicines free three times a week. Financial pressures forced him to move to **Seven Dials** until he was felled by a stroke and forced to close in 1781, having treated some 35,000 children.

Arts Theatre

Opened in Great Newport Street in 1927, the Arts Theatre Club was intended for the production of unlicensed and experimental plays for audiences of subscribing members, its seating limited to just over three hundred. Several of its productions transferred to commercial theatres, most notably Gordon Daviot's gorgeously-costumed *Richard of Bordeaux* (1932), directed by **John Gielgud**. In 1942 the Arts was taken over by Alec Clunes (1912-70) who produced over a hundred plays in a decade, raising the establishment to the status of a 'pocket national theatre'. His successor (Sir) Peter Hall (1930-) staged the English premiere of Samuel Beckett's *Waiting for Godot* (1955), which left audiences bemused but ran for three hundred performances. In 1960 the Arts also presented the first performance of *The Caretaker* by Harold Pinter (1930-2008). The theatre changed to a commercial operation in Great Newport Street in 2000. The Arts Theatre Club is now at 50 **Frith Street**.

(www.theartstheatreclub.com)

Astoria, 157 Charing Cross Road

Built (1927) as the Astoria Cinema on the site of the former premises of **Crosse & Blackwell**, the building was almost inevitably nicknamed 'The Jam Factory'. Adapted as a theatre, it reopened in 1977 with a musical *Elvis*. Since then its chequered history has included periods of closure, internal rebuilding (1986) and use as a venue for popular music. Now closed, it will be demolished to allow a reconstruction of Tottenham Court Road station .

The Arts Theatre in Great Newport Street.

Jane Austen

From 1806 until 1816 No.10 **Henrietta Street** was occupied by the bank of Austen, Maunde and Tilson , of which Henry Austen, Jane's elder brother, was a partner. Royalties from Jane's books were paid into her account there. Jane stayed with him twice at this address which she brightly described as "all dirt and confusion but in a promising way". The first time was a hectic three days in 1813, packed with parties, shopping and nightly visits to the theatre – *Don Juan* at the **Lyceum** and *The Merchant of Venice* at the **Theatre Royal Drury Lane**. Writing to her sister Cassandra, she declared "We have not had a quarter of an hour to spare ...I am going to write nothing but short sentences ... There shall be two full stops in every line." Returning to a snow-bound city the following year, she was delighted to see the celebrated **Edmund Kean** at **Drury Lane** – "I cannot imagine better acting" – but disappointed with the *farceur* Robert Elliston, "There was nothing of the *best Elliston* about him. I might not have known him, but for his voice." Foul weather limited her excursions and she passed her time indoors, devouring novels and dealing with the proofs of *Mansfield Park.* The only known contemporary likeness of Jane Austen, a pencil and watercolour sketch by her sister Cassandra, can be seen in the **National Portrait Gallery**.

(Claire Tomalin, *Jane Austen – A Life* Penguin 2003)

J C Bach

The eleventh of the thirteen children of Johann Sebastian Bach, Johann Christian (1735-82) arrived in London in 1762, having left his native Leipzig to study, perform and compose in Berlin, Bologna and Milan. Lodging with his fellow-countryman Carl Fridrich Abel in **Meard Street** and **Carlisle Street,** Bach collaborated with him to inaugurate a highly successful series of subscription concerts at **Carlisle House** for **Mrs Cornelys** in 1765-7. In 1768 Bach performed the first ever piano solo in England and did much to popularize the instrument. The Bach-Abel concerts transferred to Almack's assembly rooms and after 1775 to a purpose-built venue, the Hanover Square Rooms, the expense of which caused Bach to die burdened with huge debts.

Francis Bacon

"I always think of friendship as where two people can really tear each other to bits." Francis Bacon Francis Bacon (1909-92) remained an *enfant terrible* all his life. The son of a brutal Irish father – ex-military and failed race-horse trainer - he was thrown out at sixteen in reaction to his precocious homosexuality. After drifting through Berlin and Paris, Bacon settled in London in 1928. Working as an interior decorator, he taught himself to paint, taking his inspiration from sources as varied as the films of Sergei Eisenstein, the pioneering motion photography of Edweard Muybridge and the writings of Aeschylus and T S Eliot, but subsequently destroying much of his early work. Bacon's *Three Studies for Figures at the Base of a Crucifixion* (1944) brought him an instant notoriety, which was confirmed by his adaptation of Velazquez' celebrated depiction of Pope Innocent X to create a series of portraits of 'Screaming Popes', terrifying icons of nightmare and terror. Bacon turned up at the **Colony Club** the day after it opened and was rewarded by **Muriel Belcher** with £10 a week and free drinks for recruiting new customers. Bacon's artistic preoccupations with isolation, degradation, contortion and distortion were reflected in a personal life of eccentric squalor, which was knowingly captured in a biography by his friend **Daniel Farson**, aptly titled *The Gilded Gutter Life of Francis Bacon.* In May 2008 the triptych painted by Bacon between 1974 and 1977 in memory of the suicide of his lover George Dyer was sold for £43 million, a world auction record for a British artist. Michael Peppiatt, who knew Bacon over a period of thirty years, published an authoritative biography, *Anatomy of an Enigma* (1997) and, a decade later, *Francis Bacon in the 1950s* (2006) and *Francis Bacon : Studies for a Portrait* (2008). Peppiatt's central contention was that Bacon spent his life searching for a cruel father like the one who had rejected him, hence his obsession with depicting demented authority figures.

(www.francis-bacon.cx)

Robert Baddeley

First a cook, then a valet, Robert Baddeley (1733-94) became a member of the **Theatre Royal Drury Lane** company and was the first to play Moses in **Sheridan**'s *School for Scandal.* Having undertaken the Grand Tour for three years he had picked up a knowledge of foreign languages, enabling him to specialise in comic broken English and servant's roles. He was briefly married to the beautiful, extravagant, promiscuous actress Sophia Snow

(1745-86), who was painted by **Zoffany**. Baddeley was obliged to fight a duel with **Garrick**'s brother in defence of her honour, though the outcome was fortunately bloodless. He is chiefly remembered for his will in which he bequeathed property to found a home for needy actors and a sum to pay for wine and cake to be served in the Green Room at Drury Lane Theatre on Twelfth Night, a custom that is still observed. He was buried at **St Paul's, Covent Garden**. His ghost is said to haunt the Opera Tavern on **Catherine Street.**

Bagnios

Ostensibly a bath-house on the lines of a Turkish 'hammam', the bagnio (from the Italian for bathing house) also came to offer ancillary sexual services, similar in range to those available in its more recent incarnation, the massage-parlour. In 1679 a Duke's Bagnio and Bath was established at Salisbury Stables, **Long Acre** with a coffee house adjacent. Hummums opened in 1683 on the **Piazza** in Covent Garden at the south-west corner of **Russell Street.** The price for a bath was 5/6d or 8/- for two persons in a room. An overnight stay cost 10/-. In 1701 it was announced that the establishment had "for several years been neglected and abused by those persons that had the care and management of them, whereby several persons of quality have been disgusted and have left off coming thither to sweat and bathe as formerly". Henceforth, it was promised, a new management, having "refitted the same and rectified all those neglects and abuses", would guarantee a return to respectability. The establishment later became an ordinary hotel, Hewitt's, but another bathing establishment, Lovejoy's, existed next door. There were plenty of others. **Hogarth** depicted buxom Mother Douglas (died 1761), proprietor of another Piazza bagnio, in *The March to Finchley*, ostentatiously praying for the safe return of the soldiers – her customers. She also appears in *The Idle Prentice*, toasting the prentice in gin as he prepares to be hanged at Tyburn.

Bagnios were also a feature of the Leicester Square area where one became the setting for the notorious **Mary Tofts'** scam.

Turkish temptation – the Old Hummums (bagnio) at Hewitt's Hotel for Gentlemen in the Piazza, Covent Garden.

John Logie Baird

Baird (1888-1946) gave the first demonstration of true television in an upper room at 22 **Frith Street** on 26 January 1926 before an audience of fifty scientists. A blue plaque marks the building. Baird trained as an electrical engineer before seeking his fortune as variously the inventor and promoter of a patent sock, jam, honey and soap, each venture dashed by the ill-health which dogged his life. Turning to the machine which would broadcast images over distance, he made a primitive device from such materials as cardboard, a biscuit tin, darning-needles, string and sealing-wax. By 1928 Baird had managed to develop television systems which could broadcast across the Atlantic, to a ship in mid-ocean, in colour and in stereovision. In 1929 he broadcast the first television programme from No. 133 **Long Acre.** In 1930 he demonstrated a 'big screen' technology at the **London Coliseum** and in Paris, Berlin and Stockholm and in 1931 broadcast live coverage of the Derby. The BBC began experimental broadcasting with a Baird system in 1935 but dropped it in 1937. Undeterred, Baird continued experimenting until his early death. Baird's Frith Street apparatus can be seen in the Science Museum at South Kensington. There is a bronze bust of Baird in the **National Portrait Gallery**.

(Antony Kamm and Malcolm Baird *John Logie Baird: A Life – A Personal Biography* NMSE Publishing 2002)

Sir Joseph Banks, botanist and intellectual giant.

Sir Joseph Banks

Sir Joseph Banks (1743-1820) of 32 **Soho Square** had accompanied Captain Cook's exploratory voyage of 1768-71, returning with 3,600 plants, a third previously unclassified. Banks became co-founder of Kew's Botanical Gardens and President of the Royal Society (1778-1819). His controlling disposition and promotion of himself may have frustrated younger colleagues but he received honours rare for a scholar – a baronetcy, the Order of the Bath and being sworn of the Privy Council. No. 32 housed London's best scientific library and became the home of the Linnaean Society (1821-57), the Dental Hospital of London (1860-73), the National Hospital for Diseases of the Heart and Paralysis (1874-1913) and an antique dealers until demolished in 1937.

(Edward Smith *The Life of Sir Joseph Banks* University Press of the Pacific 2002; www.kew.org/collections/banks.html)

Dr Nicholas Barbon

The most notoriously unscrupulous – and successful – property developer in London during the hectic building-spree which followed the Great Fire of 1666, Barbon (1637/40-1698/9) was responsible for the development (1675-85) of **Gerrard Street**, **Litchfield Street**, **Rupert Street** and **Newport Market** and parts of **Dean Street**. A trained doctor, Barbon was the son of a radical Puritan preacher who christened him Nicholas Unless-Jesus-Christ-Had-Died-For-Thee-Thou-Hadst-Been-Damned Barbon. Barbon also established London's first fire insurance company and has belatedly been recognised as an original economic thinker, the first to realise that market value could be affected by such ephemeral factors as mere changes in fashion.

Sir Joseph Barnby

The foremost Victorian choral conductor, Barnby (1838-96) was a choirmaster at twelve. Serving as adviser to **Novello**, at **St Anne's Soho** (1871-86) he inaugurated musical services unprecedented at parish level. In 1892 he was knighted and became second principal of the Guildhall School of Music.

E M Barry

Edward Middleton Barry (1830-80) was the third son of Sir Charles Barry, the architect of the Houses of Parliament and took on the responsibility for their completion following the sudden death of his father in 1860. Barry junior had already established his reputation with the Gothic St. Giles' National School in **Endell Street**, which led to his election as an Associate of the Royal Academy. Barry's other works include the present **Royal Opera House** and the adjacent Floral Hall in **Bow Street,** and Charing Cross Station hotel and the Eleanor Cross which stands in front of it. Elected Professor of Architecture at the Royal Academy, the workaholic Barry was embittered by his failure to be awarded the commissions for the Albert Memorial and the Royal Courts of Justice. He died suddenly of heart failure, aged just fifty.

Beak Street

"A characteristic Soho street". (Pevsner)

Beak Street, originally, Silver Street, began building up ca. 1668 and was renamed for Thomas Beake, who developed the eastern section up to **Kingly Street** ca. 1689 and later served Queen Anne as a Royal Messenger. Nos. 65-73 and 77-79 are re-fronted houses of ca. 1719. By the time **Dickens** wrote *Nicholas Nickleby* (1838-9) he saw Beak Street as "tumbledown ... with two irregular rows of tall meagre houses". At the corner with James Street, at No. 40, once stood the Crown Inn, recommended by Newman Noggs in Dickens' novel and probably the one used by Philip Carey and his

An unusual green-tiled warehouse in Beak Street, built in 1904-5.

friends in Somerset Maugham's *Of Human Bondage*.

No. 75 is a former pub of 1847. The Old Coffee House pub was originally built as a 'temperance tavern' for Reid's brewery. The Sun and Thirteen Cantons pub (1882) alludes to Soho's old-established **Swiss community**; Pevsner describes its architecture as "Gothic and Queen Anne piratically mixed" but admires the green-glazed warehouse of 1904-5 at Nos. 50-54. No. 40 was built (1909-10) as a Metropolitan Police section house. The former home of the painter **Canaletto** at No. 41 is marked by a blue plaque. Flamboyant South African poet Roy Campbell (1903-57) lived at No. 50 from 1920 to 1922. No. 5 was the site of **Blanchard's** restaurant ("ladies not after 5 p.m. Good wines'). No. 79, with a shopfront of ca. 1850, was until recently the premises of John Wilkes, Soho's last gunmakers.

An attractive building in Beak Street, now a bistro.

The Sun and 13 Cantons in Beak Street is a reminder of the area's strong links with a Swiss community.

The Beatles

From 1964 to 1967 the Beatles' manager Brian Epstein had the headquarters of his business, NEMS, on the fifth floor of 5-6 **Argyll Street**, next door to the **London Palladium**. In 1966 Paul McCartney first met Linda Eastman at the then Bag o' Nails pub at 8 **Kingly Street**. The Beatles' White Album, including *Hey Jude*, was recorded at Trident Studios at 17 St Ann's Court in October 1968. Other key tracks recorded there include George Harrison's *My Sweet Lord*, Elton John's *Your Song* and David Bowie's *Space Oddity*. The headquarters of McCartney Productions Ltd. (MPL) are at No. 1 **Soho Square**.

(Piet Schreuders, Mark Lewisohn and Adam Smith *The Beatles' London: The Ultimate Guide to Over 400 Beatles Sites In and Around London* Portico 2008; www.beatles.com)

Samuel Beazley

The first specialist theatre architect, Samuel Beazley (1786-1851), who lived at 29 **Soho Square,** designed or altered seven theatres in London, including the **Royalty** and others abroad, from Belgium to Brazil, Ireland to India. In 1816 he rebuilt the **Lyceum** and rebuilt it again in 1834; the present portico remains from this reconstruction. Beazley also built London's first railway terminus, London Bridge, and numerous smaller stations. Described as "a Victorian Vanbrugh", Beazley was a prolific dramatist and had fought as a soldier in the Peninsular War, on one occasion waking up after a battle to find himself laid out for burial.

William Beckford

Alderman William Beckford (1709-70), twice Lord Mayor of London (1762, 1769), lived at No. 22 **Soho Square** from 1751 until his death. Heir to a huge fortune derived from Jamaican sugar plantations worked by slave labour, Beckford vigorously defended the cause of a self-styled champion of English liberties, the confrontational MP John Wilkes (1727-97), even going so far on one occasion as to lecture an astonished **George III** on the fundamentals of the British constitution. This *lèse-majesté* was rewarded by the City of London by raising a statue of Beckford in Guildhall, making him the only Lord Mayor to be so honoured. Beckford's son and heir, William junior (1759-1844) was born at No. 22 and as a child received music lessons from the young **Mozart**. Over the course of a long and eccentric life the younger Beckford would become involved in a homosexual scandal, write a dazzling Oriental fantasy novel *Vathek* (in a single burst of three days and nights, in French), build an immense Gothic folly, Fonthill (which fell down) and squander almost the entire fortune he inherited. Soho in **the Fifties** would have suited him.

(Timothy Mowl, *William Beckford: Composing for Mozart* John Murray 1998)

Bedford Coffee House

According to *The Survey of London* the Bedford was the first (1726) coffee house permitted on the **Piazza**, at the north-east corner. It was much favoured by **Henry Fielding**, Goldsmith and **Hogarth** and especially the theatrical fraternity represented by Quin, **Garrick**, **Macklin** and **Sheridan**. On 7 April 1779 the Revd James Hackman (1751-79), who had, as a young soldier eight years previously, fallen hopelessly in love with Lord Sandwich's mistress, Martha Ray, a woman fifteen years his senior and a mother of nine children, lurked in the Bedford until she came out of **Covent Garden theatre** after a performance of **Arne**'s *Love in a Village*. He then shot her dead as she went to her coach. When his second pistol failed to fire he attempted to club himself to death with the butt. Taken before **Sir John Fielding**, he was subsequently hanged at Tyburn. Henry Angelo, son of Domenico of **Carlisle House**, saw Hackman's corpse dissected at Surgeons' Hall and claimed to have been put off pork chops for life. A novel based on the incident, *Love and Madness*, was rushed out by Herbert Croft in 1780 and was an immediate success. The Bedford was subsequently home to a Shakespeare Club whose members included **Dickens** and **Macready**. The house finally closed in 1858

Bedford House

Bedford House was built by Edward Russell, third Earl of Bedford, and occupied the site of what is now Southampton Street, facing towards the Strand. An area of twenty acres to the rear and sides was enclosed by a wall in 1613. Francis Bacon (1561-1626) – the lawyer and philosopher, not the anarchic artist – went to live at Bedford House after 1621. He stayed there until 1623 and during his residence completed and translated into Latin his essay on *The Advancement of Learning*. Bedford House was demolished in 1706 when the Russells moved to Bloomsbury.

Bedford Street

The earliest residents of Bedford Street included several titled persons, notably **Sir Francis Kynaston** who founded an academy of "arms and arts" in his house. The street became notable for its concentration of publishers, including Edward Arnold, **Frederick Warne, Heinemann, Macmillan,** and **J M Dent** and the editorial offices of *The Lady*, a sedate magazine renowned for its small ads for nannies and live-in companions. Its most famous member of staff, in the late 1920s, was the young Stella Gibbons who was to achieve fame in 1932 with her comic novel *Cold Comfort Farm*, much to Virginia Woolf's outrage. Bedford Street was also the first home of **Moss Bros**. The **Civil Service Stores** stood at the junction of Bedford Street and the Strand. In 1873 and again in 1875 the Dutch painter Vincent Van Gogh was employed at the art-dealer, Goupil's, at No. 25 until his curmudgeonly manner got him summarily transferred to Paris.

The elegant offices of The Lady *magazine in Bedford Street, built as a tea warehouse in 1861.*

Bedfordbury

"a wretched little haunt ... a devious, slimy little reptile of a place, whose tumbledown tenements and reeking courts spume forth plumps of animated rags ... I don't think there are five windows ... with a whole pane of glass in them."

Bedfordbury, by Francis Shepherd (1819-78), probably mid-19th century, before the area was demolished and rebuilt.

George Sala's contemptuous dismissal was written in 1859 when an estimated two thousand people were crammed into this thoroughfare and the seven courts which then gave off it. (Four now remain). In 1861 an imposing Gothic Bedfordbury Mission House, designed by Arthur Blomfield, was built in polychromatic brick to bring some vestige of civilization to the area. In 1878, however, it was still characterised as "a nest of low, dark and crowded streets, which form a blot and disgrace on our metropolitan administration".

First built up between 1627 and 1635, Bedfordbury was drastically widened in 1880 by extensive demolition of its eastern side and the construction of Peabody Buildings as **model housing** to accommodate some 700 people. These were rebuilt in 1982 as the present **Duval** Court and Davey's Court.

Beefsteak Society

Established in 1735 by John Rich, manager of **Covent Garden Theatre**, the Beefsteak Society was a dining club of twenty-four members which met on Saturday evenings from November until June to consume liberal quantities of beef as a symbol of Englishness. Its foundation was a riposte to the establishment in 1733 of the Italophile Society of Dilettanti for alumni of the Grand Tour. Members included **Hogarth**, **Johnson**, **Garrick** and **Sheridan**. **Peg Woffington** was for many years the only female member. The club, later known as the Sublime Society of Beefsteaks, met at Covent Garden Theatre until 1808, then at the **Lyceum** (1809-30), the **Bedford Coffee House** (1830-8) and again at the Lyceum (1838-67) until its demise in 1867.

William Behnes

William Behnes (1795-1864) broke away from the family trade of piano-making to become a sculptor of precocious, prize-winning talent. Proving to be a brilliant maker of portrait busts, Behnes enjoyed such rapid success that in 1823 he bought 91 **Dean Street,** a building quite unsuitable for his needs. The expense of creating a modelling room high enough to admit massive statues crippled him financially and, aggravated by his personal extravagances, threw him into the arms of moneylenders. In the ten years that Behnes was in Dean Street he completed twenty funerary monuments and over thirty portrait busts, including those of such prestigious sitters as Earl Grey, the Duke of Kent, Princess Victoria and **John Nash**. Although his life was set on a downward spiral Behnes went on to make busts of Disraeli, Peel, Wellington and some forty other Victorian *eminenti*. His most prominent London work is the statue of General Sir Henry Havelock in **Trafalgar Square**. Bankrupted in 1861, Behnes died in the Middlesex Hospital having been found lying in a gutter with threepence in his pocket.

Jem Belcher

Bristolian by birth and a butcher by trade, Jem Belcher (1781-1811) became England's champion bare-knuckle boxer at twenty but in 1803 lost an eye playing rackets and took over the Jolly Brewers pub in **Wardour Street**. Provoked out of retirement, he gamely fought three more punishing contests but failed to regain his title from Tom Cribb. He died at the Coach and Horses in **Frith Street**, which he left to his widow.

As well known in his day as the Duke of Wellington, Belcher was similarly commemorated by an article of attire, the 'belcher', a neckerchief, originally spotted blue and white but later applied to any parti-coloured handkerchief worn loosely round the neck. In chapters 10 and 15 of Arthur Conan Doyle's novel *Rodney Stone* (1896) Belcher is eulogised for both his manly character and handsome looks.

Muriel Belcher

Formidable and foul-mouthed, autocratic and capricious, Muriel Belcher (1908-79), the proprietor of the **Colony Club**, presided over its proceedings from its foundation until her death. She knew nothing of art but had a telling eye for artists. **George Melly** described her as "a handsome Jewish dyke ... a benevolent witch, who managed to draw in all London's talent up those filthy stairs. She was like a great cook, working with the ingredients of people and drink. And she loved money" A **Francis Bacon** portrait of Muriel Belcher, *Seated Woman*, was sold at Sotheby's in Paris in 2007 for 13,700,000 euros.

Sir Charles Bell

A sometime resident of **Soho Square,** Bell (1774-1842) achieved immortality in the medical profession by discovering the function of the nerves, arguably the greatest physiological breakthrough since William Harvey's discovery of the circulation of the blood. Bell's *New Idea of the Anatomy of the Brain* (1811) has been hailed as "the Magna Carta of neurology". Bell lectured at the **Great Windmill Street** school of anatomy and provided specialist attention to the wounded of Corunna and Waterloo.

In 1830 he published the then authoritative account of *The Nervous System of the Human Body*. In 1829 Bell received the first ever Gold Medal to be awarded by the Royal Society and was knighted in 1831. Never at ease in London medical circles Bell returned to his native Edinburgh with relief in 1836 to take up a professorial chair.

Jeffrey Bernard

Born in Hampstead, Jeffrey Bernard (1932-97), the celebrated alcoholic and columnist, was the offspring of an architect and an opera singer. He made Soho his base and the **Coach and Horses** his virtual home from early youth. Bernard's cast-list of drinking acquaintances included Dylan Thomas, **Francis Bacon**, **John Minton**, **Dan Farson** and **Nina Hamnett**. A passion for the turf enabled Bernard to write a racing column in *Queen* magazine and then go on to Fleet Street journalism. Bernard was warned as early as 1965 that he could drop dead if he touched another drink. It took the vodka another thirty-two years to confirm the prediction. An article, appropriately on alcohol addiction, brought semi-regular commissions from the *New Statesman*, followed by a regular column with the *Spectator*, aptly headed *Low Life*. Bernard's drinking led to irregular contributions, signalled by the notification to readers that 'Jeffrey Bernard is unwell'. Nevertheless he managed to turn out over a thousand *Low Life* columns, invariably about himself, described by Jonathan Meades as "a suicide note in weekly instalments".

Bernard was married and divorced four times before diabetes and drink led to his demise from kidney failure in his one-room home at 45 Kemp House, **Berwick Street**. Keith Waterhouse's play *Jeffrey Bernard is Unwell* (1989), starring Peter O'Toole in the name part, was a West End hit. Bernard wrote "the immediate success of the play was heady stuff for me and although it didn't accelerate my drinking, my intake was a steady two years of celebration. First night after first night." Bernard's – predictably posthumous – memoir was suitably titled *Reach for the Ground: The Downhill Struggle of Jeffrey Bernard*.

Berwick Street

The street was laid out by James Pollett, a Catholic, in the turbulent years when his patron, the Duke of Berwick, a bastard son of the ousted **James II,** was fighting in Ireland to retrieve his father's lost throne. The southern half up to Broadwick Street was first

Berwick Street Market c. 1905. The smart clothes of the children suggest an organised outing.

built up between 1687 and 1703, the northern from 1707. Strype in 1720 described it as "a pretty handsome straight street, with new well built houses much inhabited by the French, where they have a church." There were two **Huguenot** places of worship – L'Ancienne Patente and L'Eglise du Quarre. Residents included James Giles, a china painter and Joseph Duffour, 'Carver and Gilder' and pioneer manufacturer of papier-mâché. Houses were already being rebuilt in 1734-41. Nos. 26, 31-32, 46-48, 50-52, 69-71, 77 and 79-81 are all surviving properties from the 1730s. A pub has stood on the site of the Green Man since 1738 and another on the site of the Three Blue Posts since 1739. Kemp House (built 1959-62) was the home of **Jeffrey Bernard**. No. 24 was built as a pub in 1826, Nos 27-9 as a warehouse ca. 1890.

The street market emerged in the course of the eighteenth century but was not officially recognised until 1892. A Berwick Street trader, Jack Smith, is supposed to have introduced the grapefruit to Londoners ca.1890. Selling mainly fruit and vegetables, the market is open from Monday to Saturday between 9.00 am and 6.00 pm. A plaque at No. 22 marks the birthplace of entertainer **Jessie Matthews** (1907-81). In the 1940s Berwick Street was much-favoured for the swift disposal of black market luxuries and the organisation of bent card games. The street was the location for the cover photograph of the 1995 Oasis album *'(What's the Story) Morning Glory?* an indirect tribute to the number of specialist outlets for recorded music still flourishing then along the street.

Thomas Betterton

Betterton (formerly Brownlow) Street commemorates a theatrical superstar without good looks who could not sing or dance, but who was, according to fellow thespian Anthony Aston, "a superlative good actor" who "enforced universal attention, even from the fops and orange-girls". Thomas Betterton (1635-1710), a great favourite with **Pepys**, never did farce but performed over two hundred roles. A competent theatre manager, he also had a profitable sideline in teaching voice production to ambitious clergymen. A model of respectability, married to the same wife for forty-eight years, Betterton was buried in Westminster Abbey.

(John Doran *Their Majesties' Servants: or, Annals of the English Stage, from Thomas Betterton to Edmund Kean; Actors, Authors, Audiences* BookSurge Publishing 2001)

Elizabeth Billington

Born in **Litchfield Street**, Elizabeth Billington (1768-1818) was, according to her original entry in the *Dictionary of National Biography*, " the greatest singer England has ever produced". Her mother was a pupil of **J C Bach**, her father a theatre violinist. At fifteen Elizabeth married James Billington, a double-bass player at **Theatre Royal Drury Lane**. After a brilliant debut in Dublin, she stunned the Covent Garden audience in 1786 with her performance in *Love in a Village* by **Thomas Arne**. Her unhappy marriage was compromised by many infidelities which gained her the nickname of "the **Poland Street** man trap" and in 1794 she fled abroad to escape the scandal whirling around her. The sudden death of her husband abroad also gave rise to gossip, although she was almost certainly innocent of any wrongdoing in this. Nor did it compromise her career as she sang her way round the courts of Europe. Returning in 1801, with an even less suitable second spouse in tow, she was hired by both Covent Garden and Drury Lane and made an estimated £10,000 to £15,000 in a single season. In 1806 she appeared in *La Clemenza di Tito*, the first opera by **Mozart** ever to be staged in England. Retiring in 1811, she foolishly took back the worthless brute from whom she had previously freed herself and may well have died from a blow from his hand. **Reynolds** painted Mrs. Billington as Saint Cecilia, the patron saint of music. As he was doing so Haydn called at his house and observed that "you have painted Billington listening to the angels; you should rather have made the angels listening to her."

William Blake

Blake (1757-1827) grew up and began his career and happy married life in Soho. A tower-block now covers the site of his birthplace at No. 28 (later 74) **Broadwick Street**, where he claimed the face of God pressed against the window of his father's shop. Sent to drawing-school at ten, at fourteen he was apprenticed to Basire, engraver to the Society of Antiquaries, who had him copy monuments in Westminster Abbey. A forceful bust of Blake, by Joseph Epstein, is now in Poets' Corner in the Abbey. Entering the Royal Academy Schools at twenty-one, Blake loathed its suave president, **Reynolds**. In 1784 he began selling prints at No. 27 (then 72) Broadwick Street, but later (1785-91) was at 28 **Poland Street**. Blake experimented ceaselessly to translate his mystical visions into precise visual

The Artist's Artist – William Blake by John Linnell.

form, using line with great precision but colour non-naturalistically. Hazlitt opined that Blake was "ruined by vain struggles to get rid of what presses on his brain – he attempts impossibles." Blake summarised his self-imposed quests as wanting:

To see a World in a Grain of Sand,
And Heaven in a Wild Flower.

Impatient with conventional boundaries Blake is now venerated as an original genius in both art and literature. Although his nonconformity cost him success it won him devoted friends like **Flaxman** and **Swiss** exile Henry Fuseli, who introduced him to the work of Swedish mystic Emanuel Swedenborg, which greatly influenced Blake. Many important works by Blake can be seen at Tate Britain and his portrait by Thomas Philip is at the **National Portrait Gallery**.

(Peter Ackroyd *Blake* Vintage 1998)

Blanchard's Restaurant

Established in 1862, this **Beak Street** establishment was also a noted 'wine office'. Shortly before his death **Dickens** attended a birthday party at Blanchard's in honour of his mistress, Ellen Ternan. By the 1890s it had become an imposing venue, occupying four adjoining buildings. Blanchard's passed out of family ownership in 1923 when it was converted to a night club.

The Blitz

Although many Soho properties suffered slight to moderate damage from enemy action during World War Two the area as a whole got off relatively lightly. The greatest loss of lives was at the **Café de Paris** and the Madrid restaurant in **Dean Street,** where seventeen were killed. The worst single building loss was the destruction of **St Anne's** church and the area immediately to its north, along either side of **Old Compton Street**. The southern end of **Carnaby Street** was also badly hit, as was the northern end of **Newport Place**. **Thurston's** billiards establishment was another loss. Only one V-1'doodlebug' flying bomb hit Soho, at the junction of Sherwood Strreet and **Brewer Street**, and one V-2 rocket bomb, demolishing the block to the east of Leicester Place.

Covent Garden was similarly fortunate, although V-1 rocket bombs did land on the Peabody estate in Drury Lane and at the eastern end of **Betterton** Street.

(Philip Ziegler *London at War 1939-45* Sinclair-Stevenson 1995; Sayre Van Young *London's War: A Traveller's Guide to World War Two* Ulysses Press 2004)

Peter Boizot

Peter Boizot opened Britain's first pizza restaurant at 29 **Wardour Street** in 1965 and went on to develop the Pizza Express chain with more than 300 branches. In 1980 he acquired control of **Kettner's**. A formidable entrepreneur, he has also been a generous supporter of jazz, hockey and the football club and cathedral of his native Peterborough, as well as raising funds for the restoration of threatened buildings in Venice and the UK and promoting Soho through an annual **Soho Festival**. (www.pizzaexpress.com)

Book Trade

Soho's connections with the book trade probably arose less from the presence of a few eminent writers than from its convenient location between scholarly Bloomsbury and the commerce of the West End. In 1860 Dulau & Company, founded by a Benedictine refugee from the French Revolution, prospered on the sale of textbooks by the French master at Eton and Baedeker's classic tourist

Browsers at a bookstall near St Anne's church c. 1900.

guides. Mitchell & Hughes, established in **Wardour Street** in 1797, excelled in the printing of family histories and pedigrees and pioneered the (posthumous) publication of the works of the Swedish mystic, Emanuel Swedenborg (1688-1772). Pettit & Cox of **Old Compton Street** became leading suppliers of business diaries. Howlett & Son of **Frith Street** specialised in printing gold on everything from menus and opera programmes to labels for boxes of patent pills. Kimpton's of Wardour Street was, in the mid-nineteenth century, one of only three specialist medical booksellers in the whole of London.

Routledge enjoyed a huge success with Harriet Beecher Stowe's *Uncle Tom's Cabin* while in **Soho Square** and also in the Square settled two leading Scottish publishers, Chambers and A & C Black together with Rupert Hart-Davis. More recently Bloomsbury Publishing, the publishers of the Harry Potter books by J K Rowling, are at no. 36.

Bookshops – new, secondhand, specialist (art, crime, gay) and remainder – now line both sides of **Charing Cross Road.** Indeed, Tim Waterstone, after leaving W H Smith, set up Waterstone's in the road in 1980 and from this evolved a successful national chain of shops. **Foyle's**, now rejuvenated, is still the largest bookshop in Charing Cross Road, and in **Long Acre Stanford's** specialises in travel books and maps.

(Robin Myers, Michael Harris, Giles Mandelbote (eds) *London Book Trade: Topographies of Print in the Metropolis* British Library Board 2003)

A makeshift plaque at 70 Charing Cross Road commemorates Shipley Books 'A Mecca for art lovers frequented by the likes of John Berger, Peter Blake, Annie Liebowitz and Susan Sontag'.

Andrew Boorde

The name of Andrew Boorde or Borde (?1490-1549), is commemorated as a street in the shadow of **Centre Point**. He was admitted to the Carthusian order under age but eventually managed to get himself released from his vows, which was probably just as well because he had been accused of being 'conversant with women', which scotched his appointment as suffragan bishop of Chichester. He wrote numerous publications including the first recorded account of the gypsy language, Romany.

Boorde appears to have lived at some time in the former house of the master of the hospital of **St Giles-in-the-Fields**, hence his commemoration in a nearby street. In 1547 he was accused of keeping three harlots in his rooms and consigned to the Fleet Prison, where he eventually died.

James Boswell

Famous as Dr Samuel Johnson's acolyte and self-appointed biographer, the Scottish lawyer and landowner James Boswell (1740-95), first met his hero in Davies's bookshop at No. 8 **Russell Street,** Covent Garden, where a blue plaque commemorates their encounter. Boswell's *London Journal* also records that in the same year, 1763, he prowled nervously around Covent Garden **Piazza** before approaching one of its numerous ladies of easy virtue. Boswell later lodged at 22 **Gerrard Street.**

during his annual visits to London in 1775 and 1776 and was a member of **'The Club'** which met in that same street.

(Peter Martin *A Life of James Boswell* Yale University Press 2000)

Boulestin's

Two visits to London made (Xavier) Marcel Boulestin (1878-1943), a French cook, sufficiently anglophile to acquire an alleged penchant for mint and mince pies and to eulogise the curry at **Romano's**. While living in a flat in Southampton Row Boulestin became friendly with Dorothy Todd, editor of *Vogue* and cooked his favourite French dishes for her.After he had arranged a spectacularly successful lunch for Virginia Woolf the guests agreed that he should open a restaurant. One of them, wealthy Leo Myers, put up the money and the Restaurant Français opened in **Panton Street** in 1925, moving to the corner of **Southampton Street** and **Henrietta Street** in 1927.

Boulestin, who had been an interior decorator – as well as music critic, picture dealer, novelist and soldier – installed contemporary Parisian décor featuring fabrics designed by Dufy. His mission was to bring true French haute cuisine to a city too frequently bamboozled by cheaper Italianate variants. He also ran cookery classes at Fortnum & Mason and wrote food columns for *Vogue* and the *Evening Standard*. Believing that "food which is worth eating is worth discussing", he also reached a wider audience with a stream of influential cookbooks, to which he brought a designer's eye – large type, thick paper, stout binding and a jacket designed by Jean Laboureur, who had supplied painted panels for his restaurant. Boulestin's *Simple French Cooking for English Homes* was first published in 1923 and reprinted six times within ten years. Other Boulestin titles included the aptly titled *A Second Helping* (1925), *What Shall We Have Today?* (1931), *127 Ways of Preparing Hors D'Oeuvre* (1932), two companion volumes on eggs and potatoes, *What Shall We Have To Drink?* (1933) and the *Evening Standard Book of Menus* (1935), which contained a lunch and dinner menu for every day of the year. Boulestin was forced to be prolific with his pen because his restaurant, one of the most expensive in London, still did not pay. Perfection exacts a high price.

In 1937 Marcel Boulestin gave the first ever TV cookery demonstration, on BBC's *Cook's Night Out* programme, maintaining a mystique of Gallic gravity with such pronouncements as " it is not really an exaggeration to say that peace and happiness begin, geographically, where garlic is used in cookery" and "Cookery is not chemistry. It is an art. It requires instinct and taste, not exact measurements." *Panache*, anyone?

In 1936 Boulestin published an autobiography, *Myself, My Two Countries*, but for all his Anglophilia Boulestin never considered naturalization and died in Nazi-occupied France. In 1952 his publisher, **Heinemann**, honoured him with the posthumous accolade of an anthology, *The Best of Boulestin*.

The restaurant survived under other management until 1994 when the premises were bought by Pizza Hut.

Bourchier Street

Built on an alignment dating back to before the seventeenth century, this street was before 1838 known as Milk Alley, then Little Dean Street before being renamed in tribute to the Revd Basil Bourchier (1881-1934), rector of **St Anne's**. Its main architectural feature is a block of white-rendered flats of 1995-8, described by Pevsner's successors as "strongly articulated, with elements of De Stijl and 1920s Corbusier".

Retro chic – flats in Bourchier Street, 2009.

Proceedings at Bow Street magistrates' court, depicted by Rowlandson and Pugin c. 1808.

Bow Street

Now dominated by the the **Royal Opera House** and **Floral Hall**, Bow Street was built up between 1633 and 1677. **Will's** coffee house was an important cultural rendezvous for over half a century. Although Strype in 1720 characterised it as "well inhabited and resorted unto by gentry for lodgings", by 1743 the street also had eight licensed premises.Long-term residents have included **Grinling Gibbons, Dr Radcliffe** and **John Fielding**. More briefly Bow Street has also been home to the publisher Jacob Tonson (1707), dramatist William Wycherley (1715), actors **David Garrick** (1742-4) and **Charles Macklin** (1743-8), novelist **Henry Fielding** (1749-53) and theatre manager John Rich (1754-61).

The artist Marcellus Laroon (1653-1702), another resident, was employed by Kneller to paint the draperies in his portraits but is chiefly remembered for his series of engravings of street-sellers, *The Cryes of London*. Doubtless based in large part on the many vendors who thronged Covent Garden market to buy the fruit and flowers they cried through the capital, Laroon's 'Cryes' were still being reprinted a century after his death. Marcellus Laroon the Younger (1679-1772) was born in his father's house in Bow Street and grew up to be a painter, an actor at **Theatre Royal Drury Lane**, an army officer and a friend of **Hogarth**.

Licensed premises have been at the site of the Marquis of Anglesey pub, once Edward Miles' coffee house, since 1663. The Marquis, Henry Paget (1768-1854) commanded the British cavalry at the Battle of Waterloo where he was wounded in the knee in the very last stage of the battle. His amputated leg was buried at a village nearby and its resting-place became a tourist attraction. The Marquis survived to become a Field Marshal.

Bow Street Magistrates' Court

The first court was established in 1740 at No. 4, the house of Col. Thomas de Veil, venial predecessor of **Henry Fielding**. The court on the west side of the street was demolished in 1887, by which time its business had been transferred to purpose-built (1879-81) premises on the eastern side of the street. In April 1895 **Oscar Wilde**, having been arrested at the Cadogan Hotel, was charged with gross indecency and spent a night in the cells. Breakfast of tea, toast and eggs was brought over from the

Tavistock Hotel. In 1915 the Bow Street bench found D H Lawrence's *The Rainbow* an obscene publication. In 1928 Radclyffe Hall's pioneering lesbian novel *The Well of Loneliness* met the same fate, despite the evidence of forty defence witnesses including Virginia Woolf, who thought it inferior in literary terms but felt duty bound to oppose any effort at censorship. The book remained banned until 1949. Judged incapable of modernisation, the court was closed in 2006 to await redevelopment.

Bow Street Runners

The Bow Street Runners, an early police force, were established informally in 1749 by playwright and magistrate, **Henry Fielding**. They were greatly strengthened when, following the **Gordon Riots** (1780), a part-time force of sixty-eight, armed with cutlasses, was raised by Fielding's successor, Sampson Wright, to patrol the streets of London by night. From 1783, with government funding, Wright was also able to revive a Horse Patrol on a permanent basis. In 1792 an Act of Parliament established seven more offices modelled on Bow Street, each with three salaried magistrates and up to six paid police officers.

In 1805 chief magistrate Richard Ford upgraded the establishment to a uniformed force of fifty-two, armed with pistols, truncheons and handcuffs. In 1806 a Bow Street Foot Patrol began to watch the streets by night. Increased to a hundred in 1821, they were supplemented n 1822 by a daytime patrol. The Metropolitan Police, established in 1829, absorbed the Horse Patrol as its Mounted Branch in 1836. The Bow Street Runners and foot patrols were absorbed in 1839.

(T F Banks *The Thief-Taker: Memoirs of a Bow Street Runner* Dell Publishing Co. 2002)

A rather portly Bow Street Runner.

Brewer Street

Brewer Street was laid out by Sir William Pulteney between 1664 and 1670. Nos. 80 to 84 on the northern side are from the late seventeenth century. Nos. 49 and 51 are early eighteenth century, refronted ca. 1860.

The street takes its name from two breweries which once stood on its northern side. The first brewery, opened in 1664, belonged to Thomas Ayres (hence nearby Air Street) and continued brewing until 1826. Davies's brewery adjoined it to the west and lasted from 1671 to the 1740s.

Despite Pevsner's assertion that it was "never a smart street" the Scottish novelist Tobias Smollett (1721-71) lodged there in 1765 to write up his recent odyssey as the caustic *Travels through France and Italy*. In the same year the eight-year-old **Mozart** (1756-93) was performing improvisations in the afternoons at **Hickford's Rooms**. Between 1767 and 1769 the Scottish philosopher David Hume (1711-76) lodged at No. 40 while serving as under-secretary of state, a post he did not enjoy. No. 38 (now 71) was the home of the transsexual **Chevalier D'Eon** for thirty-three years. Apart from breweries Brewer Street also once had a saltpetre works. In 1826 No. 41 was the premises of George Smith "Upholsterer and Furniture Draughtsman to His Majesty" and publisher of *The Cabinet-Maker's and Upholsterer's Guide, Drawing Book and Repository*. What had been from 1730 the Coach and Horses public house was rebuilt ca. 1876 to become the present Glasshouse Stores. Nos. 72-74 were built in 1922 for Burberry's, suppliers of the

Regency relic – an elegant shop at 14a and 14b Brewer Street c. 1907.

iconic rainwear, then recently popularised as the favoured garment of British army officers serving in the trenches during the Great War. (Hence the trade-mark epaulettes and brass rings for attaching binoculars, map-cases etc.) The Art Deco Lex Garage was built in 1928-29, on the former site of Ayres' brewery, to the designs of J J Joass. Its original features included a clubroom for chauffeurs and dressing-rooms where their employers could change into evening dress or country clothes, as appropriate.

Charles Bridgeman

A plaque at 54 **Broadwick Street** marks the home of royal gardener Charles Bridgeman (died 1738) from 1723 until his death. Bridgeman was one of the first English gardeners to defy the tyranny of the Franco-Dutch imperative of symmetry in garden design. Horace Walpole also credited him with popularising the 'haha' or sunken fence, a simple but revolutionary device which enabled the garden designer to mark a boundary without impairing a vista. An adviser to Alexander Pope and mentor to William Kent and 'Capability' Brown, Bridgeman is chiefly remembered for creating the Serpentine in Hyde Park and laying out the gardens between it and Kensington Palace for Queen Caroline of Ansbach, consort of **George II**.

The Art Deco Lex garage in Brewer Street.

The British Lying-In Hospital for Married Women

Britain's first obstetric hospital was established, with the support of surgeon **William Hunter**, in **Betterton** (then Brownlow) Street in 1749. Heavily oversubscribed – women were chosen by lottery, using a bag of coloured balls – the hospital had just twenty beds. Inmates were admitted in the last month of pregnancy and allowed to stay for three weeks after the birth. The institution was rebuilt in the 1840s and closed in 1913. Used as a military hospital in World War One, in 1921 it became St. Paul's Hospital for Diseases of the Genito-Urinary Organs and Skin, finally closing in 1948.

Broadwick Street

Broadwick Street, built up between 1686 and 1736, only acquired its present name in 1936 when its eastern part, Edward Street (a reference to Edward Wardour) was united with the former Broad Street, originally intended as a hay market. The harpsichord business founded by Jacob Kirkman was at No. 54 from 1750 to 1832. The Lion brewery was here from ca. 1801 to 1937. There has also been a percussion-cap factory.

The surviving Georgian terrace (Nos. 48-58) dates from 1722-23 and was home to royal gardener **Charles Bridgeman**. The public house (No. 39) renamed in 1956 for **Dr John Snow** was formerly (ca. 1870) the Newcastle-upon-Tyne. Trenchard House, named for the founder of the Royal Air Force and commander of the police college at Hendon, was built as a police section-house in 1938-40. The Ingenia offices at the south-west corner of the street (1998-2000) are by the Richard Rogers Partnership.

Broadwick Street was the birthplace of **William Blake** and the polymath Peter Mark Roget (1779-1869) who became secretary of the Royal Society and a founder of the University of London. Roget's famous *Thesaurus*, undertaken as a retirement project, was first published in 1852 and went through twenty-eight editions before his death. Later editions were updated by members of the Roget family until 1953.

John Broadwood

Broadwood (1732-1812) is said to have walked from his native Scotland, intent on making his fortune in London as a cabinet-maker. Finding employment with Burkhardt Tschudi, a Swiss harpsichord-maker of **Great Pulteney Street**, Broadwood married his boss's daughter and took over the business in 1769. He established a European reputation for the excellence of the pianos produced on Great Pulteney Street. and in 1795 passed control to his son, James Tschudi Broadwood.

The Builder

Founded in 1842 by the architect J A Hansom, inventor of the hansom cab, in 1844 *The Builder* came under the editorial direction of George Godwin (1815-88) who made it the conscience of the architectural profession. The former offices, purpose-built in 1874, at no. 4 **Catherine Street** survive. While also conducting a successful architectural practice, Godwin used *The Builder* to raise standards in the building trade and to campaign against slums and in favour of improved sanitation. A man of wide interests, from Greek antiquities to the stage, Godwin wrote a successful farce and was an acknowledged expert on both basic aspects of the Victorian architect's business like concrete and church restoration and recherché topics like obelisks and mason's marks. A blue plaque marks Godwin's home at 24 Alexander Square, SW3. His flamboyant memorial in Brompton Cemetery bears his portrait, embellished with the tools of his trade.

The former offices of The Builder *magazine in Catherine Street.*

Burford's Panorama

In 1787 the Irish artist Robert Barker (1739-1806) was granted a patent with the exclusive right to exploit for fourteen years his "new contrivance or Apparatus which he calls *La Nature a coup d'oeil* for the purpose of displaying views of Nature at large by Oil painting…". In 1793 Barker acquired a site at the junction of Leicester Place and **Cranbourn Street** where he erected a circular building whose main chamber, ninety feet in diameter and fifty-seven feet high, was to be used to display painted panoramas, the first being *A View of the Grand Fleet regularly moored at Spithead.*

The venture proved so immediately successful that Barker was able to buy out all his backers and to finance his son, Henry Aston Barker (1774-1856) to travel to Turkey and Paris to sketch new scenes. Henry took over the business at his father's death and profited immensely from the public appetite for scenes of victory from the ongoing wars against France. Fame-seeking **Nelson** had personally

Burford's Panorama in Cranbourn Street, advertising a spectacular panorama of the 1858 Relief of Lucknow.

thanked Barker senior for his depiction of the *Battle of the Nile*, asserting that it prolonged the glory surrounding his name for at least an extra year. The *Battle of Waterloo* netted no less than £10,000. Also at the Panorama were views of historic cities. Henry Barker's last effort was a representation of the coronation procession of **George IV**.

Retiring in 1826, Barker handed over management of the business to his assistant John Burford and when he died the following year, it passed to his brother, Robert Burford (1791-1861). Robert carried on, finding profitable new subject-matter. Leading art critic John Ruskin praised the Panorama as "an educational institution of the highest and purest value ... one of the most beneficial school instruments in London." Burford's panorama closed following the death of its proprietor and the site was subsequently acquired for the building of the **Notre Dame** church.

Edmund Burke

"*the greatest man since Milton*". T B Macaulay

A plaque at No. 37 **Gerrard Street** marks the lodgings of Anglo-Irish statesman Edmund Burke (1729-97) between 1787 and 1790. Having established a literary reputation with his *Philosophical Enquiry into the Sublime and the Beautiful* (1757), Burke co-founded the *Annual Register* (1759), became an MP (1765) and a member of '**The Club**'. Sympathising with the grievances of Britain's rebellious American colonists, he also spoke up for freer trade, Catholic Emancipation, the abolition of the slave trade and more accountable government in India. Burke is, however, chiefly remembered for his *Reflections on the Revolution in France* (1790), composed during his Gerrard Street years, in which he correctly predicted that the popular uprising against supposed tyranny would eventually lead to an even worse one. Critic Matthew Arnold hailed him as almost unique in bringing "thought to bear on politics".(Conor Cruise O'Brien *Edmund Burke* 2002)

Dr Charles Burney and Fanny Burney

Pioneering musicologist Dr Charles Burney (1726-1814) lived at 50 **Poland Street** from 1760 until 1770, making it the childhood home of his daughter, Fanny (1752-1840). Writing in 1832 Fanny remembered it as not "as it is now, a sort of street that, like the rest of the neighbourhood, appears to be left in the lurch" but one in which her neighbours had included several titled persons, including a

Reluctant courtier, Fanny Burney.

Duke, and, most memorably, a visiting Cherokee chief. Dr Burney's scholarly reputation rested on a four volume *History of Music* published between 1776 and 1789, by which time the Burneys were living at **Newton**'s former home at 35 St. Martin's Street. Fanny, the fourth child, grew up on the fringe of **Dr Johnson's** circle and in 1778 stunned literary London with *Evelina, or The History of a Young Lady's Entrance into the World*. An epistolary novel, published anonymously, it remained unacknowledged by its author until, standing next to her own father, she heard it extravagantly praised by Johnson himself. Fanny Burney's fame led to an appointment at the court of **George III** where she endured much petty spite and even more boredom until released after five years on grounds of ill-health. In 1793, long after she would have been considered of a still marriageable age, she wed a refugee royalist French general and became Mme. D'Arblay. Fanny Burney went on to have children, to survive a double mastectomy (without anaesthetic) and to leave a lively literary legacy in the form of her journals and letters (10 vols 1972-81). Her three major novels were admired by **Jane Austen**. From 1822 to 1825 Fanny Burney lived at 29 **Soho Square**. She is commemorated in Soho in the name of D'Arblay Street.

(Claire Harman *Fanny Burney: A Biography* Flamingo 2001)

Burying Grounds

The burying-ground of St James's Piccadilly is shown on **Rocque**'s map of 1746 as lying between **Poland Street** and Marshall Street. It was by then already full and overlooked by a newly-built workhouse for the poor. It now lies partly under the multi-storey garage in **Poland Street,** extending as far back as Foubert's Place.

Drury Lane Gardens, off **Drury Lane**, originated as a burying-ground for **St Martin-in-the-Fields** and was then entered from Crown Court. It became scandalously "saturated with dead" to the point where bodies were simply tipped into an open pit covered with boards. It may well have been the inspiration for the hideous graveyard described in **Dickens**' *Bleak House* where Lady Dedlock is found dead. In 1877 it became the first Westminster burying-ground to be converted to public use as a garden. Although it has been a children's playground for more than a century the old watch house – a primitive lock-up – and mortuary, where bodies were kept prior to burial, still remains.

The gardens of the red brick flats on **Tavistock Street** are the remains of a burying-ground of St Mary-le-Strand. Once notorious for rats, it was closed in 1853 and asphalted over in 1886.

(Robert Bard – *Graveyard London: Lost and Forgotten Burial Grounds,* Historical Publications 2008)

Samuel Butler

Variously employed as a clerk, secretary and steward, Samuel Butler (1613-80) found instant celebrity in 1662 with the first instalment of *Hudibras*, a satirical mock romance. Surviving copies bear the signature of **Charles II**, who gave them to favoured courtiers. Further instalments appeared in 1663 and 1680. Loosely modelled on *Don Quixote* and hailed by **Hazlitt** as having "more wit than any other in the language", *Hudibras* rambles over academic pedantry, theological hair-splitting, the civil wars, witchcraft, alchemy, astrology and marriage. Despite its success Butler remained in obscurity, plagued by poverty. Dying of consumption in Rose Street, Covent Garden, he was buried in the churchyard of **St Paul's** nearby. In 1721 Butler was belatedly honoured with a memorial in Westminster Abbey,which inspired an ironically satirical tribute:

The poet's fate is here in emblem shown,
He ask'd for bread, and he receiv'd a stone.

An oasis of peace in busy Covent Garden – Drury Lane Gardens in Drury Lane, a former burial ground of St Martin-in-the-Fields.

Button's

Button's coffee house, at no. 10 on the south side of **Russell Street**, was opened in 1712 by Daniel Button, a former servant of the wealthy Countess of Warwick, whose second husband, the essayist and wit Joseph Addison (1672-1719) set him up in the business. Addison's was not a happy marriage and he was more than content to pass long hours at the establishment, using it as the office for the gossipy publications which carried his writings, *The Spectator* and its less well-known successor The *Guardian*. Contributors were invited to deposit their efforts via a letter-box shaped like a lion's head. Other patrons included Swift, Pope, **Kneller** and Dr. John Arbuthnot, inventor of 'John Bull' as the archetype of Englishmen. Addison's death led to a decline in Button's fortunes and he died in 1731 in receipt of parish relief. The lion's head letter box eventually ended up at Woburn Abbey, country home of the Dukes of Bedford.

The Lion's Head letterbox at Button's coffee house in which contributors were invited to post items for The Spectator *magazine.*

Café de Paris

The former Rialto cinema at Nos.3-4 **Coventry Street** was built with a large basement restaurant in 1912-13. This was subsequently (1924) converted into a nightclub, the Café de Paris, which, in its inter-war heyday, was patronised by the kings of Greece, Norway, Spain and Portugal, the Aga Khan, Edward, the Prince of Wales and Lord and Lady Mountbatten. Its cabaret starred such names as Cole Porter, Marlene Dietrich and Maurice Chevalier and its dance hostesses included Merle Oberon and Norma Shearer. The décor was based on the Palm Court of the ill-starred luxury liner *SS Lusitania*. The subterranean Café – advertised during the **Blitz** as "the safest place to dance in town" – proved as vulnerable as the liner to the fortunes of war, receiving a direct hit from a German bomb on 8 March 1941. The eventual death toll was eighty.

Reopened in 1948, the Café de Paris re-established itself as London's most glamorous nightclub for London's most glamorous people, notably Princess Margaret and her circle. The demise of traditional 'Society' meant that this lasted only until the sixties, when the establishment became a mere dance venue. Reopened as a nightclub in 1996, it now also hosts award ceremonies, showbiz celebrations and fashion shows. In the film version of Colin MacInnes novel *Absolute Beginners* (1986) the Café de Paris is the setting for a fashion show fronted by svelte Henley (James Fox). It was the setting for a nightclub scene in *Scandal* (1988), the cinematic account of the disgrace and downfall of War Minister John Profumo, Mandy Rice Davies (Bridget Fonda) and Christine Keeler (Joanne Whalley) who, in real life worked as hostesses in Murray's Club in **Beak Street**. In *The Krays* (1990) the brutal Ronnie and Reggie are shown in the Café de Paris revelling in their celebrity status. The Rialto cinema closed in 1991.

Café Royal, Regent Street

When the Café Royal finally closed in December 2008 it was announced that the resultant sale of effects would consist of items ranging from brandy caskets to a blood-spattered boxing-ring. The establishment had begun modestly in 1865 as a conventional café at 15-17 **Glasshouse Street**. The proprietor, Daniel Nicholas Thévenon (1833-97), later anglicised as Daniel Nichols, was a youthful Parisian wine-merchant who had already been bankrupted once. But the times and the site favoured his new enterprise, which by 1870 had

The Café Royal in its 1920s heyday – seven uniformed staff on duty!

expanded into premises with a **Regent Street** frontage and later added such amenities as private dining rooms and billiards in the basement. The original café was complemented by a luncheon bar and a more formal Grill Room and soon attracted the sort of arty clientele which shopped at **Liberty's**, like the flamboyant and witty American painter James Whistler. **Oscar Wilde**, who could make an affectation out of punctuality, lunched at one precisely. Other artistic patrons, like Walter Sickert, Augustus John and Aubrey Beardsley, were less regular because less regularly in funds. There was also a strong literary element represented by Max Beerbohm, George Bernard Shaw and D H Lawrence. Enid Bagnold, author of *National Velvet*, claimed to have lost her virginity to the permanently priapic Frank Harris in a room at the Café Royal. The lawyer, historian, diplomat and thriller-writer John Buchan was another habitué, as was his creation, the mining engineer turned secret agent Richard Hannay, hero of *The Thirty-Nine Steps*. In *The Adventure of the Illustrious Client* Sherlock Holmes is attacked outside the Café Royal, his assailants escaping through the main restaurant and out into **Glasshouse Street** at the rear. In 1894 a real life mystery occurred when night porter Marius Martin was found dying with two bullets in his head. Not everyone, however, was convinced by the air of cosmopolitan sophistication which was assumed to pervade the lush dining salon. Actor-manager Sir Herbert Beerbohm Tree observed tartly that "if you want to see English people at their most English, go to the Café Royal where they are trying their hardest to be French."

The Café Royal offered an enticing combination of opulence, smooth service and excellent food but unconstrained by the stuffiness normally associated with such delights. The wines, drawn from what was plausibly claimed to be the greatest cellar in London – Frank Harris claimed "the best ever seen on earth" – were outstanding.

It was estimated that the cellars, stretching out under Regent Street, held 50,000 bottles. Around 1900 a dinner for two, cooked under the supervision of Cavaliere Augusto Oddenino, cost £2 4s. 6d., including caviare, *foie gras*, quails, champagne and a liqueur.

The Café Royal was rebuilt in 1923-4 as part of the general redevelopment of **Nash**'s Regent Street. Features of the original décor, such as its celebrated red velvet benches and marble-topped tables, were reincorporated. Baedeker characterised it as "an artistic and Bohemian rendezvous", still worthy of a star. Court photographer Cecil Beaton thought the Grill Room the most beautiful dining room anywhere in London. Regular patrons by then included two future sovereigns, the exuberant Prince of Wales (Edward VIII) and his far more diffident younger brother, the Duke of York (George VI). A standing order in the waiters' instruction book decreed, with reference to the royal princes, "Always plain food. No fuss. Call head waiter at once and notify manager." By the 1930s there was a new literary coterie – drama critic and autobiographer James Agate, prolific crime writer Edgar Wallace, lawyer turned playwright A P Herbert, poets T S Eliot and Stephen Spender and influential reviewer Cyril Connolly. The new generation of avant-garde artists was represented by David Bomberg, Paul Nash and Jacob Epstein.

In 1948 the Café Royal was uniquely complimented by being selected as the venue for the first Officers' Reunion Dinner of the Army Catering Corps. In *The League of Gentlemen* (1960) Jack Hawkins recruits a team of misfit ex-officers for a bank heist over lunch in a private room there.

Bought by hotelier Charles Forte in 1954, the Café Royal was given yet another thorough refurbishment to extend its banqueting and conference facilities through eight storeys. Where Whistler once baited Wilde there now convened members of the education committee of the Guild of Architectural Ironmongers and earnest disciples of retail automation. Perhaps it was, indeed, time to call time ….

Cecil Calvert – Founder of Maryland

Cecil Calvert, second Baron Baltimore (1606-75), a convert to Roman Catholicism, promoted the development of the colony of Maryland, the first to offer toleration to Christians of all stripes. Circumstances – political and familial – prevented Calvert from ever actually going there in person. He is buried in **St Giles-in-the-Fields**, where there is a handsomely-lettered modern monument in his honour.

Cambridge Circus – Home of 'The Circus'

John le Carré's spymaster George Smiley has a room on the fifth floor in the building at the south-west corner from which he ran the ring of secret agents known as 'The Circus'. Cambridge Circus is dominated by the **Palace Theatre**. Nearby is the **Marquis of Granby** public house. The former bookshop at 84 **Charing Cross Road** which inspired the book and film of that name is now a café-bar.

Cambridge Theatre

Opened in Earlham Street, **Seven Dials** in 1930, the Cambridge enjoyed intermittent success with French plays and touring companies, including the Comedie Française, seasons of opera and operetta and foreign dance companies. Notable triumphs have included *Billy Liar* (1960), starring a young Albert Finney, and *Half a Sixpence* (1963), a musical version of H G Wells' *Kipps*, starring Tommy Steele. In 1965 film star Ingrid Bergman played opposite Michael Redgrave in Turgenev's *A Month in the Country.* 1970 was a golden year as John Hanson successfully revived romantic musical comedy with *The Desert Song* and *The Student Prince*, Maggie Smith led in an Ingmar Bergman production of Ibsen's *Hedda Gabler* and Laurence Olivier played Shylock in Jonathan Miller's staging of *The Merchant of Venice.* In 1979 the American musical *Chicago* began a long run, followed by others in the 1990s for *Fame* and *Grease.*

(www.cambridgetheatre.co.uk)

Canaletto – Master of Light

Venice was the birthplace, the home and the subject-matter of Giovanni Antonio Canal (known as Canaletto) (1697-1768), who built up a lucrative business selling views of his native city to well-heeled English *milords* on the Grand Tour, encouraged by the patronage of the British consul, Joseph Smith. Thanks in part to the disruption of the Grand Tour by the war of Austrian Succession (1740-8), Canaletto decided to move to London in May 1746, settling at 16 Silver Street (now 41 **Beak Street**) in the house of a cabinet-maker, Richard Wiggan. Apart from an eight-month return to Venice in 1750-51 he was to remain for a decade producing superbly-executed views of the Thames, St. Paul's, Westminster Bridge etc. **George III** acquired Consul Smith's entire collection of Canaletto's work – some fifty canvases and 142 drawings – for the royal collection in 1762. While he was in London Canaletto placed a newspaper advertisement inviting "any Gentleman that will be pleased to come to his House, to see a Picture done by him, being *A View of St. James's Park*" – which now, thanks to the capacious (£10,000,000) wallet of Andrew Lloyd Webber, can be seen – free – at Tate Britain. Another large collection of Canaletto drawings is in the British Museum. His paintings can also be seen in Sir John Soane's Museum and the **National Gallery**.(*Canaletto in England. A Venetian Artist Abroad 1746-55* Yale 2006)

Billie Carleton

Brought up by her aunt as a supposed orphan, elfin Flora Leonora Stewart (1896-1918) became teenage actress Billie Carleton, appearing in a Cochran revue at the **St Martin's Theatre**, a musical at the **Adelphi** and a farce at the **Prince of Wales's.** By August 1918 she was at the Haymarket, the West End's youngest leading lady. She was also involved with at least three rich men and had become a regular drug user. Billie Carleton died the day after a victory ball at the Albert Hall, probably of depressants taken for a cocaine-induced hangover. **Noel Coward**, who knew her, acknowledged her story as the inspiration for his first major stage success, *The Vortex*, which was ostensibly about drugs, though later interpretations insist that the real, unspoken issue was homosexuality, then impossible to present on stage.

Carlisle House

Two properties, one in Soho Square and the other nearby, have been known as Carlisle House.

The first Carlisle House, whose site is now covered by **St Patrick's,** was built ca. 1685 for the 2nd Earl of Carlisle and remained in the hands of the Howard family until 1753, when the lease was sold to the upholsterers Bradshaw and Saunders. They used the outbuildings as workshops but let the house (1754-8) to the Neapolitan ambassador. The house became notorious during the tenancy of **Mrs Cornelys** and continued as a place of entertainment after her downfall until its demolition in 1791. Of the two dwellings built on its site one survives as the presbytery of St Patrick's.

The second Carlisle House, bombed in 1941, stood virtually opposite, at the far western end of Carlisle Street. Built ca. 1685-7, it passed through the hands of titled tenants until occupied by the Countess of Carlisle, estranged wife of the 3rd earl. She lived there for almost thirty years until her

Carlisle House, Soho Square, when used by the forerunner of St Patrick's church.

A Promenade at Mrs Cornelys' home at Carlisle House, Soho Square.

Carlisle House in Carlisle Street, destroyed in the last war.

death in 1752. The house was subsequently bought by Domenico Angelo Malevolti Tremamondo (1716-1802), better known as Domenico Angelo.

Italian by birth, Angelo had studied fencing and horsemanship in Paris under the finest masters in Europe before arriving in England ca. 1755. He rapidly attracted the attention and approval of **George II** and was appointed tutor in arms to the future **George III**. In 1763 he published a handsomely-illustrated treatise on swordsmanship which was recognised as definitive. Carlisle House gave Angelo the space to cash in on his fame and it soon became the most fashionable school of arms and manners in all London. He built a riding-school in the back-garden and took in boarding students at 100 guineas a year.

Angelo's son, Henry Angelo (1760-1839), was sent to Eton, carried on the business and wrote an amusing, if somewhat selective, volume of memoirs. By then the Angelo academy had long since relocated to fashionable St James's, where it remained as a family business until 1897.

Carlisle House was, from the 1780s, sub-divided into workshops for craftsmen restoring pictures or carving woodwork. A Freemasons' lodge met in the former ballroom. In 1860 the building became a boarding-house for 'Clerical, Medical and Law Students', then Whittaker's Private Hotel. From 1873 to 1936 it was used as an antiques warehouse. It was then occupied by the British Board of Film Censors until it was destroyed in the last war. During the 1960s the new-built Carlisle House was occupied by a firm of printers called CAPS, which helped to revolutionise lithographic printing in London and elsewhere.

Carlisle Street

This short street of 1685-7 once terminated in **Carlisle House**. Nos. 4, 5 and 6 are of late seventeenth century. No. 6, once the home of musician **J C Smith**, is the editorial office of ***Private Eye***. The Partisan café at No. 7 – self-styled as "an anti-espresso bar' – offered its patrons the rival delights of agitprop chatter, folk song, poetry and chess. Founded in 1958 by Raphael Samuel (1934-96), pioneer of 'history from below', the café's menu was an intriguing combination of the proletarian and the provincial – borscht, Irish *peasant* stew, frankfurters, Breconshire mutton with caper sauce, apple dumplings, Viennese coffee etc. Above the Partisan café were the editorial offices of the ultra-left magazine *Black Dwarf*, a creation of the activist litterateur Tariq Ali, the poet Christopher Logue and the feminist historian Sheila Rowbotham.

Carnaby Street

In 1683 bricklayer Richard Taylor put up Karnaby House on the east side of what was soon built up as Carnaby Street and largely rebuilt in the 1720s (e.g. Nos 22, 23, 40). Many early inhabitants were **Huguenots**. Inderwick's at No. 45 is England's oldest pipe manufacturer, established in 1797. In 1820-5 the former Carnaby Market was built over to make the present east side of the street (e.g.

A plaque in Carnaby Street to commemorate John Stephen whose shops made the street famous for fashion.

Above, shoppers in Carnaby Street, 2009. 'A victim of its own hype' – Rough Guide
The mural at the corner of Broadwick Street and Carnaby Street celebrates Soho and its famous residents.

Nos. 21, 24-29) and the still attractive side-streets leading off it. By the mid-nineteenth century the street was predominantly commercial rather than residential. The first 'boutique' was opened in 1957 by John Stephen. Within a decade the name of Carnaby Street had been recognised by the *Oxford English Dictionary* as a synonym for "fashionable clothing for young people". The street was pedestrianised in 1963. Epitomising London's 'Swinging Sixties', Carnaby Street soon got stuck in its own self-created time warp. As early as 1968 one of its own shopkeepers moaned to a *Sunday Times* reporter that it had ceased to be a genuine showcase for trend-setting fashion and had descended into "a tourist attraction – nothing more." In *Bend It Like Beckham* Jess (Parminder Nagra) buys her football boots at sports superstore Soccer Scene at No. 46 and then relaxes at the **mock-Tudor** Three Greyhounds on Greek Street. Recently a whole new shop and restaurant quarter has been built between Carnaby Street and **Kingly Street**. (www.carnaby.co.uk)

The ornate Opera Tavern in Catherine Street.

Catherine Street

Laid out ca. 1631, Catherine Street was originally Brydges Street with the 1673 southern extension to the Strand named for the consort of **Charles II**, Catherine of Braganza. The name was applied to the whole street from 1873. The Fleece which stood (1632-88) at the corner of **Tavistock Street** had a reputation for murderous violence. The Rose Tavern (demolished 1775) was the setting for Tom Rakewell's drunken debauch illustrated in Plate 3 of **Hogarth**'s *The Rake's Progress*.

The **Theatre Royal**, Drury Lane opened in 1663.

For two centuries the street was notorious for its prostitutes. The offices of the ***Morning Post*** were here and at No. 4 ***The Builder***, whose purpose-built premises survive. **Thurston's** billiards equipment works was here from 1814 to 1901. The Opera Tavern at No. 21 was built in 1879 to the designs of prolific pub architect George Treacher. Mark Girouard commends it as a "nice example of vulgar stucco classicism". The **Duchess Theatre** opened in 1929.

The Edith Cavell statue, St Martin's Place

After working (1886-90) as a governess in Brussels, Edith Cavell (1865-1915) returned to England to train as a nurse at the London Hospital in Whitechapel. In 1906 she was invited back to Brussels to set up the Berkendael Medical Institute to train Belgian nurses. When war broke out in 1914 she cared for both Allied and German casualties but, once Brussels was occupied by the Germans, she also assisted some hundreds of British and French soldiers to escape. Arrested, she was held in solitary confinement for ten weeks and then court-martialled. Despite widespread pleas for mercy, notably from the neutral United States, Edith Cavell was shot at dawn on 12 October 12 1915. Her monument, directly opposite the **National Portrait Gallery**, is inscribed with her last words as recorded by the Revd Stirling Gahan who visited her on the eve of her death – "Patriotism is not enough. I must have no hatred or bitterness

National Icon – the Edith Cavell monument opposite the National Portrait Gallery.

Pedestrian paradise – Cecil Court, 2009, a place for quiet browsing.

for anyone." Three others convicted with her, two of them women, were reprieved following personal appeals from the Pope and the King of Spain. In Britain the rate of volunteering for the armed forces doubled in the two months after her execution. The *Daily Telegraph* mounted an appeal to collect money for a memorial statue. After the war Nurse Cavell's body was reinterred in Norwich Cathedral. The monument was unveiled by Queen Alexandra, a tireless worker for nursing causes, in March 1920. Even at the time it was not thought to be one of Sir George Frampton's more accomplished creations. 'The Norfolk Heroine' is also memorialised in the name of a mountain in the Canadian Rockies.

(Christine Farenhurst *A Cup of Cold Water: The Compassion of Nurse Edith Cavell* P & R Publishing 2007; Jack Batten *Silent in an Evil Time:The Brave War of Edith Cavell* Tundra Books 2007; www.edithcavell.org.uk)

Caves de France

The Caves de France in Dean Street stood next door to the **Colony Club** and was its antithesis in the sense that clientele tended to patronise either the one or the other. It promoted itself as a "social club for French-speaking people and meeting place for poets, painters, writers and artists."

Cecil Court

Now a pedestrian precinct famed for specialist bookshops, Cecil Court is named for Robert Cecil, Earl of Salisbury, who masterminded James VI of Scotland's accession to the throne of England after the death of Elizabeth I. The street was severely damaged by fire in 1735 but swiftly rebuilt. **Mozart** lodged here above Couzin's barbershop in 1764. Cecil Court was rebuilt to assume its present form in 1888-90. In 1961 a bungled robbery at No. 23, Louis Meier's antiquities shop, led to the fatal stabbing of shop assistant Mrs. Elsie May Batten. The police issued an 'Identikit' likeness of the suspect which led six days later to the arrest of Edwin Bush in **Old Compton Street**. Bush was found guilty and executed, the first murderer to be caught by the use of this novel technique.

Centre Point

" ... *barren phallus of egg-boxes without eggs*"
Alan Brownjohn *Ode to Centre Point*

The West End's most obtrusive skyscraper, designed by the prolific and unloved Col. Richard Seifert, was built between 1959 and 1966, the first in London to be put up without scaffolding. Its thirty-four storeys stand 385 feet (117 metres) high. Centre Point was deliberately kept unoccupied until 1975, by which time it was worth four times what it cost to build, making it the most profitable speculation in London's history. Unsurprisingly, it was reviled by the left-wing intelligentsia as a repellent symbol of rampant capitalism, totally out of scale with its surroundings and serving no useful purpose except capital appreciation for its begetter, the property developer Harry Hyams. It was refurbished in 2002 and was listed Grade II in 2003. A suffragette bookshop once occupied the site.

Centre Point – a 'repellent symbol of rampant capitalism'.

Sir William Chambers RA

Born in Sweden, Chambers (1726-96) voyaged to China as a teenager, then studied art and architecture in Italy and Paris before settling in **Poland Street** ca. 1755. Here he established the foundations of a brilliant career. Coming to the notice of Princess Augusta, creator of Kew Gardens, he adorned her pet project with *faux* Roman temples, fake ruins and the 200-foot high Chinese pagoda which stands to this day. Appointed tutor in architectural drawing to the future **George III**, Chambers consolidated his reputation with the publication of his *Treatise of Civil Architecture*.

In 1768 he became a founder member and first Treasurer of the Royal Academy and in 1771 was knighted by the king of Sweden. By 1772 he was ready to move on to Marylebone. Chambers' chief London legacy is Somerset House on the **Strand**, the first purpose-designed government office building in Britain. A portrait of Chambers by **Reynolds** is in the **National Portrait Gallery**.

(John Harris and Michael Snodin *William Chambers: Architect to George III* Yale University Press 1996)

Charing Cross Hospital

In 1815 Benjamin Golding (1793-1863), while still a medical student, opened his house to the poor to dispense free medical treatment from eight in the morning until one. By 1818 he had moved into premises at 16 Suffolk Street and in 1826 to 28 Villiers Street where the accommodation consisted of twelve beds. With the support of the public-spirited and scholarly Duke of Sussex in 1834 Golding was at last able to open a new hospital on the Strand, built to the designs of Decimus Burton and with accommodation for sixty beds. By 1904 there were 278 beds. Students at its prestigious medical school would include the missionary-explorer David Livingstone and 'Darwin's bulldog', T H Huxley. Charing Cross Hospital relocated to Fulham Palace Road in 1973. Afterwards, the building was briefly used as a hostel for the homeless and then converted to become a police station in 1974.

Charing Cross Road

"*I went first of all to Charing Cross Road; but couldn't find any book I really wanted to buy.*"
Arnold Bennett *Journal* 1926

This road is, like **Shaftesbury Avenue** which it crosses, a relatively new road. Parliamentary

Charing Cross Road bookstores in the 1920s. Though there are today fewer bookshops, there is still a good mix of new, secondhand and remainder stores.

permission for its construction was given in 1877 but the work was not completed until late in the following decade. Essentially a widening of the existing Crown Street and Castle Street, it also involved the demolition of some of the capital's most noisome slums. Despite the fact that the project was entrusted to the Metropolitan Board of Works' distinguished architect, George Vulliamy, and its engineer, Sir Joseph Bazalgette, the outcome was aesthetically disastrous.

Charing Cross Road is best-known as a street of bookshops – most famously **Foyle's** – and especially secondhand bookshops, though their number has declined in the last decade. The post-war correspondence between the American writer Helen Hanff and Marks & Co. was recast to become her 1971 best-seller *84 Charing Cross Road,* later filmed with Anthony Hopkins and Anne Bancroft in the leading roles. Regular customers of Marks & Co. (now no longer in existence) included George Bernard Shaw and Sigmund Freud. The proprietor's son, Leo Marks, was so intrigued by the shop's secret pricing code for rare books that he went on to become chief code-breaker for the Special Operations Executive during World War Two.

A flat at No. 20 Burleigh Mansions was used by T S Eliot (1888-1965) as a refuge from his deranged first wife, Viv.

Charles I statue

All statues are more or less visual untruths, in the case of Charles I (reigned 1625-49) markedly so. Unique as the first equestrian statue of an English monarch, the statue depicts him in armour and carrying the baton of a marshal. Small, shy, Scottish and stammering, Charles I, while an accomplished horseman and by no means lacking in personal courage, was far more interested in art than in the arts of war. Sculptor Hubert le Sueur (ca. 1595-ca.1650) took his inspiration for the pose from the masterly canvases of the king on horseback by his court painter Sir Anthony van Dyck, now to be seen in the **National Gallery**. These invariably fudged the issue of the king's diminutive stature by showing him on a 'great horse', with the viewer's perspective from below. Le Sueur's 'solution' was

The mounted statue of Charles I, at the south of Trafalgar Square. Aquatint by Rowlandson and Pugin, c.1808. In the centre of the picture is a pillory used for the punishment of offenders whose crimes were believed to have provoked general public indignation. However, when the writer Daniel Defoe was pilloried in 1703 for a satirical pamphlet about the church, he was pelted with flowers by a supportive populace.

foisted on him and specified in his contract – just make the king a whole foot taller. The most technically challenging piece of bronze casting ever attempted in England up to the time (1633), the statue was originally commissioned at a cost of £600 by Richard Weston, first Earl of Portland, who died in 1635. By 1644 Weston's estate at Roehampton – and the statue – had passed to the royalist Sir Richard Dawes, who had his possessions seized following the execution of the king and the abolition of the monarchy in 1649. The statue was bought for a knock-down price of £150 by three men from the parish of **St Paul's, Covent Garden**, who gave it temporary sanctuary in the churchyard. In 1655 the statue was sold on to John Rivett, a Holborn brazier for £215, to be melted down as scrap. This he did not do – but he did sell items, purportedly made from its metal, which were bought by parliamentarians as trophies and by royalists as relics. Rivett's ruse was sufficiently plausible to allay suspicions of his loyalty to the republican regime until its demise so that, at the Restoration in 1660, he was able to return the statue, intact – after an unfortunate misunderstanding which saw him arrested for falsely appropriating Crown property – to a delighted **Charles II**. After Charles II completed his purchase of the statue he commissioned his Master Mason, Joshua Marshall (1629-78) to carve a pedestal of Portland stone, designed by Sir Christopher Wren and elaborately embellished with trophies, shields and arms. The statue was finally erected at its present location in 1676, on the site of the former Eleanor Cross – thus enabling Charles I in effigy to stare down Whitehall to the site of his own execution outside the Banqueting House. Each year on 30 January, the anniversary of his death, wreaths are still laid to his memory at the statue by loyalists who venerate him as 'Charles the Martyr'. The more vengeful among them doubtless recall that, on the same spot, several of the regicides who had signed the king's death warrant, themselves suffered the horrendous death reserved for traitors, being hanged, drawn and quartered. **Pepys** was an eyewitness to the death of Major-General Harrison, sardonically observing that he looked as cheerful as a man could be expected to in the circumstances.

(Christopher Hibbert *Charles I: A Life of Religion, War and Treason* Palgrave 2007; Richard Cust *Charles I: A Political Life* Longman 2007; www.skcm.org)

Charles II statue

Charles II (1630-85), having spent much of his youth in exile, was famously determined never to go on his travels again. The same cannot be said of the statue of him in **Soho Square**. First erected in 1681, it was the work of Caius Gabriel Cibber, a Dane and father of the actor **Colley Cibber**, and originally formed the centre-piece of a grandiose monument probably modelled on Bernini's fountain on the Piazza Navona in Rome, with four flanking classical figures – 'old fathers with wet beards' – representing the Rivers Thames, Severn, Tyne and Humber. The whole thing became badly decayed and was swept away in the name of 'improvement' in 1875-6. Thanks, however, to the intervention of a local pillar of the community Mr T Blackwell of **Crosse and Blackwell**, whose premises overlooked the square, the statue was rescued and relocated in the grounds of Grimsdyke the extravagant pseudo-medieval pile built at Harrow Weald for the artist Frederick Goodall RA. The house was subsequently acquired by W S Gilbert (of Gilbert & Sullivan) whose widow bequeathed the statue back to it original location in 1938. By then its original central site had been usurped by the faux-Tudor kiosk (1925-6) which masks an electricity sub-station and is used by the square's maintenance crew to store their equipment. So the present location of the mobile monarch, sadly shorn of his aqueous courtiers, is to the north of its intended position. Even the cement wash inflicted on the king in 1987 has failed to obliterate entirely the louche air of a time-worn but successful survivor, an impression confirmed by Edward Hawker's depiction of the monarch on display in the **National Portrait Gallery**, slumped, rather than sitting, on his throne and regarding the onlooker with an air of quizzical ennui.

(Tim Harris *Restoration: Charles II and his Kingdoms 1660-85* Penguin 2006)

Mobile monarch – the statue of Charles II in Soho Square.

Chinatown

Although there were Chinese restaurants in Soho by the inter-war period the Chinese presence around **Gerrard Street** and **Lisle Street** is largely a post-war phenomenon. As late as 1950 *The Wonderful Story of London* observed that "not many Chinese live in Soho, though they run several restaurants there and in the vicinity." Chinatown then and before the last war was centred on Limehouse, in the East End.

The Communist Party's accession to power in China in 1949 caused a huge flight of refugees from Shanghai and Canton, thousands of whom came, via British-controlled Hong Kong, eventually to London. The uncertain future direction of post-war Soho deterred many British from investing in businesses there but sufficient Chinese were willing to take the risk and were rewarded with the patronage of ex-Servicemen who had acquired a taste for Chinese food 'out East', by students looking for a cheap meal and, more profitably, by theatre-goers pleasantly surprised to find restaurants still open after a performance.

Celebrations of Chinese New Year began in Soho in 1973. The three gateways on Gerrard Street date from 1985. The darker side of Chinatown –

Promoted to Imperial rank for the occasion, a Soho resident celebrates Chinese New Year.

exploitative labour conditions, illegal gambling, criminal Triad gangs etc. – was exposed in Timothy Mo's novel *Sour Sweet* (1982), published in the same year as seven people died in the firebombing of an illegal gambling den in Gerrard Street.

Although only a tiny percentage of London's Chinese population actually lives in Chinatown it is an important centre for the entire metropolitan community for specialist shopping, family reunions and celebrations and dining out, especially on Sundays. Soho's Chinatown also accommodates the headquarters of the Chinese Chamber of Commerce and the offices of the extensive Man, Pang and Cheung clans. Guanghua bookshop on Newport Market offers the capital's largest selection of Chinese publications.

(www.chinatown-online.co.uk)

Thomas Chippendale

Nos. 60-61 **St Martin's Lane** were leased by Thomas Chippendale (1718-79) in December 1753. In 1754 he published *The Gentleman and Cabinet Maker's Director*, the comprehensive furniture catalogue which made his name famous and ensured that his designs would be widely imitated. A second edition followed in 1759 and a third in 1762. Both Catherine the Great and Louis XVI are known to have had copies of the work. Chippendale also designed wallpaper, carpets and brassware. Chippendale's many prestigious clients included **Garrick**, **Mrs Cornelys** and Robert Adam.

Following Chippendale's death, the business passed to his son, also Thomas, who took over No. 62 as a personal residence and carried on the business until 1813. Despite the gibes of Thomas Sheraton, who judged Chippendale's designs to be "wholly antiquated", the entire stock was auctioned off in just two days.

(www.thechippendalesociety.co.uk)

Colley Cibber

Actor, manager, dramatist and Poet Laureate, Colley Cibber (1671-1757) was the son of the distinguished Danish sculptor who carved the statue of **Charles II** in **Soho Square.** Shrill-voiced, hatchet-faced, vain, tactless, snobbish, sycophantic and a shameless social climber, Cibber wrote a superb part for himself – the foppish rake-cum-hero Sir Novelty Fashion – in his very first play *Love's Last Shift, or The Fool in Fashion* (1696). In 1699 Cibber cobbled together a version of *Richard III* which imported whole passages from other Shakespeare plays and remained the definitive version for more than a century. As an extremely conscientious manager of **Theatre Royal Drury Lane** he produced a skilful adaptation of *Tartuffe* and completed

A verse printed beneath this 18th-century depiction of the Cider Cellars in Maiden Lane refers to the habituées as 'Sublimed with liquid fury'. But smoking appears to have been quite as important as cider.

Vanbrugh's unfinished last play as *The Provok'd Husband* (1728). As Poet Laureate (1730) Cibber was mercilessly attacked by **Henry Fielding** for allegedly committing an assault on the English language.

Cider Cellars, Maiden Lane

Established on the south side of **Maiden Lane** in 1730, the Cider Cellars attracted a clientele notably diverse in class and age but overwhelmingly male, including Disraeli, Thackeray and Louis-Napoleon Bonaparte, the future French emperor, Napoleon III. The consumption of cider was accompanied by the singing of raucous and risqué ballads.

The Cider Cellars closed in 1858 to make way for the enlargement of the **Adelphi** theatre.

Civil Service Stores

Established in 1864 by post office employees as a consumers' co-operative for bulk-buying tea, and then other groceries, at a discount, this venture was extended to other civil service employees the following year. Retail premises were opened, initially on Victoria Street, but relocated to No. 425 Strand in 1877. In 1927 the business severed its specific links with the civil service and was relaunched as a public company and general department store. A disastrous fire in 1982 put it out of business.

Willy Clarkson

Former actor Willy Clarkson (1861-1934) found his métier as a theatrical wig-maker. Such was his standing in thespian circles that the foundation stone for his business at 41-43 **Wardour Street** (see p.12) was laid by Sarah Bernhardt and the coping stone by **Henry Irving**. A further endorsement of Clarkson's reputation is the fact that the celebrated wife-murderer Dr Crippen wore a Clarkson wig when fleeing to Canada by ocean liner in 1910. The building, an inventive compound of Baroque and Art Deco by H M Wakley, architect of the Spice of Life pub on **Cambridge Circus**, is described enthusiastically by Pevsner as "a finer show in its small compass than some London theatre fronts". Clarkson's business carried on until 1940. The premises are now occupied by Wong Kei, the largest restaurant in **Chinatown**, capable of seating over five hundred diners.

The Club

Subsequently known as The Literary Club, this weekly meeting for elevated conversation (excluding politics) was co-founded in 1764 by **Dr Samuel Johnson** and **Sir Joshua Reynolds**. Members foregathered at the **Turk's Head Tavern** in **Gerrard Street** on Mondays at seven while Parliament sat. The original membership of nine included **Edmund Burke**, Oliver Goldsmith and the bibliophile Topham Beauclerk. This later expanded

"You're barred" – the Coach and Horses in 2009.

to thirty-five, embracing such luminaries as the actor-manager **David Garrick**, Johnson's biographer, **James Boswell**, the radical Charles James Fox, the dramatist **Richard Sheridan** and the philosopher Adam Smith. By the 1790s The Club had shifted its meetings to Sackville Street and included the historian of the Roman empire, Edward Gibbon, the orientalist and philologist Sir William Jones and the scientist **Sir Joseph Banks**.

Coach and Horses, Greek Street

The present pub dates from 1847. Its most celebrated habitué was the columnist **Jeffrey Bernard**. Others have included the actors Tom Baker, best known as a flamboyant incarnation of 'Dr. Who', John Hurt and Michael Elphick. The editorial staff of ***Private Eye*** meets for a fortnightly lunch in an upstairs room. The famously grumpy landlord, Norman Balon, who retired in 2006, published his own autobiographical account of the establishment under the singularly appropriate title of *You're Barred You Bastards.*

Cockpit Theatre

Built in 1609 as a cockfighting venue and converted into an indoor playhouse in 1616, the Cockpit stood on the site of the Peabody housing in Wild Street. Destroyed by a Puritan mob in 1617, it was rebuilt in 1618 as the appropriately named Phoenix. Closed (1642-60) by order of Parliament, it reopened in 1660 as The Cockpit. **Pepys** saw the *Merchant of Venice* there. It closed as a theatre c. 1664.

Coffee Bars

The coffee bars of the sixties were described as "varied, international, stimulating". They represented both a reaffirmation of the area's Italian community and the emergence of a sub-culture of youth, students and devotees of rock'n'roll. Imported from Italy, the novel Gaggia Espresso coffee machine produced an enticingly frothy beverage distinct from the dismal liquid Britons were used to. As the Gaggia company's headquarters was at No. 10 **Dean Street**, Soho's pre-eminence was a foregone conclusion. The Moka at No. 29 **Frith Street**, opened by Italian film star Gina Lollabrigida, claimed to be "London's first Espresso coffee bar. Patronised by over fifty nationalities." **Old Compton Street** alone mustered the Amalfi (noted for its murals, it closed in 2005), the Prego Bar Restaurant, Act One, Scene One ("Real French coffee. Where the film and theatrical celebrities gather"), the Pollo, Heaven and Hell ("Visit the unusual décor of the dive basement) and, most famously at No. 59, the Two I's, run by a couple of Australians but named for the original proprietors, the Irani brothers. The Two I's had the distinction of launching the rock'n'roll careers of Tommy Steele, Cliff Richard and the Shadows. Other notable establishments included the Source Café at No. 78 **Brewer Street**, the Café Rio at No. 58, which had a historic family archive on its walls and Lina Stores at No. 18; Bar Italia at No. 22 Frith Street and A. Angelucci at No. 23b; Lorelei at 21 **Bateman**

A plaque at No. 59 Old Compton Street celebrating the famous 2i's coffee bar.

Street and Bar Bruno at 101 **Wardour Street**. The New Piccadilly, established in 1951 at No. 8 Denman Street by Pietro Marioni was reckoned "a cathedral amongst caffs". In Covent Garden the Nucleus on Monmouth Street offered modern **jazz** until the early hours of the morning.

The function of the coffee bar was primarily social rather than nutritional, an autonomous arena of expression for that phenomenon, the teenager. In Dean Street Les Enfants Terribles offered "Music, songs and laughter a la Française". In **Carlisle Street** the Partisan was a centre for left-wing discussion and personalities.

(www.classiccafes.co.uk)

Coffee Houses

First opened in the 1650s, London's earliest coffee houses were concentrated in the City and frequented by men of business. After the Restoration of **Charles II** they proliferated in the Covent Garden area as centres of conversation and culture. Notable amongst them were the **Bedford**, **Button's**, **Old Slaughter's**, **Tom's** and **Will's**. Many local residents were periodic or short-term visitors, like **James Boswell**, lodging in single rooms or garrets scarcely suitable for entertaining friends, much less new acquaintances they wished to impress. Seeking congenial company they were content to pay the penny that secured their entry – and kept the riff-raff out. Apart from drinks and snacks the attractions invariably included a warm fire and a selection of (taxed and therefore quite expensive) periodicals and, often, the opportunity to play chess or cards.

(Anthony Clayton – *London's Coffee Houses: A Stimulating Story* Historical Publications 2003)

Colony Club

Founded in 1948 by **Muriel Belcher**, this famed drinking-hole is accommodated in unprepossessing upstairs premises at 41 **Dean Street** and has long been favoured by artists, actors and alcoholics. **Daniel Farson**'s *Soho in the Fifties* treats the Colony as the focal point of Soho's bohemian life. In Colin MacInnes' novel *England, Half English* the club features, thinly disguised, as Mabel's. Noted 'regulars' have included **Francis Bacon**, painter Lucian Freud, comedian **Peter Cook**, actor Trevor Howard and, more recently, avant garde artists Damien Hirst and Tracey Emin. Following Belcher's death in 1979, ownership passed to the equally aggressive barman Ian Board, who died in 1994, since when the tone of cross-counter venom has moderated somewhat. The Colony Club was re-created in a studio for John Maybury's *Love is the Devil*, in which Derek Jacobi played Francis Bacon and Tilda Swinton Muriel Belcher.

Communist Party of Great Britain

The headquarters of the CPGB were at No. 16 King Street from 1920 until 1980.

A raid on the building in 1925 led to prison sentences for a dozen, mostly high-ranking, party members on charges of sedition and incitement to mutiny. The party's national organizer, Douglas Springhall, lived at No. 11, a house owned by the CPGB. Springhall had been expelled from the Royal Navy for agitation, was imprisoned for the same offence during the General Strike of 1926 and served as the political commissar of the British component of the International Brigade during the Spanish Civil War. He was expelled from the Party in 1943 after being convicted of espionage in relation to Britain's efforts to develop the jet engine.

(www.cpgb.org.uk; www.communist-party.org.uk)

Joseph Conrad

Born of Polish parents in Russian-dominated Ukraine, Jozef Teodor Konrad Korzeniowski (1857-1924) settled in England in 1894 after twenty years at sea. Writing in English, his third language, he published his first novel at thirty-eight.

Conrad was a member of the literary circle which met at the Mont Blanc restaurant on **Gerrard Street** and a more occasional patron of the 43 Club. Soho is the setting for the pornographic bookshop managed as a front by the villainous Verloc in *The Secret Agent* (1907). Conrad's works were published by **Heinemann**.

(www.josephconradsociety.org)

Peter Cook

Peter Cook (1937-95) first came to public notice as a member of the cast of *Beyond the Fringe* at the **Fortune Theatre**. Initially created for the Edinburgh Fringe, it starred Cook, Dudley Moore, Jonathan Miller and Alan Bennett, then all recent Oxbridge graduates. It had no sets, costumes, music or girls and was a triumphant success, skilfully subverting the self-satisfactions of post-war Britain. On the strength of this success Cook started the ironically named Establishment Club in **Greek Street.** Modelled on the satirical nightclubs of Weimar

Joseph Conrad, an habitué of the Mont Blanc in Gerrard Street and of the 43 Club.

Germany, which as Cook sardonically observed "did so much to prevent the rise of Adolf Hitler", it was another triumph, prompting Cook to open a branch in New York. He also became a co-founder of *Private Eye*, of which he eventually became proprietor. In his absence the Establishment Club collapsed from financial pressures. In partnership with Dudley Moore, Cook made a series of television programmes *Not Only ... But Also* (1965-71), which were arguably the most inspired and sustained comedies ever broadcast. Cook passed his last decade gambling, golfing, watching television but, despite the best efforts of a devoted third wife, succumbed to alcoholism and boredom. (www.petercook.net)

John Singleton Copley RA

J S Copley (1738-1815), protégé and fellow-countryman of **Benjamin West**, lived at 28 **Leicester Square** from 1774 until 1783, during which period he was elected to the Royal Academy and painted *The Death of Chatham* (**National Portrait Gallery**), a massive group portrait of the House of Lords, and *The Death of Major Peirson* (Tate Gallery), a huge, dramatic depiction of the repulse of French troops from Jersey, which won

A plaque at 18 Greek Street commemorating Peter Cook. It reads: "Comedian and 'only twin' co-founded and ran the Establishment Club here 1961-1964".

immense acclaim. Copley, despite his successes, eventually declined into debt and dementia, eased by the comfort of a loving family. His son, as Lord Lyndhurst, became Lord Chancellor of England.

The American exile, John Singleton Copley, painted c. 1783 by his fellow American Gilbert Stuart.

Mrs Cornelys

Theresa Cornelys (1723-97) was born in Venice as Theresa Imer. Having married an Italian, been the mistress successively of a Venetian senator, a German nobleman and a Dutch merchant, this actress/singer/dancer and theatre manager also gave birth to two children, one of which claimed to be the offspring of Casanova, who certainly wrote of her in detail in his *Memoirs*. Settling in England in 1759 in the company of a cellist (and con-man), John Freeman (*aka* Fermor), she rented and refurbished **Carlisle House** on **Soho Square.** as a venue for polite assemblies. Beginning with modest entertainments, consisting of dancing and cards, she escalated her offerings to include masquerades and a programme of concerts directed by **J C Bach** and built a ballroom and banqueting room onto the back of the house. Entry by subscription and pre-paid tickets gave Mrs Cornelys' entertainments an air of spurious exclusivity, for the occasions were often immensely overcrowded. Young **Fanny Burney** was dazzled by the décor and the company but appalled by the crush and the heat. Even the blasé Horace Walpole felt bound to attend, if only to sneer. Mrs Cornelys reached her apogee in 1768 when her patrons included the Prince of Monaco and the King of Denmark. According to Casanova she had a country place at Hammersmith, kept six horses and had an entourage which included a companion, a mute, three secretaries and thirty-two servants. Recklessly extravagant and defiant of respectable opinion, Mrs Cornelys made enemies, not least among her long-suffering creditors and the proprietors of rival attractions. Repeatedly fined for keeping "a disorderly house", her fate was sealed by the opening of the **Pantheon** on Oxford Street, which lured away much of her clientele. By 1772 she was bankrupt and imprisoned for debt. Although she returned to Carlisle House for its new owners, her decline was irreversible. A pathetic attempt to set up a business in Knightsbridge selling asses' milk got her on the wrong side of creditors again and she died in the Fleet Prison.

A vicious caricature of Mrs Cornelys by stage designer Philippe Jacques de Loutherbourg (1740-1812), dated 1776.

Country Life

The **Tavistock Street** office of *Country Life* magazine was the first (1904) major building to be designed by Sir Edwin Lutyens (1869-1944). Lutyens' work was assiduously promoted by the magazine, for whose eccentric proprietor, Edward Hudson, the architect had designed (1899-1902) a majestic Arts and Crafts mansion, Deanery Gardens at Sonning in Berkshire. Lutyens also designed the clock on the former **Newnes** building in **Southampton Street**.(www.countrylife.co.uk)

Covent Garden Market

"*...fruit women screamed, carters fought, cabbage stalks and rotten apples accumulated in heaps at the thresholds of the Countess of Berkshire and the Bishop of Durham.*" T B Macaulay

When the Covent Garden fruit and vegetable market moved out to Nine Elms in November 1974 horrendous plans existed to transform the Covent Garden area into a hotel/conference/commercial complex. These were successfully fought off and the old market buildings became the centre of the area's renaissance as a shopping, eating and tourist centre.

The market began informally in the 1650s as a cluster of stalls in the **Piazza** behind the back wall of **Bedford House**, a mansion on the north side of The Strand. The Earl of Bedford, having decided to turn a nuisance into a source of income, in 1670

View of Covent Garden Market, looking towards St Paul's church, before the erection of the present market buildings. Aquatint by Rowlandson and Pugin c. 1808. Thomas Archer House (see p. 5) may be seen on the right – the first house beyond the colonnaded prremises.

got a licence from **Charles II** to hold a market every day except Sunday and Christmas Day. In practice the market was held three times a week. The closure (1737) of the Stocks Market in the City greatly boosted the trade of Covent Garden and a substantial rebuilding took place in 1748.

Transient residents of the area could not only buy their provisions but also lavender to sweeten their lodgings and hedgehogs to rid them of bugs and beetles. Continued expansion led to the erection of **Charles Fowler's** handsome market buildings in 1828-30. The Jubilee Market to the south was built (1904) for the sale of imported flowers. A Flower Market was built in the south-east, a building which now houses the London Transport Museum. The Floral Hall, a private venture, was built adjacent to the Royal Opera House in Bow Street, but in 1887 this was bought by the Bedford family and used for a foreign fruit market. It is now part of the facilities of the Royal Opera House.

Even in the early 20th century the market was a byword for traffic congestion and confusion and in 1918 the 9th Duke of Bedford was grateful to sell out his interest to the Covent Garden Estate Co., a private company owned by the family of Sir Thomas

A Covent Garden porter in the 1920s, carrying 25 empty vegetable baskets.

Beecham, the conductor and artistic saviour of the **Royal Opera House**. In 1961 the Company was superseded by a Covent Garden Market Authority established by Act of Parliament.

Covent Garden Theatre, Bow Street

What is now the **Royal Opera House** began as a theatre, built in 1732 for John Rich, famed for his playing of Harlequin, who had made a fortune out of John Gay's smash hit *The Beggar's Opera* (1728). The most luxurious theatre built in London to date, its opening was celebrated in an engraving by **Hogarth**. Star performers at Covent Garden included **Garrick**, **Macklin** and **Peg Woffington**. **Sheridan** had a great success with *The Rivals* (1775). Substantially rebuilt in 1792, the theatre burned down in 1808 and was rebuilt by 1809 to designs by **Sir Robert Smirke**. The management's attempt to offset the rebuilding costs by raising ticket prices led to 'Old Price Riots' for 61 nights until the management caved in. In 1812 **Mrs Siddons** gave her farewell performance. Opera was introduced, including the first English performances of **Mozart**'s *Don Giovanni* (1817) and *Marriage of Figaro* (1819). Under **Charles Kemble** the theatre came near to financial ruin. In the year of Kemble's retirement, **Kean** collapsed with a stroke while playing *Othello*. In 1847 Covent Garden was reopened as the Royal Italian Opera under Italian composer Giuseppe Persiani. Frederick Gye took over in 1849 and staged the English premieres of Verdi's *Rigoletto* (1853) and *Il Trovatore* (1855). In 1855 John Anderson took a sub-lease and on the last day of his lease, in 1857, the theatre was destroyed by fire. *(See **Royal Opera House** for its subsequent history)*

Coventry Street

Built up from 1681 and named for Henry Coventry, Secretary of State to **Charles II**, Coventry Street had become primarily commercial by the nineteenth century. Linking **Leicester Square** and **Piccadilly Circus**, it has been more notable for establishments of recreation and refreshment than for its residents – notably Scott's fish restaurant, the first Lyons' Corner House, the **Trocadero**, the **Café de Paris** and the **Prince of Wales** theatre.

Covent Garden Theatre depicted c.1808. The audience seems more interested in itself than the stage.

A Talent to Amuse – Noel Coward.

Noel Coward

A lifelong man of the theatre, the ultra-versatile (Sir) Noel Pierce Coward (1899-1973) is memorialised by a bar at the **Phoenix** theatre and a statue at the **Theatre Royal Drury Lane.** A regular patron of **The Ivy restaurant**, he was often guest of honour at the parties of his friend, **Clemence Dane**. Coward's financial security was assured from 1951 when he appeared in cabaret, singing his own songs, at the **Café de Paris**. Three more sell-out seasons followed, and then a month's booking in Las Vegas which paid $140,000 and opened up the lucrative world of American television and film. A portrait by Edward Seago is in the Phoenix Theatre and the **Garrick Club** and another by Clemence Dane in the **National Portrait Gallery**.

(www.noelcoward.net)

Noel Coward Theatre, St Martin's Lane

Built in 1903, this opened as the New Theatre, enjoying early success with Baroness Orczy's *The Scarlet Pimpernel* (1905) which then became a novel and later a film. Landmark productions have included **Noel Coward**'s first West End play (1920), the first London staging of Shaw's *St. Joan* (1924), Gielgud's triumphant *Richard of Bordeaux* (1933), (Sir) Ralph Richardson's commanding performances in the name roles of *Peer Gynt* (1944) and *Uncle Vanya* (1946), T S Eliot's *The Cocktail Party* (1950), Dylan Thomas's *Under Milk Wood* (1956), *Gigi* (1956) and Lionel Bart's *Oliver!* (1960-66), based on **Dickens**' *Oliver Twist,* which ran for 2,618 performances. During World War Two the theatre offered a temporary home to both the Old Vic and Sadler's Wells companies. In 1973 the name was changed to The Albery in compliment to past manager Sir Bronson Albery (1881-1971), stepson of Charles Wyndham and co-founder of the **Arts Theatre**. The present name was adopted in 2006.

Cranbourn Street

Built up from the 1670s, this was where **Hogarth** served his apprenticeship to the engraver Ellis Gamble. It was famous for the sale of cheap straw bonnets and millinery. The street was widened and extended in 1843. The Warner Cinema stands on the site of **Daly's Theatre**. A plaque at 38-44 records the birthplace of the socialist intellectual and activist Sidney Webb (1859-1947) who was one of the founders of the Fabian Society, the *New Statesman* and the London School of Economics. A plaque at Nos. 77-8 marks the site of **Old Slaughter's** coffee house.

Crosse and Blackwell

"Throughout the world Soho Square ... is now chiefly known as the place of the principal factories and offices of Messrs. Crosse and Blackwell."

In 1830 the company known as West and Wyatt, which could trace its origins back to 1706, was bought out by two former apprentices Edmund Crosse and Thomas Blackwell. Specialising in preserved foodstuffs, such as pickles, sauces and condiments, which could survive long distances and hot climates, the new firm found a ready market for its products not only at home but among culinary exiles in Britain's vast colonial empire. Mustard pickle was an early success. Canned soups were introduced in 1862, followed by mango chutney and marmalade in 1866.

The firm received its first royal warrant in 1837 on the accession of Queen Victoria. The main office was at 21 Soho Square. In 1876 an imposing block of stables was built on Crown Street to the designs of R L Roumieu but these were subsequently demolished to make way for the construction of **Charing Cross Road**. Other Roumieu buildings for the firm survive on Charing Cross Road as Nos. 114-16 (1888) and 147-155 (1877-85). By the end of the century the company had 2,000 employees, its own wharves at Lambeth and Millwall, a plant in the Caledonian Road producing a million gallons of vinegar a year and a 'lemon squeezing factory' at Vauxhall. The five-storey factory flanked by Sutton Street and facing onto Charing Cross Road was demolished in the 1920s to make way for the **Astoria** cinema. Thomas Blackwell held practically every parochial office in Soho, becoming a JP and High Sheriff for Middlesex. Together with his partner he also "took the lead in discountenancing the dangerous artificial colouring of green fruits and vegetables" which was rife in the Victorian food-processing industry. The name of Crosse and Blackwell became synonymous with such British staples as salad cream and baked beans. The firm also built up a portfolio of brands to control such household names as Kieller's marmalade, Gale's honey, Typhoo tea, Rowntree's jelly, Sarson's vinegar and Branston pickle. Taken over by Nestlé in 1950, in 2002 the UK side of the business became part of Premier International Foods. (www.crosseandblackwell.com)

Crown and Two Chairmen, Dean Street

The Crown and Two Chairmen is claimed to have acquired its unique name because "it was here that sedan chairmen waited when Queen Anne was sitting for her portrait at **Sir James Thornhill's** house, No. 74, still standing on the opposite side of the street."

Thornhill was employed by Queen Anne to decorate several of the royal palaces and according to the first edition of *The Dictionary of National Biography* did live at No. 75 Dean Street – though this now seems doubtful. Even if he did, it seems unlikely that the Queen should have come to him rather than vice versa and even less plausible that she should come by sedan chair, rather than a carriage.

Given his proclivity for a pint or two **Karl Marx** might well have popped in to seek solace from his squalid lodgings next door. George Orwell and Graham Greene were also patrons, though many other Soho watering-holes could claim the distinction of their custom.

The Crown and Two Chairmen in Dean Street.

Edmund Curll

"odious in his person, scandalous in his fame"
Weekly Journal 1718

Publisher, pornographer, pamphleteer, publicity-seeker, peddler of patent medicines and literary pirate, Edmund Curll (1683-1747) managed to provoke enmity from antagonists ranging in scale from Alexander Pope to the boys of Westminster School.

Publication of *Venus in the Cloister; or the Nun in her Smock* and *De usu Flagrorum* cost him a spell in the pillory at Charing Cross and five months in prison. Printing pornography became known in his day as *Curlicism*. Between 1723 and his death Curll lived variously "over against **Catherine Street**", and in **Bow Street**, Burleigh Street and **Rose Street.**

John Harrison Curtis

An early specialist in the treatment of ear problems, and more noted for his confidence than his qualifications, John Curtis (1778-1860) in 1816 founded the Dispensary for Diseases of the Ear at 38 **Carlisle Street**, Britain's first such specialist establishment. Licensed doctors considered Curtis a quack but his wife was wealthy and well-connected, enabling him to attract many patients of means and position. The hospital proved so successful that in 1820 it moved to larger premises at 10 **Dean Street** and gained the patronage of

George IV. In 1838, at the peak of his career, Curtis wrote a letter to *The Lancet* claiming that one of the commonest causes of deafness was a deficiency of earwax, which could be remedied by treating the ear with creosote. The outrage this display of ignorance provoked set Curtis's career on a downward spiral which ended in debt, flight and death in a Manx asylum. Curtis's hospital moved to **Frith Street** in 1876 and in 1904 to new buildings at 42-43 Dean Street, when it was renamed the Royal Ear Hospital. It moved out to Huntley Street, Bloomsbury in 1926. The ground floor is now a Malaysian restaurant and the upper floors are the premises of the **Groucho Club**.

Daly's Theatre, 2 Cranbourn Street

This 600-seat theatre was initially under the direction of the American manager and dramatist Augustin Daly (1839-99). Apart from Shakespeare's comedies, its early presentations included *La Dame aux Camelias* and *A Gaiety Girl*. Under the masterly George Edwardes (1852-1915) Daly's put on a succession of cheery musical comedies to become one of the West End's most fashionable venues. Its greatest triumph, however, came with *The Maid of the Mountains* (1917), which ran for 1,352 performances. After almost two decades of indifferent success Daly's was demolished in 1937 to make way for the Warner cinema.

A poster by Alick Ritchie. Posters for London Underground by the same artist can be seen in the London Transport Museum.

Faithful friend – Clemence Dane by Frederic Yates, c. 1917.

Clemence Dane

Clemence Dane was the pen-name of Winifred Ashton (1888-1965). Initially trained as a painter, she was also an actress and teacher before becoming a full-time writer, who produced ten novels, thirty plays and won a screenplay Oscar (1946), although she never again managed to match the success of her first play *A Bill of Divorcement* (1921), which ran for 401 performances at the **St. Martin's Theatre**. Ashton's prolific output also included work for radio and television as well as detective stories, and an affectionate if rather rambling history of Covent Garden, *London has a Garden* (1964). Dane was a member of the **Detection Club** and a close friend of the much-travelled **Noel**

Coward, whom she taught to paint and for whom she frequently threw 'welcome home' parties in the modest **Tavistock Street** flat where she passed most of her adult life. Clemence Dane was the inspiration for the medium Madam Arcati in Coward's *Blithe Spirit*. Her portrait and bust of Coward are in the **National Portrait Gallery**. Her own memorial is in St Paul's, Covent Garden.

Marianne Davies

A prodigy, Marianne Davies (1743-?1816) made her musical debut at **Hickford's Rooms**, aged seven, playing a flute concerto and then harpsichord concerto by Handel. At the time her family lived in **Long Acre**. In 1762 she gave the world premiere performance of Ben Franklin's glass 'armonica', of which she thereafter had a monopoly. She was subsequently overshadowed by her younger sister, the singer Cecilia Davies (?1750-1836). After enjoying success and acclaim amongst the crowned heads of Europe the sisters returned to London ultimately to die in poverty and obscurity.

John Deakin

Originally an aspirant painter, John Deakin (1912-72) passed World War Two in Malta as a sergeant in an army film and photographic unit. Deakin later proved mediocre as a fashion photographer but excelled at portraiture, his subjects including Yves Montand, Dylan Thomas, Maria Callas and Picasso. His most outstanding portraits were however, of his Soho circle, totally uncompromising in their avoidance of the slightest flattery, what **Daniel Farson** called "prison mugshots taken by a real artist". One of **Francis Bacon's** most constant drinking companions, Deakin lived on **Berwick Street**, was an habitué of the **French House** and, until barred, the **Colony Room**. His life's work, subsequently honoured with an exhibition at the **National Portrait Gallery**, was literally salvaged from under his bed. Daniel Farson's *Soho in the Fifties* devoted almost a third of its text to the sayings and doings of John Deakin, whom **George Melly** described as "a vicious little drunk of such inventive malice and implacable bitchiness that it's surprising he didn't choke on his own venom". Examples of Deakin's work can be seen in the **National Portrait Gallery** and on the website of **The French House**.

(Robin Muir *A Maverick Eye* Thames and Hudson 2002)

75 Dean Street, supposed home of Sir James Thornhill.

Dean Street

Built up ca. 1678- 1697, partly by **Barbon** and **Frith**, Dean Street may have been so named in compliment to Henry Compton, Bishop of London, who was also Dean of the Chapels Royal. No. 29 is of ca. 1692. Survivors from the major rebuilding of the 1730s include Nos. 26-8, 33, 39-41, 67-8, 69-70, 76-9 and 94. No. 90 is of 1756-67 and No. 88 has a delightful bow-front of 1791. No. 75, once supposed to have been the home of the painter **Sir James Thornhill** was wonderfully painted with *trompe-l'oeil* effects. In 1914 it was the subject of the first Preservation Order under the terms of the Ancient Monuments Act (1913) but the house was nevertheless demolished in 1923. The stair-case and ground-floor rooms were reconstructed at the Art Institute of Chicago but the paintings were lost for ever.

Sculptor and skinflint Joseph Nollekens (1737-1823) was born at No. 29. Actress **Peg Woffington** lived at No. 78 in 1740-48. **Karl Marx** lived at Nos 64 and 28.

By the late eighteenth century Dean Street had become something of an artistic colony with residents including history painter Francis Hayman RA (1708-76), from 1765 until his death, decorative painter Jean-Francois Rigaud RA (1742-1810) from 1774 to 1777, architect Thomas Hardwick (1752-1829) in 1783 and William Beechey (1753-1839), best known for his portrait of **Nelson**, in 1791. An artistic coterie attached to the fashionable architect **James 'Athenian' Stuart** (1713-88) gathered at the Blue Posts public house. In the 1790s the Italian

The Soho Theatre in Dean Street.

composer Domenico Corri ran a music publishing and **musical instrument** business at No. 90 with his son-in-law the Czech musician J L Dussek.

Sculptor **William Behnes** lived at No. 91 between 1823 and 1833. This site was rebuilt (1911-13) for the West End Hospital for Nervous Diseases (which actually treated venereal infections).

No. 23 became Morland's Hotel, run by Henry, brother of artist **George Morland** in 1798. From 1813 to 1849 No. 33 was Walker's Hotel. The Royal Ear Hospital, established at No. 10 in 1816, returned to occupy purpose-built premises at Nos. 42-3 between 1904 and 1927. The **Royalty Theatre** was at the site of Nos. 73-4.

Public houses include the **Crown and Two Chairmen**, Golden Lion and **French House** and the Bath House (1899). Other noted places of refreshment include the **Colony Club** at No. 41 and the **Groucho Club** at No. 44, which occupies the former site of Gennaro's, claimed to have been Soho's first Italian restaurant.

No. 21 was the site of the Venetian Ambassador's chapel, then (1748-63) Caldwell's Assembly Rooms, where **Mozart** played, later a dancing academy, an auction room and warehouse and St Anne's National School (1872-1939). In 1944 it became the West End Great Synagogue and was rebuilt (1961-3) to incorporate the Ben Uri Art Society Gallery before being converted (1999-2000) to become the Soho Theatre.

Denmark Street

Built up ca. 1687, London's 'Tin Pan Alley' is named for George of Denmark (1653-1708), adored consort of Queen Anne, a man judged so stupid by his contemporaries that he was, despite much pleading, never permitted command of any military force. The accomplished painter **Johann Zoffany** lived for a while at No. 9, and **Augustus Siebe** was at No. 5.

Initially dominated by music publishers, this short street later became notable for its recording studios and is now known for the sale of musical instruments. The Rose Morris music shop at No. 11 went into business in 1919. The *Melody Maker* weekly music magazine was launched at No. 19 in 1926; taken over by Odham's in 1929, it survived until 2000. No. 20 was the offices of Mills Music Ltd, where in 1965 Elton John earned £5 a week as an office boy; in the same year the firm turned down the offer of recording Paul Simon's songbook. Lionel Bart worked as an in-house songsmith at No. 21, next door, writing hits for **Adam Faith** and Marty Wilde. Rhodes Music at No. 22 supplied guitars to Pete Townshend and Eric Clapton; the Tin Pan Alley studio in the basement was used by Manfred Mann and the Small Faces. Denmark Productions at No. 25 managed the quintessential London band, The Kinks. On the opposite side of the road the Rolling Stones recorded their 1964 debut album at the Regent Sound Studios at No. 4; other recording artists who used this facility included Elton John and Steven Georgiou *aka* Cat Stevens *aka* Yusuf Islam, who was born minutes away on New Oxford Street.

At No. 5 the *New Musical Express* had its first offices in 1952. No. 7 was the home of Box and Cox music publishers whose greatest hit was *I've Got a Lovely Bunch of Coconuts*. The coffee bar at 9a, formerly La Gioconda restaurant, was a favoured hangout of David Bowie, the Small Faces and the Clash.

De Hems, 11 Macclesfield Street

London's pre-eminent Dutch pub stands on the site of a coaching inn of 1685 known as the Horse and Dolphin, which was pulled down in 1890. Originally named The Macclesfield, De Hems was designed by specialist pub architects Savile and

De Hems in Macclesfield Street.

Martin. When De Hem, a retired Dutch sea captain, took over he began to sell oysters, saving the shells (300,000 of them!) to decorate the walls, an aesthetic statement thankfully consigned to a skip in the 1950s. During World War II the pub served as a rendezvous for Dutch refugees and resistance fighters. The name was formally changed to De Hems in 1959. The pub sells imported Dutch beers and genevers and Dutch equivalents of tapas.

Thomas De Quincey

De Quincey (1785-1859) ran away from his Manchester mercantile family at seventeen, drifted through Wales and finally pitched up in Soho, where he shared an untenanted house at No. 61 **Greek Street** with a waif from the streets. By his own account de Quincey would have starved to death but for the kindness of Ann, a teenage prostitute, whom he met in **Soho Square** and who, when he fell faint from hunger, spent her last sixpence on wine to revive him. De Quincey, having managed to raise a loan from an acquaintance at Eton, arranged to meet Ann on Oxford Street but the rendezvous failed. Despite frantic searching he never saw her again, although the impression she had made on him remained lifelong. Reconciled with his family, de Quincey went up to Oxford where his brilliance was recognised but his intellect was not engaged. During a visit to London, cursed with toothache and facial neuralgia, he bought

Thomas de Quincey in 1855 – "a little, artless, simple-seeming body"

laudanum to soothe the pain from a druggist's "near the Pantheon". This marked the beginning of a lifelong addiction. Returning to London in 1821 in search of literary work de Quincey settled at No. 36 **Tavistock Street** (then 4 York Place) and began writing the stylistic masterpiece that was to make him famous - *Confessions of an English Opium Eater*, which contains a vivid account of his relationship with mysterious, merciful Ann. (www.queens.ca/english/tdq/)

The Detection Club

Emerging in the late 1920s the Detection Club was a self-selecting coterie of mystery writers who met in rooms on the first floor of 31 **Gerrard Street**. New members were initiated at the annual banquet, which was presided over by a 'Ruler', clad in Chinese robes, a post held by G K Chesterton (1874-1936), Dorothy L Sayers (1893-1957), Agatha Christie (1890-1976), Julian Symons and H R F Keating. *The Rite of Initiation*, written by Sayers, a committed Anglican and churchwarden at **St Anne's**, was a parody of *The Book of Common Prayer*, which required candidates to pledge themselves to maintain the purity of the mystery genre by never writing plots which depended on "Divine Revelation, Feminine Intuition, Mumbo-Jumbo, Jiggery-Pokery, Coincidence or the Act of

Charles Dickens, based on a photograph taken when he was writing David Copperfield, *his favourite book.*

God", to be moderate in their invocation of "Gangs, Conspiracies, Death-Rays, Ghosts … Trap-doors, Chinamen", and "utterly foreswear Mysterious Poisons unknown to Science". After World War Two Dorothy Sayers' church connections enabled the club to acquire the use of a room in **Kingly Street**. Dorothy Sayers' fictional hero, Lord Peter Wimsey, dines (dreadfully) at the mythical 'Soviet Club' in Gerrard Street, which was based on the Detection Club.

Charles Dickens

From 1859 until his death, the London home of Charles Dickens (1812-70) was over the offices of *All the Year Round* at No. 26 **Wellington Street**. His contributors included Mrs. Gaskell and his friend Wilkie Collins, whose pioneering detective thriller, *The Moonstone*, first appeared in *Household Words* as a serial. Dickens' fascination with the Covent Garden area began as a boy when he read a description of the area by the hack playwright George Colman:

"Centrick, in London noise, and London follies,
Proud Covent Garden blooms, in smoky glory;
For chairmen, coffee-rooms, piazzas, dollies,
Cabbages, and comedians, famed in story."

According to Dickens' friend and first biographer, John Forster, "he remembered snuffing up the flavour of the faded cabbage-leaves as if it were the very breath of comic fiction". When his father was imprisoned for debt when he was twelve, Dickens took employment in Warren's blacking factory at 30 Hungerford Stairs. (The location is now marked by a plaque in Chandos Place). Wrenched from the familiar comfort of home, family and school Dickens passed his days pasting labels onto bottles of blacking, enduring a "grief and humiliation" softened only by the kindly protection of his young supervisor, Bob Fagin, whose name he would later appropriate for his most famous villain.

Dickens returned to Covent Garden under happier circumstances when he established the editorial offices of his magazine, *Household Words*, at No. 16 Wellington Street.

Covent Garden figures prominently in *Little Dorritt*, for whom it was "a place of past and present mystery, romance, abundance, want, beauty, ugliness, fair country gardens, and foul street gutters; all confused together". The market also features in *Sketches by Boz* (*'The Streets – Morning'*), *The Old Curiosity Shop*, *Martin Chuzzlewit*, *Our Mutual Friend* and *The Uncommercial Traveller*. In *Oliver Twist* Bill Sikes refers to it as 'Common Garden', a place where he can recruit accomplices for a night's nefariousness from a tribe of more than fifty feral youths. **Bow Street Magistrates' court** features in both *Oliver Twist* and *Barnaby Rudge*. Hummum's Hotel figures in *Sketches by Boz* and *Great Expectations*.

Sketches by Boz also contains accounts of *'Seven Dials'* and *'Meditations in Monmouth Street'*. **Monmouth Street** was the centre of the trade in second-hand clothes but **Seven Dials** haunted Dickens as the location of "wild prodigies of wickedness, want and beggary". In *Nicholas Nickleby* Mantalini is discovered, turning a mangle, in a cellar "in the "labyrinth of streets which lies between Seven Dials and Soho", while Ralph Nickleby lives in **Golden Square**. In *Great Expectations* the offices of the manipulative lawyer, Mr Jaggers, are in **Gerrard Street** in "a stately house of its kind but dolefully in want of painting."

In June 1857 Dickens gave the first of his celebrated public readings at **St Martin's Hall** in

Long Acre. The occasion was organised to raise funds for the family of his friend, the author and journalist Douglas Jerrold, who had recently died, leaving his wife and children in straitened circumstances. Dickens' chosen text was, despite the season, *A Christmas Carol*. So many were turned away that he had to undertake a repeat performance. Dickens, a keen participant in amateur dramatics, not only enjoyed the experience immensely but realised that it strengthened his relationship with his readers and could also make him a very great deal of money. In April 1858 Dickens returned to the same venue to read *The Cricket on the Hearth* in the first of the paid public performances which he would henceforth undertake for the rest of his life and the strain of which would, in the opinion of many, so undermine his health that they would contribute directly to his early death.

In the **National Portrait Gallery** is a portrait of Dickens at twenty-seven, by Irish painter Daniel Maclise. Thackeray thought it "as a likeness perfectly amazing". Dickens' first marital home, at 48 Doughty Street in Bloomsbury, the only one of his London residences to survive is now the Dickens Museum, about twenty minutes brisk walk from Covent Garden.

(Peter Ackroyd *Dickens* Sinclair Stevenson 1990; Paul Schlicke (ed) *Oxford Reader's Companion to Dickens* Oxford University Press 1999; www.dickensfellowship.org; www.dickensmuseum.org)

Sir Kenelm Digby

A Renaissance man in his versatility, the exceptionally handsome and well-spoken Sir Kenelm Digby (1603-65) defeated a Franco-Venetian fleet in Scanderoon harbour when he was just twenty-five, wooed and won the celebrated beauty Venetia Stanley, killed a French lord in a duel for insulting the name of **Charles I**, served as an agent for Cromwell and still managed to secure the post of chancellor to the dowager queen, Henrietta Maria. Digby also wrote works of theology, enjoyed the friendship of Ben Jonson, John Evelyn, Thomas Hobbes and Rene Descartes and, as a founder member of the Royal Society, made his home in **King Street** a lively centre of scientific discussion. Not bad for the son of an executed Gunpowder Plot conspirator.

Dog and Duck, Frith Street

Recalling Soho's past as a hunting-ground, the name of the Dog and Duck was first recorded in 1743. The present pub dates from 1897 and has exuberant interior décor featuring ceramic tiles and mirrors. George Orwell (1903-50) was a regular.

Donmar Warehouse

In the 1870s what is now a 250-seat theatre at No. 41 Earlham Street was a brewery vat room and hop warehouse. By the 1920s it had been the first film studio to use colour and was being used as a depot for ripening bananas. In 1961 it was rebuilt by the Donmar company formed by Donald Albery and Margot Fonteyn to be used as a rehearsal studio by the London Festival Ballet. From 1977 the building was the London home of the Royal Shakespeare Company and then (1981-9) a base for touring companies. The Donmar's emergence as an outstanding centre of theatrical excellence in its own right dates from the appointment of Oscar-winning Sam Mendes as Artistic Director in 1990. Comprehensively revamped in 1990-92, with a distinctive thrust stage, it has attracted such talents as Judi Dench, Sir Ian McKellen, Nicole Kidman, Gwyneth Paltrow, Derek Jacobi, Kenneth Branagh

Theatrical gem – the Donmar Warehouse in Earlham Street.

and Jude Law. Apart from revivals of accepted classic plays, the Donmar has also commissioned numerous new translations of foreign works and enjoyed much success with musicals. Its limited performing space has led to the transfer or initiation of productions to other, larger houses, such as Wyndham's. (www.donmarwarehouse.com)

Drury Lane

Originally the Via de Aldwych, this thoroughfare was already referred to as 'old' in 1199. A pub has stood on the site of the White Hart since the fifteenth century. Sir Thomas Drury had a house here in the sixteenth century and John Donne after his clandestine marriage had rooms there. The site of the **Cockpit Theatre** is now covered by the Wild Street Peabody housing estate (1880-1). Oliver Cromwell and **Nell Gwyn** both had lodgings in the road but by the eighteenth century Drury Lane had become so disreputable that **Hogarth** used it as the setting for Plate 3 of *The Harlot's Progress* and **Dickens** as the location of 'A Gin Shop' in *Sketches by Boz*. Although the Lane had become the lowest of slums by the nineteenth century, the first branch of Sainsbury's was still opened here in 1869. Drury Lane was extensively remodelled by the Metropolitan Board of Works in 1877 when the burial ground of **St Martin-in-the-Fields** became the first in Westminster to be converted into public gardens (see page 32).

John Dryden

The plaque on No. 43 **Gerrard Street** in honour of Poet Laureate John Dryden (1631-1700) was placed there by the Royal Society of Arts. Unfortunately Dryden actually lived at No. 44 next door, from 1687 until his death there from gout and gangrene. During this period he wrote *A Song for St. Cecilia's Day* (1687), which has been much anthologised and lasted rather better than the plays he wrote. A masterly translator of Virgil, Dryden was also a brilliant versifier, a discerning critic and a savage satirist. Praised by Congreve, Pope and **Johnson**, Dryden has been called "the literary dictator of his age". *The Cambridge Guide to English Literature* hails him as the first master of 'modern English prose' and "a professional in the modern sense of the word."

If Dryden had his admirers he also had his enemies; in 1679 he was mercilessly beaten by three thugs in Covent Garden. Who paid them and why remains a mystery, though the ultra-debauched but poetically gifted Earl of Rochester is the usual suspect. Another suspect was one of **Charles II's** mistresses. Having managed to get away with praising both Cromwell and Charles II, Dryden converted to Catholicism at the height of an outbreak of Protestant bigotry and remained doggedly loyal to **James II**, though it cost him posts of profit and honour, including the Laureateship. Nor could Dryden look for much consolation in his domestic life, for his wife accused him of preferring his books to her company and vowed to transform herself into a library volume to get her due share of attention. Dryden advised her to make it an almanac so he could at least change her annually. He had his literary revenge in a pithy epitaph:

"Here lies my wife: here let her lie!
Now she's at rest, and so am I."

John Dryden – the first Poet Laureate and the first to have a 'blue' plaque – actually green.

In 1921 Dryden's home became the premises of the 43 Club, run by the Irish divorcee Mrs Kate Meyrick (1875-1933), who evoked the dead poet as a guardian angel of her dubious enterprise. Mrs. Meyrick's clientele did include a few cultural lions, including the aged novelist **Joseph Conrad**, the youthful sculptor Jacob Epstein and the then thrusting journalist J B Priestley. More characteristic of her preferred patrons was Lancashire millionaire Jimmy White, who turned up one night with six Daimlers full of showgirls and binged £400 on champagne. Just opposite the 43 was a restaurant run by 'Brilliant' Chang, who also supplied more stimulating substances than noodles to Mrs Meyrick's guests. The 43 was first raided by the police in 1922 for out-of-hours drinking and in 1924 Mrs M served six months in Holloway for selling liquor without a licence. Despite this she battled gamely on, marrying all three of her daughters into the peerage. A victim of police corruption and the puritanical Home Secretary Sir William Joynson-Hicks, Mrs Meyrick served two further gaol terms in 1930-31, which broke her health. Having been worth £500,000 at one point, with interests in three night-clubs, she died worth just under £800. A colourful memoir *Secrets of the 43* appeared posthumously (1933). The 43 was the model for the Old Hundredth club in Evelyn Waugh's *A Handful of Dust* (1934).

Dufour's Place

Dufour's Place takes its name from its builder, Paul Dufour, who may have been the Captain Defour or Defaux who lived on **Poland Street** from 1705 to 1740. Its most prominent feature is the T-shaped block of offices and flats built (1983-4) by Quinlan Terry, judged by Pevsner to be "an implicit critique of Modernist tower blocks but too personal and peculiar to have had much influence … of true load-bearing brick but tall enough to confound polite Georgian proportions". The building of this block helped to fund the restoration of the Georgian terrace in **Broadwick Street** which it overshadows.

Offices and flats in Dufour's Place, designed by Quinlan Terry.

Duke of York's Theatre, St Martin's Lane

Built (1891-2) to the designs of Walter Emden, this was originally the Trafalgar Square Theatre but changed its name in 1895. In 1893 the first English performance of Ibsen's *The Master Builder* was staged here. American Charles Frohman, manager from 1897 until his death in 1915, had two major successes with new plays by J M Barrie – *The Admirable Crichton* (1902) and *Peter Pan* (1904) which became an annual Christmas fixture for a decade. (www.dukeofyorkstheatre.co.uk)

Claude Duval

Born in Normandy, Duval (1643-70) became a footman in Paris and in that capacity came to England at the Restoration of **Charles II** in the train of the Duke of Richmond. He soon turned highwayman and gained an additional reputation as a womaniser. A celebrated anecdote records that he once waylaid the coach of a married couple carrying £400 in cash but returned £300 to them after dancing with the lady in the moonlight. Almost two centuries after this alleged event the Victorian genre painter W P Frith immortalised it on canvas. Duval was captured while drunk at the Hole-in-the-Wall (now the **Marquis of Granby**) in Chandos Street and condemned to the gallows on six counts. Charles II resolutely refused a pardon despite many pleas. After his hanging Duval was given a 'lying-in-state' at the Tangier Tavern in **St Giles**. His character and exploits figure prominently in **Samuel Butler's** *Hudibras*. A memorial plaque in the nave of **St Paul's,** Covent Garden warns the onlooker as follows:

Here lies Du Vall; Reader, if male thou art,
Look to thy purse; if female, to thy heart.

He may, however, actually be buried at St Giles-in-the-Fields.

(www.stand-and-deliver.org.uk)

Staging a revival of Tom Stoppard's Arcadia, *the Duke of York's Theatre in St Martin's Lane in 2009.*

Empire Cinema, Leicester Square

Built (1927-8) for MGM by a leading American cinema architect, Thomas W Lamb of New York, and seating 3,226, the Empire Cinema on the north side of **Leicester Square**, when opened, boasted the largest auditorium ever seen in the West End and a paybox open to the street, American style. It is on the site of the **Empire Theatre**. In the week of 11-18 May 1929, 82,849 patrons paid to see *The Broadway Melody*, the most successful week in any West End cinema ever. The show then ran for another eight weeks. On Tuesday 27 December 1939, 14,388, the biggest daily attendance ever achieved at the Empire, came to see *The Citadel*, a miners and medics saga based on the novel by A J Cronin. *Gone With the Wind* ran for twelve weeks. The Empire was rebuilt in 1962 and sub-divided in 1989. (www.empirecinemas.co.uk)

Empire Theatre, Leicester Square

The Royal London Panorama was built on the site of **Savile House** and opened in 1881 with a depiction of *The Charge of the Light Brigade* on 15,000 square feet of painted canvas. In 1884 the building was reincarnated as a theatre and initially enjoyed huge success with a programme of burlesques and extravaganzas. In 1887 it became the Empire Palace of Varieties under the joint management of George Edwardes and **Augustus Harris**. Under the inspiration of Adeline Genee, the Empire became renowned for spectacular ballet productions and its promenade as a pick-up point for prostitutes. In 1894 this 'haunt of vice' was targeted by a 'Purity Campaign' led by a Mrs Ormiston Chant. When screens were put up to separate the promenade from the auditorium they were torn down by a rioting audience, egged on by a youthful Winston Churchill, then a cadet at the Royal Military Academy, Sandhurst. He wrote excitedly to his brother "Did you see the papers about the riot at the Empire last Saturday? It was I who led the rioters – and made a speech to the crowd – "Ladies of the Empire, I stand for Liberty!" The exuberant author was unaware that, even as he wrote them, his own beloved father was succumbing to the ravages of syphilis. The 'victory', moreover, was brief and temporary as the recently-established London County Council insisted, as a precondition of relicensing the premises, that the notorious promenade area be altered to frustrate soliciting.

The Empire Theatre in Leicester Square in the late 19th century. Rebuilt in 1928, it closed as a theatre in 1961.

The Empire was reconstructed in 1904 by Frank Verity and moved forward into a new era of uplifting balletic spectacle under the gracious influence of Adeline Genée. A new theatrical format, the revue, made its first appearance at the Empire shortly before the Great War. A series of successful musical comedies began in 1918 and ended with *Lady, Be Good!*, with music by George Gershwin and starring Fred and Adele Astaire. Closure was followed by demolition and conversion into the Empire Cinema *(see above)*.

Endell Street

Laid out by royal surveyor Sir James Pennethorne (1801-71) in 1843-46 to clear a slum, Endell Street soon became home to several public institutions including baths and washhouses, the St Giles parish workhouse and the National School which had a soup kitchen and industrial school in the basement and established the reputation of **E M Barry**. There was also a stained-glass factory of 1859 at No. 22 and at No. 79 the **Swiss** Protestant church, completed in 1853 to the designs of George Vulliamy. The street was named for the Revd James Endell Tyler, rector of **St Giles's**. Nos. 51-59 and 63-69 are survivors from the late eighteenth century.

The Chevalier d'Eon

Soldier, spy, swordsman, diplomat and gender bender, Charles-Genevieve-Louis-Auguste-Andre-Timothee Eon de Beaumont (1728-1810) first passed himself off as a woman on a secret mission to Russia, then reverted to masculinity to serve as a captain of dragoons. Ordered to London in 1762, a quarrel with the French ambassador left him in fear of assassination and he took refuge in the house of a Belgian wine merchant at 38 (now 71) **Brewer Street**. Eventually the French, fearing d'Eon might use his insider knowledge to damage Anglo-French relations, decided it was cheaper to pension him off. The Chevalier was a popular guest at dinners and receptions but became the subject of rumour as a result of his fine features, soft voice and apparent indifference to women. In 1777 he

The handsome former stained-glass factory in Endell Street.

The statue of Eros in Piccadilly Circus. It commemorates compassion, not erotic love, but it helped to bankrupt its sculptor, Sir Alfred Gilbert

appeared to confirm conjecture by appearing in public in a gown and, on going to France, being received at court as a woman. Returning to England, d'Eon found that the outbreak of revolution in 1789 deprived him of his French state pension and the income from his family properties. Now permanently dressed as a woman, d'Eon scraped a living by playing exhibition fencing and chess matches. Seriously wounded in a bout at sixty-seven, s(he) lived out an enforced retirement on the charity of a compassionate Frenchwoman. An autopsy conducted two days after d'Eon's death confirmed his masculinity. The Beaumont Society is a support group for transsexuals and transvestites. (www.beaumontsociety.org.uk)

Eros statue, Piccadilly Circus

London's most celebrated statue is one of the most misunderstood. It does not represent Eros as the spirit of erotic love but is a tribute to the disinterested compassion for the poor of the 7th Lord Shaftesbury, after whom **Shaftesbury Avenue** is named. Designed by Sir Alfred Gilbert (1854-1934) it was London's first aluminium, and first one-legged, statue and made a £4,000 loss for the sculptor, a procrastinator and perfectionist who took seven years to make it, never got a proper contract for the job and boycotted the unveiling (1893) after his original design had been changed. By 1902 Gilbert was bankrupt. Expelled from the **Garrick Club** for failing to pay his subscription, he fled to exile in Bruges for the next quarter of a century. (Richard Dorment *Alfred Gilbert* Yale 1985)

L'Escargot

L'Escargot was founded at No. 48 Greek Street in 1927, originally as the Escargot Bienvenu, by Georges Gaudin, a native of Bourges. Its speciality, as its name proclaims, was snails – originally farmed in the basement. Gaudin was also responsible for introducing London to his favourite aperitif – chambery. In true French, and Soho, style Georges was succeeded in the business by his son, Alex. During the 1980s the restaurant was owned by the wine writer Jancis Robinson. At the time of writing it is part of a chain of six elite eateries controlled by celebrity chef Marco Pierre White. Patrons of L'Escargot have included the playwright A P

The emblematic insignia of L'Escargot restaurant in Greek Street.

Herbert, **Clemence Dane** and Lord Woolton, controller of Britain's rationing programme during World War Two. L'Escargot was awarded its first Michelin star in 1996. Apart from its menu, L'Escargot is renowned for its décor which includes works by Miro, Matisse, Chagall, Hockney, Warhol and Picasso. (www.lescargotrestaurant.co.uk)

Exeter Hall, Strand

Built in 1829-31 for public meetings, Exeter Hall was variously used by the Anti-Slavery Society, the Ragged School Union, the Bible Society and the Temperance Society. The main auditorium could hold three thousand people. 'Exeter Hall' in Victorian parlance became the equivalent of 'readers of *The Guardian'* in terms of public attitudes. The self-educated star preacher Charles Hadding Spurgeon (1834-92) also preached there to large congregations. Choirs six hundred strong performed the works of Handel. In 1856 Jenny Lind, 'the Swedish Nightingale', gave a benefit concert in aid of the medical fund promoted by Florence Nightingale and drew an audience of almost two thousand at a guinea a head. Exeter Hall was acquired by the YMCA in 1880 and demolished in 1907. The Strand Palace Hotel covers the site

Adam Faith

'Sixties pop star Adam Faith (1940-2003) began his showbiz career at the 2i's **coffee-bar** on **Old Compton Street** as lead singer of a skiffle group, the Worried Men. His film debut came in *Beat Girl* (1960), set in Soho, which he subsequently dismissed as "a disastrous teenage exploitation movie which bore little or no relation to Soho or the youth it was supposed to represent". No great

Arena of conscience – Exeter Hall in the Strand.

shakes as a singer, Faith eventually proved by far the best actor of the rock 'n' roll generation. Soho provided much of the background for Faith's TV series, *Budgie*, in which he played a small-time crook but a 1987 stage musical version flopped. (www.adamfaith.org.uk)

Daniel Farson

The son of an American journalist, Farson was the product of a troubled Transatlantic upbringing, but National service in the US armed forces made him aware of the possibilities of photography and journalism. The **National Portrait Gallery** collection includes Farson's photographs of Soho contemporaries such as **Nina Hamnett** and **Francis Bacon**, literary lions like Kingsley Martin and Cyril Connolly and theatrical figures Richard Burton and Joan Littlewood. Other memorable images include a hung-over **Jeffrey Bernard** at the foot of the **Charles II statue** in **Soho Square** and Gaston Berlemont opening a bottle for patrons of '**The French**'. Farson came to public notice between 1957 and 1964 as the detached presenter of offbeat documentaries on unconventional or problematic

Two houses on the north-east side of Soho Square. On the left is Fauconberg House, and on the right the former headquarters of Crosse and Blackwell (see p. 53).

aspects of British society, ranging from naturism, body-building and witchcraft to illiteracy and interracial marriages.

A legacy enabled Farson to buy The Waterman's Arms pub on the Isle of Dogs, where he tried to revive the Victorian music hall tradition of boisterous live entertainment. This venture imploded in a year, losing £30,000, a sum which at the time would have bought an entire row of terraced houses or guaranteed his financial security for life. Farson retreated to his father's former home in Devon where he lived a semi-reclusive life, punctuated by periodic forays to London – and Turkey – in search of casual homosexual liaisons, laced with drunken excesses and occasional violence. Given Farson's remarkable range of talents, his was a life of spectacular under-achievement and unhappiness, riddled with unfocused guilt and blighted by alcoholism. Farson's portrayal of *Soho in the Fifties* (Pimlico 1993) is one of his best books, an affectionate account of the non-judgmental microcosm in which he felt least alienated.

Fauconberg House, Soho Square

Fauconberg House stood in the north-east corner of the square and is now remembered by Falconberg Mews, off Sutton Row. From 1683 to 1700 it was the home of Thomas Belasyse, 1st Earl of Fauconberg. Although coming from a royalist family, Belasyse switched sides during the civil war and became a fierce supporter of Cromwell, marrying one of his daughters. At the Restoration he was able to switch allegiances back again to become a Privy Councillor and Captain of Charles II's Guard. In 1689 he betrayed Charles's brother and successor, **James II**, by becoming one of the cabal which invited his son-in-law, William III to take the throne – for which he was raised to the rank of earl. From 1753 to 1761 Arthur Onslow, Speaker of the House of Commons, was the occupant of the house, followed from 1762 to 1770 by the 4th Duke of Argyll. A later owner, John Grant commissioned the leading architect-designer of the age, Robert Adam, to make improvements, most notably a radical remodelling of the frontage. After Grant's death the building became Wright's Hotel and Coffee House, then (1810-57), the premises of a firm of pianoforte makers, Dalmain & Co. In 1858 **Crosse & Blackwell** acquired it for use as a bottling and labelling plant for their range of preserved foods. They demolished it in 1924 to make way for new offices, initiating similar developments in other parts of the square. The warehouse at the rear of these premises, built after the formation of **Charing Cross Road** in the 1880s, was later converted to make the **Astoria Cinema** and Dance Salon.

Henry Fielding

The career of Henry Fielding (1707-54) followed a unique parabola which took him from scourge of government to crusader against crime. Educated at Eton, he enjoyed a youthful success with *Love in Several Masques* at **Theatre Royal, Drury Lane** (1728) before studying at the University of Leyden. Over the course of just eight years, he produced twenty-five theatrical pieces including burlesques, farces, ballad opera and adaptations from Moliére until *The Historical Register for 1736*, an attack on the policies and conduct of the administration of Sir Robert Walpole, proved so provocative that the government responded by passing the Theatrical Licensing Act (1737), investing the Lord Chamberlain with powers of censorship over plays which were only abolished in 1968. More immediately this brought Fielding's theatrical career to an abrupt end, turning him to journalism and reading for the bar. In 1741 he published *An Apology for the Life of Mrs Shamela Andrews,* a parody of Samuel Richardson's sentimental novel of virtue, *Pamela*. This was followed by a novel *The Adventures of Joseph Andrews* (1742) and a play *The Wedding Day,* produced by **Garrick**. Severely depressed by the death of his devoted wife of ten years Fielding then shocked many of his circle by marrying her maid.

In 1748 Fielding was appointed a magistrate, working from 4 **Bow Street**, and launched a campaign to eliminate the baneful influence of venial 'trading justices' who used their office as a source of personal profit, often acting in collusion with the criminal gangs who were Fielding's other main target. He also campaigned for a more effective and just system of poor relief and against public hangings.

In 1749 Fielding published his masterpiece, *The History of Tom Jones, a Foundling*, which was received with general acclaim, though Dr Johnson dismissed it as 'vicious'. In 1750 he published his *Inquiry into the Causes of the Late Increase in Robbers*, an analysis of the crime-wave which followed the ending of the War of Austrian Succession in 1748. Fielding put most of the blame on the ready availability of cheap gin corroding the health and morals of the poor. In 1752 Fielding used *The Covent Garden Journal* to satirise contemporary ills – political corruption, social hypocrisy and the absurdities of fashion. In 1753 in his capacity as a magistrate he established a small force of permanent constables to assist him but as they were denied rewards due to them for effecting arrests the little force was soon disbanded. Although broken in health for the last two years of his life, Fielding continued his war on crime until he was persuaded, for the sake of his constitution, to take a voyage to Lisbon, where he died.

The 'blind beak of Bow Street', Sir John Fielding.

Sir John Fielding

Half-brother to **Henry Fielding**, Sir John Fielding (died 1780) was blind from birth. In 1755, following Henry's death, he succeeded him as the magistrate at **Bow Street** and committed himself to continue his campaign of gang-busting. In 1758 he published *A History and Effects of the late Henry Fielding's*

Police and revived his band of 'thief-takers'. Unlike traditional constables or watchmen these agents were proactive in seeking out perpetrators of crime, relying extensively on networks of informants to tip them off. Paid a weekly retainer and expenses, they also received a share of due rewards. They wore no uniforms but carried short staves with gilt crowns as proof of their office. In 1785 the *Morning Herald* referred to them as the **Bow Street Runners.**

Knighted in 1761 for his efforts, in 1763 Fielding established a system of horse patrols to protect travellers on the vulnerable fringes of the capital by policing the turnpike roads. They rapidly proved their worth but because the Treasury was too mean to pay for their upkeep they were disbanded after eighteen months. But the example had been set and patrols were set up by private citizens at Bayswater, Islington and Highbury.

The Fifties

"that dodgy never-never land, that hallucinatory enclave where we waited, consumed by angst, to cure today's hangover, by making certain of tomorrow's." **George Melly**

What were supposed to be the defining characteristics of London in the 'Swinging Sixties' – unrestrained hedonism, casual attitudes to sex, experimentation with drugs, new and challenging forms of artistic, musical and literary creativity, a cheery disregard for bourgeois conventions and 'establishment' values – were all foreshadowed, not to say, intrinsic, in the Soho of the Fifties, as subsequently chronicled by **Daniel Farson** and in Nigel Richardson's semi-fictionalised *Dog Days in Soho* (**Gollancz** 2001).

Flamingo Club, Wardour Street

The Flamingo Jazz Club opened at 33 Wardour Street in August 1952. Early appearances were made by Johnny Dankworth, **Ronnie Scott** and Sarah Vaughan. Saxophonist Benny Green (1927-98) also sang for the resident band. Green later became a popular radio presenter, with an encyclopaedic knowledge of music and a passion for cricket, which enabled him to edit a series of anthologies drawn from the pages of **Wisden.**

John Flaxman RA

Sculptor John Flaxman (1755-1826) was born and brought up in **New Row**, Covent Garden. His father had worked as a modeller for **Roubiliac**. From 1775 Flaxman gained his main living by producing

Master of Monuments – John Flaxman, RA..

classical designs for **Wedgwood**. **William Blake** was a close friend at this time. Upon marriage he moved to 27 **Wardour Street**. After spending seven years in Rome Flaxman returned to London, became Professor of Sculpture at the Royal Academy and devoted most of the rest of his life to producing funerary monuments. He was buried in **St Giles-in-the-Fields** where a memorial, based on one of his own monuments, was fixed by the Royal Academy in 1930. Flaxman's London works include the statue of **Sir Joshua Reynolds** in St Paul's Cathedral, a bust of **John Hunter** at the Royal College of Surgeons and the frieze depicting Ancient and Modern Drama on the façade of the **Royal Opera House**. There is a collection of his sculpture at University College, London.

Floral Street

Originally (ca. 1632-7) Hart Street, with middle-class tenants, this thoroughfare was taken over by the tailors and barbers who catered for the locality's more affluent residents and nine public houses which catered to their servants. **Macklin**'s attempt to run a tavern here failed, obliging him to return to the stage. Actor **Joseph Haines** died at his lodgings here. In 1703 the parish rented a house here for the poor. By the nineteenth century the street was notorious for its dunghills and 'disorderly houses'. Nos. 28-29 was built in 1833 for Messrs Turrill, coach-builders and has also been a pub. The former

The Fortune Theatre in Russell Street.

Always controversial – the Fourth Plinth in Trafalgar Square.

Parish Schools at No. 12 date from 1838. The road was extended westward into Garrick Street in 1861-5. **Odhams** began business here in 1894, before developing into the country's largest printers and publishers. Although dominated by the fruit trade, the street was renamed Floral Street in 1895. Bertorelli's restaurant was established at No. 44A in a former warehouse in 1912.

Fortune Theatre, Russell Street

Built on the site of the Albion Tavern, the historically- and optimistically-named Fortune Theatre opened in 1924. Despite its central location, with seating for just over four hundred it struggled commercially and by the 1930s it was being used by amateur companies. But small can sometimes play big. In 1957 *At the Drop of the Hat,* a two man show of humorous songs by Michael Flanders and Donald Swann ran for 733 performances. A second moment of theatrical glory arrived on 10 May 1961 when *Beyond the Fringe* opened, launching the local careers of **Peter Cook** and three university friends. *Rejoyce,* Maureen Lipman's superlative solo celebration of the talents of Joyce Grenfell, was a hit in 1988-9. (www.fortune-theatre.co.uk)

Ugo Foscolo

Famed as a tragedian before he was twenty, a professor at thirty, Ugo Foscolo (1778-1827) was also variously a translator, an epic poet, a satirist, soldier and seducer – but always a passionate Italian patriot. Fleeing the reimposition of Austrian rule in Italy, he came via Switzerland to London in 1816. The archetype of a dashing Byronic hero, he was initially feted and able to live in some style at No. 11 **Soho Square**. Writing for literary periodicals initially provided a means of support, but Foscolo's prosperity proved fleeting and he died in great poverty at Turnham Green. Following the final unification of his native country, Foscolo's body was repatriated in 1871 for a state funeral.

Fourth Plinth, Trafalgar Square

Erected at the north-west corner of the square in 1841, this plinth was originally intended for an equestrian statue of King William IV (reigned 1830-37) but as no funds were allocated for this purpose it remained empty for over a century and a half. Since 1999 it has been used to exhibit new works of art for a limited period only, and usually with much controversy. In July 2009 the sculptor Antony Gormley supervised a succession of human beings standing on the plinth. (www.londongov/fourthplinth)

Charles Fowler

The designer of Covent Garden's market buildings (1828-30) was a specialist in designing large covered market buildings. Charles Fowler (1792-1867) was an original who managed to span the rapidly widening gap between the traditional disciplines of architecture and the emerging techniques of civil engineering, making imaginative use of novel materials such as cast-iron and large-plate sheet glass. Aiming at "ORIGINALITY without the affectation of NOVELTY", Fowler was recognised by J C Loudon, himself a pioneer of glasshouse construction, as "one of the few modern architects who ... design buildings on fundamental principles instead of antiquated rules and precedents." Fowler's other market buildings at Gravesend, Hungerford Market by Charing Cross and Exeter in his native Devon, have all been demolished. In 1835 Fowler became a founder member of the (future Royal) Institute of British Architects and later its vice-president.

Foyles' bookshop in Charing Cross Road, old and new.

Foyle's bookshop, Charing Cross Road

For long hailed as "the greatest bookshop in the world", Foyle's now seems content to be merely excellent. Transformed after Christina Foyle's death in 1999, it is now a refuge for any book lover, organised and vast, but still a book store.

The business was the creation of the eccentric William Alfred Foyle (1885-1963), the seventh child of a seventh child of a seventh child, who believed himself therefore possessed of visionary and intuitive gifts. Aided by his brother Gilbert, Foyle opened his first bookshop at eighteen and by 1907 had established himself in **Charing Cross Road**. Thanks to credit from the publishing house of **Heinemann** he began dealing in new books in 1912. To accommodate his ever-expanding stock he bought premises in **Manette Street** and rebuilt his business as a modern multi-storey block (1929). Foyle's daughter Christina, meanwhile, launched a programme of high-profile literary lunches which featured the most popular writers of the day.

As 'Willie' Foyle turned to the life of a country gentleman, indulging his passions for yachting and book-collecting, the business fell increasingly under the direction of the autocratic Christina, becoming an institutional expression of her own idiosyncratic approach to the trade. The 1995 edition of the *Rough Guide to London* warned readers that Foyle's was "awesomely enormous and famously chaotic, with notoriously offhand staff and an archaic paying system which forces you to queue twice – once to part with the cash and once to pick up the book". Novels were arranged by publisher rather than by author, the shop having auctioned premium shelf and display space to publishers. Staff turnover was rapid, many having only an imperfect grasp of English or the monetary system. Trade unions were banned and females were confined to the role of cashier. This all ended at Christina's death and since then the store has reinvented itself and has even opened new outlets. (www.foyles.co.uk)

The Freemasons' Hall in Great Queen Street in 1956, then blackened by London's coal fired atmosphere.

The French House in Dean Street, in 1994, flying the flag.

Freemasons' Hall, Great Queen Street

Freemasons' Hall is the headquarters of the United Grand Lodge of England, which was founded in 1717 as the first in the world. Freemasons have had a meeting place in Great Queen Street since 1775. The present, third, building covering two and a half acres, was built (1927-33) to the designs of H V Ashley and F W Newman as a memorial to the 3,225 Freemasons killed on active service in World War I. It is claimed to be the only Art Deco building in London preserved in its original condition and used for its original purpose. Public tours are available. (www.ugle.orh.uk)

'The French' pub, Dean Street

This legendary establishment at No. 49 **Dean Street** became a Wine House in 1910 but its German owner, one Schmidt, was dispossessed on the outbreak of the war in 1914. Ownership passed to a Belgian, Victor Berlemont, under whose patronage 'Maison Berlemont' was referred to universally as 'The French', its walls liberally festooned with photographs of visiting French celebrities like cabaret artist Maurice Chevalier and champion boxer Georges Carpentier. During World War II the pub served as a favoured rendezvous of members of the French Resistance in London. General de Gaulle drafted his famous broadcast of defiance to the Nazis – *A Tous les Francais* – in a room above the bar. The flying bomb which took out St Anne's church opposite also destroyed the pub's Victorian façade. After rebuilding the pub reverted to its original name, the York Minster.

In the '**Fifties** it was a favoured watering-hole of Soho 'characters' like **Daniel Farson, Francis Bacon, John Deakin** and **Nina Hamnett**. It also figured on the itinerary of high-profile eccentrics like Salvador Dali, Brendan Behan and Dylan Thomas. A safe refuge for tarts, 'the French' also functioned as a banker of last resort for many of its 'regulars'. Victor's son, Gaston Berlemont, who was born in the pub in 1914, retired on Bastille Day 1989, the two hundredth anniversary of the outbreak of the French Revolution. The new proprietors, journalists who had themselves been regulars, spruced the place up and changed its name to The French House. The upstairs restaurant famously serves unreconstructed French provincial cooking. The pub's stylish website features outstanding photographs by John Deakin and Daniel Farson.

(www.frenchhousesoho.com)

French Hospital and Dispensary, Shaftesbury Avenue

Opened initially on **Lisle Street**, this valuable institution moved to purpose-built premises on **Shaftesbury Avenue** in 1889. Intended to serve London's French-speaking community and French-speaking visitors, the excellence of its service soon attracted **prostitutes** of all nationalities. Closed down for lack of finances in 1966, it became the Shaftesbury Hospital for Urology until 1992 and is now the Covent Garden Hotel. The dispensary survives on Euston Road.

French Protestant Church, Soho Square

The French Protestant Church at the north-west corner of Soho Square was a favourite work of its designer Sir Aston Webb, best known for his Victoria & Albert Museum and the façade of Buckingham Palace. Built in 1891-3 to house the Huguenot congregation ousted from its church in the St Martin's le Grand, its façade features Franco-Flemish Gothic features in terracotta. The tympanum above the door celebrates the four-hundredth anniversary of the arrival of the first Huguenots in 1550.

Although the new church was intended for French Protestants throughout the capital there were still at that time enough in Soho itself for the minister, Pasteur Degremont, to hold an open-air service in French on Sunday evenings at the corner of Moor Street and Old Compton Street. During World War Two the church was much used by 'Free French' servicemen.

(Yves Jaulmes *The French Protestant Church of London and the Huguenots* French Protestant Church of London 1993)

The French Protestant church in Soho Square one of Sir Aston Webb's favourite works.

The bas-relief above the door to the French Protestant church, dedicated to Edward VI, who first gave Huguenots refuge in England.

Richard Frith

A bricklayer with ambitions to rival **Barbon** himself, at least as far as Soho went, Richard Frith (died 1695), after successfully putting up a few houses in St James', in 1677 undertook the development of Soho Field, which extended over nineteen acres. Alas, shortly after laying out **Soho Square**, **Frith Street** and the streets adjacent to them, he was squeezed mercilessly on the loans he had taken out to buy building materials.

Frith's involvement in building **Monmouth House** sealed his fate. When the Duke of Monmouth was executed Frith and his partner in the venture were "very great loosers by the misfortune of the said Duke". Frith was still in debt when he died ten years later.

Frith Street

Built up from ca. 1678 by Richard Frith, and also known as Thrift Street, Nos. 60-62 are of 1680-88, Other early survivors include Nos. 6-7 (1718), 5 (ca.1731), 63-4 (frontages ca. 1734), 37-8 (1781) and 44-9 (1804-7). The 'Gothick' shopfront of No. 15 was originally (1816) for a bookbinder.

The naval hero Sir Cloudesley Shovell (1650-1707), was an early resident. He captured Gibraltar but was shipwrecked off the Scilly Isles en route for home, when his fleet strayed seventy miles off course. Shovell made it to shore but, lying exhausted at the water's edge, had his head bashed in by a local woman for the sake of a fine emerald ring he was wearing. In 1764 **Mozart** lodged at No. 20. Another musical resident was Johann Christian Fischer (1733-1800), the greatest oboist of the eighteenth century.

Later the tone became distinctly arty, residents including royal drawing-master Jack Gresse (1794), actors Arthur Murphy (1801) and William Macready (1816), painter John Constable (1810-11), portraitist John Hayes (1821-47) and dramatists **Mrs Inchbald** and Mary Russell Mitford. Law reformer Sir Samuel Romilly was born at No. 18 and critic **William Hazlitt** died at No. 6. **John Logie Baird** gave the first demonstration of television at No. 22.

Furniture Makers

Furniture-making became a significant Soho trade in the nineteenth century. Thomas Sheraton (1751-1806) was established at 106 **Wardour Street** in the 1790s. Far more influential as a teacher and designer than as a maker, he made his reputation with *The Cabinet Makers' and Upholsterers' Drawing Book* issued in four parts between 1791 and 1794. Unfortunately he never made his fortune, dying in **Broadwick Street** and leaving his family in distressed circumstances. Within a generation of Sheraton's passing, Wardour Street had become synonymous with faked antiques.

Cribb and Son of **Soho Square**, by contrast, enjoyed the prestige of royal patronage and maintained a tradition of craftsmanship from their foundation in 1770 well into the machine age a century later. George Smith of 41 **Brewer Street** also claimed royal patronage as 'Upholsterer and Furniture Draughtsman to His Majesty', the discriminating if spendthrift **George IV**.

With premises in Wardour Street, Chapel Street, **Dean Street** and **Carlisle Street**, Edwards and Roberts ranked as one of the largest furniture dealers in the country. Sinclair Galleries occupied five floors at 55 **Shaftesbury Avenue** and specialised in *objêts d'art*. W & J Wright of Wardour Street specialised in carving and marquetry, while W & C Nightingale of Dean Street were specialist manufacturers of bedding.

In Covent Garden, **Thomas Chippendale** (1718-79) was established in St Martin's Lane in 1753.

Theodore Gardelle

Born in Geneva of Italian descent, Theodore Gardelle (1722-61) was encouraged to consider an international career after successfully painting and enamelling a miniature portrait of **Voltaire**. By the time he arrived in London in 1759, Gardelle had already abandoned a mistress and two children in Paris. Lodging at 37 Leicester Fields, he painted a portrait of his extrovert landlady, Mrs Anne King, which so displeased her that in the ensuing violence he cut her throat to stifle her screams. Gardelle then cut up her corpse and attempted to dispose of the various parts but was discovered, tried and eventually executed at the corner of **Panton Street**. The whole gory story can be read in detail on the engrossing Old Bailey website (www.oldbaileyonline.org) or in the online version of *The Newgate Calendar* (www.exclassics.com/newgate/ng287.htm).

The Gargoyle Club, Dean Street

One tourist website, even more cavalier with history than most, alleges that this location is haunted by the ghost of **Nell Gwyn**, on the grounds that she once lived in a house on this spot. Given that the street was built up between 1678 and 1697 this is feasible on grounds of chronology, but given that she was already a well-established mistress of **Charles II** by 1669 and had acquired a 'des res' on Pall Mall it doesn't seem likely.

The present building at No. 69 was built by John Meard jnr in 1732-3 and was home to the **Novello** music-publishing family in the 1830s. Thirty years later they added two floors to use the premises as a printing house.

The Gargoyle Club was established in 1925 by socialite the Hon. David Pax Tennant (1902-68), a descendant of William the Conqueror, and his actress wife Hermione Baddeley (1906-86), a descendant of the British general Sir Henry Clinton (1738-95) of the war of American Independence. Hermione often appeared at the Gargoyle in cabaret, began making films in the 1920s and was a principal character in *Brighton Rock* (1947). In later life she became known to US audiences as Ellen, the Irish maid in *Mary Poppins*, as a regular character in *Little House on the Prairie* and *Bewitched* and as a voice-over actress in *The Aristocats*. In her Gargoyle days, however, she was a pint-sized nymphette with a talent for wild improvization.

The Gargoyle boasted décor by Lutyens and a red glass mirror mosaic by Matisse and a clientele which, over three decades, would range from Tallulah Bankhead and **Noel Coward** to **Francis Bacon**, Feliks Topolski and Dylan Thomas. Others included Anthony Powell and Cyril Connolly, Augustus John, philosopher A J Ayer, Soviet agents Burgess and Maclean and Brian Howard, the inspiration for Anthony Blanche in Evelyn Waugh's *Brideshead Revisited*. Tennant sold up in 1952 and the establishment went rapidly down-market as a seedy drinking-den and strip club named for Nell Gwyn. From 1979 to 1982 the Gargoyle found a new incarnation as the first home of the Comedy Store and thus a launch pad for the careers of Alexei Sayle, Paul Merton, Rik Mayall, Ben Elton and Jack Dee.

David Garnett

Novelist and bookseller and co-founder of the **Nonesuch Press**, David Garnett (1892-1981) was an expert on John Galsworthy and T E Lawrence. Having once had an affair with Bloomsbury painter Duncan Grant, he subsequently married Grant's daughter, Angelica, at whose birth he had been present. Grant was horrified. Garnett's novel *Aspects of Love* (1955) provided the basis of Andrew Lloyd-Webber's hit musical of that title. Vanessa Bell's portrait of Garnett is in the **National Portrait Gallery.**

David Garrick

"His profession made him rich and he made his profession respectable." **Dr Samuel Johnson**

There are at least 450 portraits and engravings of David Garrick (1717-79), more than of any other eighteenth-century personality, royalty included. Of **Huguenot** descent, Garrick, a former pupil of Dr Johnson, was first involved in the wine-trade. In 1741 he made a sensational debut in London as *Richard III*, a role in which he was painted by **Hogarth**. Garrick's stage career was meteoric in its success, thanks to a naturalism which was in striking contrast to the stylised declamatory school of stagecraft which had long been the norm. Having conducted a liaison with the actress **Peg Woffington** and lived briefly in **King Street**, after marriage Garrick moved to No. 27 **Southampton Street** in 1749 and stayed there until his retirement.

David Garrick as Tancred in Tancred and Sigismunda.

A prominent bronze plaque marks his former residence.

As manager of the **Theatre Royal**, **Drury Lane** from 1747 until his retirement Garrick made it the leading playhouse in Europe, introducing a number of significant innovations – banishing aristocratic spectators from the stage and installing concealed lighting and naturalistic painted backdrops. In an attempt to staunch the misappropriation of theatre costumes, weapons, furniture etc. he began the practice of marking them as 'props' – property of the management. Garrick was also largely responsible for the rebirth of Shakespeare as England's national dramatist and bore the main burden of financing and organising the first Shakespeare Festival at Stratford-on-Avon. Garrick's fine country retreat at Hampton-on-Thames, severely damaged by fire in 2008, was adorned with a temple to Shakespeare designed by Robert Adam and holding a bust of the bard by **Roubiliac**.

As a member of '**The Club**' Garrick was a personal friend of **Reynolds** and **Zoffany** and built up a fine collection of some two hundred pictures, including works by **Lely**, Poussin, Watteau and Gainsborough. Apart from landholdings in Essex and shares in four newspapers, Garrick also left a personal fortune of £100,000 and an extensive collection of play scripts which he bequeathed to the British Museum. **Sir John Fielding** commended his influence and legacy – "the Chastity of Mr. Garrick as a manager of a Public Theatre and his exemplary life as a Man, have been of great service to the Morals of a dissipated Age." A cortége of fifty carriages, led by the chief mourner, **Sheridan**, followed Garrick to his burial in Westminster Abbey's Poets' Corner, where Dr Johnson was later laid beside him. Garrick was the first actor to be honoured with burial in Westminster Abbey; the next was Laurence Olivier in 1989.

(Alan Kendall *David Garrick: A Biography* St Martin's Press 1985)

The Garrick Club, Garrick Street

Named for the celebrated actor, the Garrick Club was founded in 1831 by the Duke of Sussex and was originally based in a former family hotel at No. 35 **King Street**. In 1835 the club acquired the collection of theatrical portraits assembled by the comic actor Charles Mathews, including works by **Lely**, **Kneller** and **Zoffany**. Intended as a meeting-place for actors, writers and artists, it numbered **Dickens** and Thackeray among its members and later Gilbert and Sullivan. The clubhouse at 15 Garrick Street, which it has occupied since 1864, was designed by Frederick Marrable. In 1879 the composer Sir Arthur Sullivan celebrated his birthday at the club in the company of the Prince of Wales (the future Edward VII), **Augustus Harris** and **Henry Irving**. W S Gilbert, his librettist, was notably absent from the list of guests. The party broke up just before 5am. Irascible novelist Kingsley Amis spent much time at the Garrick in his later years until the climb to the first floor bar became too challenging. A A Milne, a member, bequeathed the club part of the rights to *Winnie the Pooh*. In 1998 the Disney Corporation paid £50 million to acquire them. Despite women being among the world's greatest actors, they are still accepted only as guests, not members. (Richard Hough *The Ace of Clubs* 1986; www.garrickclub.co.uk)

Garrick Theatre, Charing Cross Road

Built (1889) for W S Gilbert to the designs of Walter Emden and C J Phipps, the theatre features a copy of Gainsborough's portrait of Garrick in its foyer. In 1895 sensation surrounded the production of Pinero's *The Notorious Mrs Ebbsmith* when a woman named Ebbsmith was found drowned in the Thames with a counterfoil of a ticket for the play in her pocket. Variously a home to Shakespeare, revue, musicals and farce, the Garrick has hosted successful transfers of productions which had already had a long run elsewhere, notably *No Sex Please, We're British* (four more years after eleven at the **Strand Theatre**) and the National Theatre's *An Inspector Calls* by J B Priestley, which had already moved once to the **Aldwych**, came to the Garrick in the mid-1990s and continued into the new century. The resident ghost is said to be that of former manager Arthur Bourchier (1863-1927), a founder member of the Oxford University Dramatic Society and himself a distinguished Shakespearean. He is said to appear as a spectre and to descend a phantom staircase from his roof-top flat to clap actors encouragingly on the back as they await their cues.

(www.garrick-theatre.co.uk)

Gay Hussar, Greek Street

London's most celebrated Hungarian – and political – restaurant was the creation of a Welsh Italian, Victor Sassie (1915-99), who was born in Barrow-in-Furness and had trained in the kitchens of Budapest and Vienna. The Gay Hussar opened at 2 **Greek Street** in 1953 in premises previously occupied by Josef, "without doubt Soho's best Jugo-Slav restaurant" and supposedly a favourite of General Eisenhower, the Queen of Siam and, less

Red restaurant – the Gay Hussar in Greek Street.

surprisingly, ex-King Peter of Yugoslavia. The Gay Hussar became a favourite venue of the bon vivant Labour MP, journalist and not-so-closet gay Tom Driberg and through him a wide circle of Left Wing intellectuals, hacks and trade union apparatchiks. Oblivious to culinary fashion, the restaurant resolutely refused to amend its original menu. Michael Foot, Roy Hattersley and Lord Pakenham all became habitués. **Jeffrey Bernard** and **Frank Norman** both worked there as dish-washers. Sassie retired in 1988, by which time the Left London he had catered for had been obliterated by the onslaught of Thatcherism. (www.gayhussar.co.uk)

Georges II, III & IV and their statues

Three of the six King Georges of Britain are commemorated in statues in the area covered by this book.

Now largely forgotten, George II – 'The Little Corporal' – had a long, successful reign (1727-60), bringing much-needed Hanoverian efficiency to his personal fixation, the army. The public, however, rightly suspected his brainy, buxom consort, Caroline of Anspach, was the real ruler:

"You may strut, dapper George, but' twill be in vain:

We know 'tis Queen Caroline, not you, that reign."

Caroline worked skilfully with the king's chief minister, Sir Robert Walpole and her death was genuinely mourned – *"O death, where is thy sting? To take the Queen and leave the King!"*

Appropriately for a military obsessive, at Dettingen in 1743, George, aged sixty, was the last king of Britain personally to lead troops into battle, exhorting his troops "Be brave, boys, fire and the French will run". They did and they did. He was buried in Westminster Abbey beside Caroline, their coffins broken open for their dust to mingle. The US state Georgia, founded as an alternative to prison for London's debtors and petty offenders, was named for him.

The statue of George II in **Golden Square** shows him conventionally dressed as a Roman general, on a plinth too low to command proper attention. **Dickens** described it as "the guardian genius of a little wilderness of shrubs". The 1988 whitewash effect imparts a melancholy ghostliness. The **National Portrait Gallery** has a portrait by Thomas Hudson, displaying the royal legs to maximum effect.

The statue of George II in Golden Square – the last monarch to be depicted in historic costume.

George III (reigned 1760-1820), also last king of America, was the first monarch whose statue was paid for by public subscription. Succeeding his *grandfather*, George II, he was the first Hanoverian to speak English as his native tongue and never went to Hanover in his life, though briefly contemplated exile there after losing the American colonies. Although derided for stinginess, George III was cultured and conscientious. His passion for agricultural improvement made him known as 'Farmer George'. Tormented by dementia and finally reduced to blindness, deafness and madness, symptoms portrayed in Alan Bennett's play (later a film) *The Madness of George III*, the King yet retained respect as a symbol of patriotism, humanity and good sense through the long wars (1793-1815) against France. Cast in bronze by Matthew Cotes Wyatt, his equestrian statue at Cockspur Street was unveiled in 1836.

George IV inherited his father's cultured tastes but not his domestic virtues. Affable and athletic in youth, he declined into extravagant self-indulgence, lavishing £25,000 on a voluminous

George III on horseback in Cockspur Street.

coronation garment to disguise his transformation into 'the Prince of Whales'. His 'official' marriage was a disaster, his love life an embarrassing shambles, chiefly involving married grandmothers. He did, however, have *some* good points. A patron of **John Nash**, Regent Street is named in his honour as is Regent's Park. A true connoisseur, he added greatly to the royal collections and supported the founding of the **National Gallery**. He also founded (1823) and funded the Royal Society of Literature. Flattering portraits by **Sir Thomas Lawrence** show him as "the first gentleman of Europe"; but he died an object of contempt to his subjects. His statue on **Trafalgar Square** by Sir Francis Chantrey, shows him considerably slimmed down. Originally intended for Buckingham Palace, it was placed in its present location 'temporarily' in 1843. (Veronica P M Baker-Smith *Royal Discord: The Family of George II* Athena Press 2008; Jeremy Black *George III: America's Last King* Yale University Press 2006; Christopher Hibbert *George III: A Personal History* Penguin 1999; Steven Parissien *George IV: The Grand Entertainment* John Murray 2001; Kenneth Baker *George IV: A Life in Caricature* Thames and Hudson 2005)

George IV, too fat to get on a horse in later life, is commemorated on horseback in Trafalgar Square. St Martin-in-the-Fields is in the background.

Gerrard Street

Gerrard Street has been at the heart of London's **Chinatown** for little more than half a century. The street was originally (1677-85) built up by **Barbon** on land, formerly the **Military Ground**, forcefully acquired by Lord Gerard of Brandon, first Earl of Macclesfield. Gerard's own house, on the south side, survived until a fire of 1887. Nos. 11-12, 17-19, 31, 41 and 47 are of the late seventeenth century. No. 16 is of 1730 and a century ago housed the Mont Blanc restaurant favoured by a loose literary coterie consisting of Belloc, Chesterton, Galsworthy, **Conrad,** Masefield, W H Davies, Ford Madox Ford and Edward Thomas. Nos 3-6 are of 1733-34 and 36 and 39 of 1737. Inhabitants of Gerrard Street have included **Dryden**, **James Gibbs**, royal silversmith **Paul de Lamerie**, **Edmund Burke**, water-colourist John Sell Cotman (1782-1842) and actor-manager **Charles Kemble** and his actress daughter Fanny Kemble (1809-93). **James Boswell** lodged at No. 22, then a tailor's house, in 1775, in "a very neat first floor room at sixteen shillings a week." No. 3 was a coffee-house, known as the Nassau, patronised by painter **Benjamin Haydon**. No. 9 was once the **Turk's Head Tavern**, later the **Westminster General Dispensary**. **The Nonesuch Press** was at No. 30.

Celebrating Chinese New Year in Gerrard Street, 2009.

Grinling Gibbons

Dutch by birth but of an English father, Gibbons (1648-1720), the outstanding decorative woodcarver of his – or possibly any – age, was, from 1671, the protégé of diarist John Evelyn, who brought him to the notice of **Charles II** and Sir Christopher Wren. Outstanding examples of Gibbons' work include the choir stalls and organ case of St Paul's Cathedral, the reredos of St Mary Abchurch in the City, the exquisite font-cover at All Hallows-by-the-Tower and the reredos of St James's, Piccadilly, of which Evelyn declared "there was no altar in England, nor has there been any abroad, more handsomely adorned." Gibbons also carved a marble monument to **Sir Peter Lely** (though this was lost when **St Paul's, Covent Garden** was ravaged by fire in 1795) and cast fine bronze statues of Charles II (at Chelsea Hospital) and **James II** (in front of the **National Gallery**). Gibbons moved to **Bow Street** in 1678 and lived there for the rest of his life. In 1701 his house fell down but none of his large family was injured and he rebuilt it on the same site.

(David Esterly *Grinling Gibbons and the Art of Carving* V & A Publications 2000)

James Gibbs FRS

The architect of two of the most prominent Anglican churches of the day, St Mary-le-Strand (1714-23) and **St Martin-in-the-Fields** (1722-6), James Gibbs (1682-1754) was an outsider on at least two counts, being both a (closet) Catholic and a Scot. After failing in Rome to become either a priest or a painter, Gibbs turned to architecture, thus becoming the first British architect to receive a professional training abroad. Returning to London he joined the academy headed by **Sir Godfrey Kneller** and became friends with **Hogarth**, **Thornhill** and **Charles Bridgeman**.

St Martin-in-the-Fields, Gibbs' masterpiece, established a combination of a temple-front portico and a steeple rising from the ridge of a roof which was to be widely imitated on both sides of the Atlantic. His original plan was for a round church, but this was dismissed as too radical. Gibbs also designed the quadrangle at St Bartholomew's Hospital (for which he would take no fee), the steeple of St Clement Dane's, the Radcliffe Camera at Oxford and at Cambridge the Senate House and the Fellows' Building of King's College. In the opinion of Sir John Summerson, Gibbs' *Book of*

The youthful John Gielgud.

Architecture (1728) was "probably the most widely-used architecture book of the century, not only throughout Britain but in the American colonies and the West Indies" – and, he added later, in India and Australia as well. One of its plates is claimed to have inspired the design of the White House in Washington. Gibbs lived at No. 18 **Gerrard Street** until 1726. (James Gibbs *Gibbs' Book of Architecture: An Eighteenth Century Classic* Dover 2008)

John Gielgud

Sir John Gielgud (1904-2000) a descendant of Lithuanian aristocracy and great nephew of **Ellen Terry**, acted *Hamlet* over five hundred times in the course of a career which made him one of the few people ever to win BAFTA, Emmy, Grammy, Tony and Oscar awards. Gielgud's gorgeously-costumed production of *Richard of Bordeaux* (1933) at the then New (now **Noel Coward**) Theatre gave early evidence of his talents as a director, confirmed by his remarkable season (1937-8) at the **Queen's**. The following year he directed and starred in what was regarded as the definitive interpretation of **Oscar Wilde's** *The Importance of Being Earnest* at the theatre now named in his honour.
(John Gielgud *An Actor in his Time* 1979; Jonathan Croall *Gielgud: A Theatrical Life* Methuen 2001)

Gielgud Theatre, Shaftesbury Avenue

Opened in 1906 as the Hicks Theatre for Sir Seymour Hicks (1871-1941), it became the Globe in 1909. The theatre's longest running productions have been *There's a Girl in My Soup* (1966), 1,064 performances and *Daisy Pulls It Off* (1983), 1,180 performances. The theatre adopted its present name in 1994 to mark the actor's ninetieth birthday.
(www.gielgud-theatre.com)

Glasshouse Street

Glasshouse Street, following the line of an ancient lane running north-west from Piccadilly, was recorded in 1391 as Suggen Lane. The area was leased in 1675 to Windsor Sandys, a supplier to the Glass Sellers' Company. He also had the contract to remove night-soil from the parishes of St Giles-in-the-Fields and St Martin-in-the-Fields. Since saltpetre (potassium nitrate) is both a by-product of night-soil and used in making glass Sandys could benefit from both his business interests, one of which gave rise to the name of Glasshouse Street, while the other may have given rise to Peter Street.

The street was dominated by the gigantic Regent Palace Hotel, built (1912-15), with an initially estimated two miles of corridors, for the Salmon and Gluckstein families which controlled the catering and food retailing empire of J. Lyons & Co. The hotel at the time of writing is being demolished prior to rebuilding.

Golden Square

Built 1675-ca. 1706, Golden Square may well have been planned by Sir Christopher Wren, although the moving spirit was Sir William Pulteney and the builders were James Axtell, John Emlyn (hence the approach roads named James and John) and Isaac Symball. Intended for "such houses as might accommodate Gentry", the square initially attracted members of the courtly elite, including **Charles II's** former mistress, Barbara Villiers, Duchess of Cleveland (1705-7), the fabulously wealthy 1st Duke of Chandos (1700-10) and the compulsive conspirator Henry St. John, Viscount Bolingbroke (1702-14). Other residents included a bishop, four peers or future peers and half a dozen army officers.

Golden Square, c.1755. The statue of George II, erected in 1753, is in the centre.

By 1720 it was described as "a very handsome place railed round and gravelled with many very good houses inhabited by gentry on all sides." The square was at various times in the eighteenth century home to the embassies of Bavaria, Brunswick, Genoa, Russia and Portugal. Anatomist **John Hunter** lived at No. 31 from 1763 to 1770. Swiss painter Angelica Kauffmann (1741-1807), a founding member of the Royal Academy, lived at No. 16 from 1767 until her return to Italy in 1781 with her second husband the Venetian artist Antonio Zucchi. The Italian-born Polish architect Michael Novosielski (ca. 1747-95) was living in the square in 1772 and went on to become master painter at the King's Theatre in Haymarket, which he subsequently rebuilt after a fire in 1789. A future President of the Royal Academy, Martin Archer Shee, lived (1796-8) at No. 13.

Surviving original properties on the west side include Nos. 21 (ca.1684-5), 23 (1684) and 24 (1675). No. 24 was refronted ca. 1730 during its occupation (1724-47) by the Portuguese Embassy, whose most famous resident was the **Marquis de Pombal**.

By the 1840s the square had become dominated by doctors, with no less than nine in residence. In 1865 the Hospital for Diseases of the Throat, the first of its kind in the world, was established at No. 32 by Sir Morell Mackenzie (1837-92); rebuilt in 1883, it finally closed in 1985, the site being rebuilt in 1987-9.

Dickens observed that "although a few members of the graver professions live about Golden Square, it is not exactly in anybody's way to or from anywhere. It is one of the squares that have been: a quarter of the town that has gone down in the world, and taken to letting lodgings. Many of its first and second floors are let, furnished, to single gentlemen and it takes boarders besides." By the 1860s there were eight hotels and boarding-houses doing business in Golden Square. By 1870 the dominant professional presence was represented by sixteen solicitors.

Although many of the older buildings remained substantially unaltered there were none left in use as private residences. Over the subsequent forty years the square, so conveniently near the epicentre of bespoke tailoring at Savile Row, became the focal point of the capital's trade in fine woollens and worsteds. There had been a tailor in one or other of the houses in the square since 1777 and Gagniere's, a French house dealing in silk and wool, had opened its London office here in 1844. Nos. 34-6 in the middle of the north side was built for them in 1913-15 and reconstructed in 1996-7 for the advertising gurus Maurice and Charles Saatchi. Messrs Farr and Jones took over No. 12 in 1868. By 1880 there were ten woollen and worsted merchants in Golden Square, by 1890 forty and by 1900 seventy. No. 17 was built (1902) for Burberry's, as were 15-16 (1907-8). By 1914 only four buildings had no connection with the trade, one a lone surviving hotel and two others warehouses for glass and pianos respectively. For a few years from 1905 Golden Square was home to Britain's first 'judokan' – 'The School of Japanese Self-Defence' – opened at No. 31 by Prof. S K Uyenishi.

By the outbreak of the Great War of the original thirty-nine domestic dwellings in the square, nineteen had been demolished to make way for commercial replacements. As the *Survey of London* noted grievingly of Golden Square's metamorphosis into a failed version of Brussels – "With a few notable exceptions, they jostle and vie with each other, and the south end, in particular, presents a jagged skyline of ill-assorted gables, a nightmare Grande Place effect." A stranded statue of **George II** stands, rather irrelevantly to its location, in the central garden.

Sir Victor Gollancz

Victor Gollancz (1893-1967) came from a brilliant family. One uncle was the first lecturer in English at Cambridge, another the first British rabbi to be knighted. Gollancz entered publishing in 1920, having been a soldier and a teacher. In 1928 he founded his own firm at 14 **Henrietta Street**. Early success came with the publication of R C Sheriff's powerful play about war in the trenches, *Journey's End*. This was reinforced by the buoyant sales achieved by such female authors as Elizabeth Bowen, Daphne du Maurier and Dorothy L Sayers. Gollancz is best known, however, as the publisher of George Orwell's first book, *Down and Out in Paris and London*. He then commissioned Orwell to write *The Road to Wigan Pier*, an exposé of the impact of depression on the industrial North of England, for The Left Book Club, which produced a monthly title for subscribers from 1936 until 1948. Orwell's acerbic chronicle of the Spanish Civil War, *Homage to Catalonia*, was, however, turned down by Gollancz as too brutally anti-Communist.

Victor Gollancz combined a scholarly mind with a flair for marketing and reconciled economy in production with imaginative design, notably in the house style of book jackets, which typically featured black and magenta typography on bright yellow paper. A spellbinding speaker and ardent campaigner against capital punishment and nuclear weapons, his private passions were for music, bridge and English pottery, of which he made a substantial collection.

(Richard Edwards, Ruth Edwards and Sophy Williams *Victor Gollancz: A Biography* Weidenfeld and Nicolson 1987)

Goodwin's Court

One of the originally seven courts which ran between **Bedfordbury** and **St Martin's Lane**, Goodwin's Court consists of a row of quaintly bijou, bow-fronted cottages, ambiguously hailed by Pevsner as "a surprisingly complete survival, paved and murky". A plaque claims they were built ca. 1690 – when the alley first appears in the rate-books – but Pevsner dates them a century later. Largely occupied by tailors in the nineteenth century, they were condemned in 1936 as unfit for residential use but allowed to survive as office accommodation.

Gordon Riots

London's worst ever civil disturbances, the anti-Catholic Gordon riots of 1780 spilled across the entire metropolis. The then Bavarian chapel in Warwick Street was sacked but saved from burning by the timely arrival of soldiers. **Savile House** was picked out for particular attention. Dozens of rioters

The diminutive Goodwin's Court c. 1926.

were tried before magistrates meeting in the **Turk's Head Tavern** in **Gerrard Street**. Soldiers escorting others accused of rioting were jeered and pelted with mud en route to **Bow Street Magistrates Court**. (Robert Shoemaker *The London Mob: Violence and Disorder in Eighteenth Century England* Hambledon and London 2004)

The Marquis of Granby, Shaftesbury Avenue and Chandos Place

Numerous pubs, including two in the Covent Garden area, are named after this marquis. After Eton, Cambridge and a 'Grand Tour' of Europe, John Manners, Marquis of Granby (1721-70) was elected an MP at twenty and became a colonel at twenty-four.

Granby's reputation as a general was made in the Seven Years War (1756-63) against France. Leading the heavy cavalry at the battle of Warburg in 1760 Granby pressed fearlessly forward, having lost both his hat and his wig, giving rise to the phrase "to go at it bald-headed", the way in which he is invariably depicted on the signs of the public houses named after him. Brave, skilful, open-handed to a fault and beloved of his men, the Marquis of Granby eventually rose to become Commander-in-Chief of the British Army. He was painted by **Reynolds** no fewer than twelve times and had a town in Massachusetts named in his honour. His later years were, however, clouded by unmerited political attacks and harassment by his creditors. He died £37,000 in debt, not yet fifty. There is a Marquis of Granby pub at 142 **Shaftesbury Avenue** and another at 51-2 **Chandos Place** (where **Claude Duval** was arrested) as well as others in Fitzrovia and Westminster. Yet more are scattered the length and breadth of England, from Norfolk to Staffordshire, from Yorkshire to Surrey.

Baron Grant

Born Albert Gottheimer, Grant (1830-99) was the most audacious and unscrupulous company promoter of the nineteenth century, responsible for losing at least £20,000,000 belonging to the naïve investors who trusted him Some of his schemes did work out, hence an Italian barony for a venture in Milan, but most of the mines, railways, waterworks and banks which attracted the savings of widows, vicars and orphans were either ill-founded or fraudulent. Elected MP for Kidderminster in 1865, Grant made a bid for public respectability by posing as a disinterested national benefactor. As such he paid for the laying out of the gardens in **Leicester Square** in their present form and the installation of the busts of its distinguished former residents and a statue of Shakespeare. Grant also bought Landseer's arresting oil sketch of Sir Walter Scott and presented it to the **National Portrait Gallery**, where it still hangs. Meanwhile he lavished money on the construction of Kensington House, the largest private residence in London, which was used just once, for a 'Bachelors' Ball'. In 1875 Anthony Trollope published *The Way We Live Now*, whose villainous protagonist, Augustus Melmotte, was a very thinly disguised portrait of the arch-fraudster. By 1877 Grant was besieged by some eighty-nine separate legal actions. Kensington House was seized on behalf of his creditors and demolished. Unlike the fictional Melmotte, Grant survived and retired to the south coast.

The Great Globe

James Wyld (1812-87), MP and geographer, recognised that the Great Exhibition would flood London with visitors who might patronise other attractions and therefore determined to realise a long-held dream, to construct "a great model of the earth's surface". In return for a ten-year lease he agreed to locate his project on the then derelict gardens of **Leicester Square** and, at the end of his term, to restore them. A prime attraction of the site must have been the proximity of the **Alhambra** and **Savile House**, which would bring him the benefit of a passing trade. A hundred men worked around the clock to build the Globe, which opened just a month after the Exhibition, in June 1851. Over the course of its existence the Great Globe was used for a wide range of lectures and exhibitions,

The Great Globe, erected in Leicester Square in 1851.

including a mock-up of a gold-mine and a moving diorama of Russia. After some legal wrangling the building was demolished in 1862. The garden was enclosed by a stone kerb and iron railing but still left much to be desired until completed by **Baron Grant**.

Great Marlborough Street

Named for John Churchill, Duke of Marlborough (1650-1722), ancestor of Sir Winston Churchill, this broad commercial street was begun in 1704, the year of Marlborough's historic victory over the armies of Louis XIV of France at Blenheim in southern Germany. Marlborough became a national idol of almost royal status and this was the first London street named to honour him. Nearby Ramillies Street and Place, honouring a Marlborough victory of 1706, were known as Blenheim Street until 1885. Scattered across London and its suburbs there are still more than forty streets and locations incorporating the name of Blenheim and forty-eight with the name of Marlborough.

The first section of the street to be built up stretched from **Poland Street** to **Carnaby Street** and was extended westward in 1736 with the building of **Argyll Street** and then westwards again in 1820 to the new **Regent Street**. In 1714 it was written that Great Marlborough Street "surpasses anything that is called a street in the magnificence of its buildings and gardens and is inhabited by all prime quality". Both pubs in the street date from 1739.

No. 47 is of ca. 1710 with a stucco front of ca. 1830. This was from 1896 a home of the Royal College of Music. No. 48 was built (1774) as 'the Casino', an intended assembly room à la **Carlisle House** but this proved short-lived. In 1869 Nos. 49 and 50 were bought up and a temporary iron church opened behind them; all were demolished to make way for the church of St John the Baptist, built (1884) in Perpendicular Gothic to the designs of Sir Arthur Blomfield. The church was demolished in 1937 and replaced by a modernistic building of 1939.

On the south side the most notable building is **Liberty's**. Just round the corner at the top of **Carnaby Street** is the mock-Tudor Shakespeare's Head pub (1928) with the Bard's balding head leaning quizzically out of an upper window.

Opposite stands Art Deco Ideal House, built (1927-9), to the designs of celebrated American architect Raymond Hood, for the National Radiator Co. Pevsner condemns it as flashy – "an architectural parallel to the Wurlitzer" (giant cinema organ) – but the stylish floral motifs at the top are an elegant offset to the austere black granite facing.

The Art Deco Ideal House in Great Marlborough Street, now styled Palladium House in Argyll Street.

The hotel at Nos. 19-21 was built (1913-16) as a Magistrates' Court and police station. In 1895 its predecessor witnessed the beginning of proceedings against the Marquis of Queensberry for libelling **Oscar Wilde.** The actual trial, resulting in Wilde's exposure, disgrace, imprisonment and exile, took place at the Central Criminal Court, Old Bailey. Between 1786 and 1798 the site had been occupied by the museum of anatomist Joshua Brookes (1761-1833), which included the corpses of executed criminals among the exhibits. The museum, which cost him some £30,000, proved impossible to dispose of in its entirety and, sold off piecemeal over twenty-two days, failed to provide him with the comfortable retirement he had intended.

Sir Walter Farquhar (1738-1819) built up a highly successful practice while living on Great Marlborough Street between 1771 and 1797, first as an apothecary, then as a physician. An army surgeon initially, he did not formally qualify as a doctor until he was almost sixty but still became physician to the future **George IV**.

The actress **Sarah Siddons** lived at No 54. **Nelson** and his new wife, the former Mrs. Frances Nisbet, took lodgings on the street shortly after their marriage. Architect Thomas Hardwick (1752-1829) lived here from 1815-25, during which time he completed the building of Marylebone parish church and served as architect to St Bartholomew's Hospital and Hampton Court Palace.

Charles Darwin (1809-82) was briefly (1837-8) resident at No. 41 on his return from circumnavigating the world aboard *HMS Beagle*. Other residents of Great Marlborough Street have included the reclusive millionaire scientist Henry Cavendish in 1782-4 and **Benjamin Haydon** who also lived at No. 41 from 1808 to 1817.

Great Newport Street

One of the first streets to be built up in Soho, the earliest houses were erected soon after 1612 but were dilapidated by 1650. Redeveloped by Richard Ryder, later Master Carpenter to **Charles II**, the street attracted aristocratic tenants. Strype observed in 1720 that the north side "hath far the Best Buildings and is inhabited by Gentry, whereas on the other side dwell ordinary Tradespeople, of which several are of the French nation", i.e. **Huguenots**. A young **Joshua Reynolds**, newly arrived in London, lived at a house on the site of Nos.10-11 in 1754-60. By 1755 he had 120 sitters a year, by 1759, 156. During this period he painted three members of the royal family and twelve dukes, as well as Horace Walpole, Laurence Sterne, **David Garrick** and **Dr Johnson**. George Romney (1734-1802) lived in the street in 1768-9 and greatly advanced his career thanks to his portrait – and the friendship – of the dramatist Richard Cumberland. **Johann Zoffany** lived here in 1779, returning from seven years in Italy. The bijou **Arts Theatre** was founded (1927) to stage unlicensed and avant-garde plays.

Great Pulteney Street

The first street, narrower and inferior to the present one, was laid out ca. 1668 and replaced ca. 1718-20. Nos. 8-13 and 35-40 are of the early eighteenth century. No. 23 (1722) was built by plasterer Isaac Mansfield for himself and refaced ca. 1780. Most of the rest were built as warehouses for the wool trade of **Golden Square**.

Harpsichord maker Jacob Kirkman had his business at No. 17 from 1739 to 1750. Josef Haydn (1732-1809) stayed at No.18 in 1791-2 in what he thought "charming and comfortable but very expensive lodgings", where he wrote six of the 'Salomon' symphonies, occasionally peering out in wonder at fog so thick "you could spread it on bread." Byron's acolyte **Dr John Polidori** was born and committed suicide at No. 38.

Great Queen Street

Built up from the 1630s and hailed as the "first regular street in London", Great Queen Street was originally a major thoroughfare linking Covent Garden and Lincoln's Inn Fields. Nos. 6, 27-9 and 33-7 are early- and mid-eighteenth century. The street was brutally truncated by the construction of Kingsway at the beginning of the twentieth century. Prominent residents have included **Kneller** (1702-23), **Arne** (1735-48) and **Sheridan** (1777-82). **Blake** was apprenticed (1771-8) to an engraver at No. 31. The gigantic **Freemasons' Hall** (1927-33) occupies the site of the Freemasons' Tavern, where the Football Association was founded in 1863 by eleven clubs including one from the War Office and another called No Names, Kilburn.

Great Windmill Street

A windmill to the north of the line of Coventry Street was recorded in 1585. After 1671 the track leading up to it was built up by **Thomas Panton**. Major features include the former home of **Dr William Hunter**, the **Windmill Theatre** and the Red Lion pub where **Karl Marx** lectured in 1850-1.

Greek Church, Soho

Driven out of their home islands by Ottoman forces, a small contingent of Greek refugees arrived in London in 1670. Here, in the uncharacteristically sympathetic words of *The Survey of London*, they made "a melancholy attempt to establish among the raw brick carcases of Soho, a shrine of Byzantium." Built between 1677 and 1681, on the western side of Hog Lane (now **Charing Cross Road**), the venture was plagued by funding difficulties, by the promoters' ignorance of the English language and of English law and by the disenchanting realisation that it had been built in the wrong location, far too far from where most Greeks had actually settled in London. Having also failed to grasp that the site had been made available on a lease, rather than freehold, Joseph

Hogarth's famous 1738 depiction of the congregation emerging from the fashionable Huguenot (formerly Greek) church to the right. A gutter symbolically segregates the decorous worshippers from the squalor and chaos of their indigenous neighbours.

Georgirenes, Archbishop of Samos, sold the building to the **Huguenot** community and felt cheated to receive far less than the cost of the building alone. From 1682 until 1822 L'Eglise des Grecs was a fashionable place of French worship, its stylish congregation illustrated in **Hogarth**'s engraving *Noon* (1738). From 1822 until 1849 the building was occupied by Calvinistic Independents. In 1850 it became, as St Mary the Virgin, an Anglican out-station of **St Anne's**. It was finally demolished in 1934, the proceeds being used to finance St Mary the Virgin at Kenton. The site was covered by **St Martin's School of Art**.

Greek Street

Mentioned in 1679 and named from the **Greek church**. Huguenot Abraham Meure lived here (1691-1714) and ran an elite academy for French and English pupils, teaching French, Latin, drawing, dancing and fencing.

Nos. 12-13 were built (ca. 1684) as a single seven-bay house and for more than twenty years housed the showrooms of **Josiah Wedgwood**. Nos. 6, 8, 50, 51 and 58 are from the 1730s. No. 48, the restaurant **L'Escargot** is in a house of 1741-2. No. 3 is from ca. 1744. The shopfronts of 17 (ca.1824) formerly (1789) Clagget's museum of **musical instruments**, Nos. 18 (1862-3) and 20 (1842) are a reminder of the street's long commercial history. No. 18 was from 1864 to 1866 the headquarters of the Central Council of the International Working Men's Association, the socialist 'First International', whose Inaugural Address was drafted by **Karl Marx**. Maison Bertaux claims to be London's oldest French patisserie, dating from 1871.

The St James and Soho Club, one of London's first working men's clubs moved into No. 19 in 1864. No. 59 was built (1884-5) as the Soho Club and Home for Working Girls to provide respectable lodgings, evening classes and recreation. A Western Jewish Girls' Free School was once at No. 6. **The Pillars of Hercules** (1935), the Three Greyhounds (1924) and the **Coach and Horses** (1847) are all noted Soho drinking-spots, the **Gay Hussar** and Au Jardin des Gourmets celebrated restaurants.

Casanova stayed here in 1764 and **de Quincey** found refuge in a deserted house. The brilliant portraitist **Thomas Lawrence** (1769-1830), a future knight and President of the Royal Academy, lived at No. 60 when he was twenty-one and had just attracted the favourable attention of **Sir Joshua Reynolds**. No. 49 was the home of the Skiffle Cellar. Soho's best example of domestic **architecture**, the former home of **William Beckford**, is at No. 1.

Groucho Club

Opened in 1985, the Groucho Club at 45 Dean Street occupies the premises of the former Gennaro's restaurant. It was intended as an antidote to the traditional men's clubs of St James's and was initiated by two leading figures from the world of publishing, Liz Calder of Bloomsbury and Carmen Callil of Virago. Its name refers to the remark attributed to the American film star Groucho (Julius Henry) Marx (1895-1977) that he would not want to belong to any club that would have him as a member. Membership has expanded over the years to embrace a wide range of recruits from the media and creative arts. (www.thegrouchoclub.com)

Nell Gwyn

Eleanor Gwyn (or Gwynn) (1650-87) probably grew up on **Drury Lane**, possibly in a brothel, and certainly had lodgings there as an adult. She began her theatrical career as an orange-seller (and is thus often depicted on pub signs) but soon graduated to the stage, making her debut at fourteen in *The Indian Emperor* by **Dryden**. **Pepys** was distinctly

Nell Gwyn, a portrait by ***Sir Peter Lely***.

unimpressed when he saw Nell Gwyn in serious or tragic roles but greatly taken by her playing a 'breeches part', Florimel in Dryden's *Secret Love* – "so great a performance of a comical part was never I believe in the world … It makes me, I confess, admire her." Speaking the witty epilogue to Dryden's *Tyrannic Love, or the Royal Martyr* brought Nell to the notice of **Charles II** whose mistress she became and to whom she bore two sons. A reclining nude of Nell with one of her children, the Duke of St Albans, as *Venus and Cupid* was painted by **Sir Peter Lely** for Charles II's personal delectation. The Nell of Old Drury pub is at 29 **Catherine Street** and the Nell Gwynne at Bull Inn Court, just off the **Strand**.

(Charles Beauclerk *Nell Gwyn: A Biography* Pan 2006).

Joseph Haines

Haines (died 1701) was an outstanding dancer, excellent comedian, compulsive practical joker and prolific composer of prologues, epilogues and lampoons which on occasion got him into trouble with the authorities. Haines played clowns and buffoons in **Killigrew**'s company and was one of the first English actors to play Harlequin. His talent as a dancer certainly impressed **Pepys** and was sufficient to gain him employment abroad. In 1670 he danced before Louis XIV in the premiere performance of Molière's *Le bourgeois gentilhomme*. A great favourite in the **coffee-houses** of Covent Garden, Haines died in his lodgings at Hart, now **Floral, Street.**

Nina Hamnett

Rejecting a respectable Welsh background in favour of Bohemian life in Paris and London, Nina Hamnett (1890-1956) knew Sickert and Picasso and the Satanist Aleister ('the wickedest man in the world') Crowley and modelled for Modigliani ("Modigliani said I had the best tits in Europe") and for Henri Gaudier-Brzeska, whose *Torso of Nina* (1913) is now in the Tate. She also painted. Incomparable in her youth, Nina Hamnett declined through alcoholism and improvidence into incontinence. A regular at the **Colony Club** until she was banned, she also drank at **The French**, the **Caves de France** and the Fitzroy and the Wheatsheaf in Fitzrovia. In 1956 a radio play about her life cut too close to the bone and days later she fell from the window of her room and impaled on the railings forty feet beneath. She survived long enough to die in Paddington General Hospital. The coroner recorded a verdict of accidental death but among her small remaining acquaintance her death was generally believed to have been suicide.

(Denise Hooker *Nina Hamnett: Queen of Bohemia* 1986; Nina Hamnett *Laughing Torso: Reminiscences of Nina Hamnett* Hildreth Press 2008)

Augustus Harris

Augustus Harris (1852-96), whose bust adorns the exterior of the **Theatre Royal, Drury Lane**, came of a great theatrical lineage. His grandfather, Joseph Glossop, had built the Coburg Theatre (now the Old Vic) and managed La Scala, Milan. His father, also Augustus Harris (1826-73), had made his stage debut at eight and managed the Princess's and **Covent Garden Theatre**. Harris himself was born in Paris and grew up speaking both French and German. Beginning as a touring actor in the provinces, he was quickly promoted to stage

'Augustus Druriolanus' by 'Spy'.

manager. At twenty-seven, on borrowed cash, he took over the lease of the **Theatre Royal**. Harris co-wrote and acted in his first melodrama, *The World* (1880); enthralling staging and effects compensated for its baffling plot. Unashamedly catering to popular taste, he devised a seasonal programme which began with melodrama and ended with 'highbrow' plays but centred on pantomime, the profits from which subsidised the other elements. Harris's pantomimes featured top-line music hall talents, including Little Tich, Dan Leno, Marie Lloyd and Vesta Tilley. The 'highbrow' productions ranged from Shakespeare to Wagner and the *Comedie Francaise*. In the interests of authenticity Harris reproduced a real cigarette factory for a staging of *Carmen*. When he wanted extras drilled in marching he hired the then Major Kitchener – the future conqueror of the Sudan and subject of the iconic Great War recruiting poster – to undertake the task. In 1888 Harris took over **Covent Garden** and bought the *Sunday Times* to use as a weapon against critics.

At Covent Garden he initiated the production of operas in their original language, not just Italian, and arranged personal visits by Mascagni and Puccini. Royal approval was indicated by the staging of command performances at Windsor Castle in 1893 and 1894. Harris also – somehow – found time to serve as a member of the newly-constituted London County Council and as Sheriff of the City of London, for which, rather than for his contributions to theatrical life, he was knighted in 1891. A combination of overwork, diabetes and cancer carried off the colourful impresario at just forty-three. His flamboyant tomb in Brompton Cemetery features a life-size Victorian beauty in an extravagant pose of mourning.

Benjamin Haydon by G H Harlow, in 1816.

Benjamin Haydon

The fact that Benjamin Haydon (1786-1846) is now best remembered as a diarist speaks volumes for his talents as an artist. He was determined, in his own words, to paint "great works and great works only." The art historian Jeremy Maas has, however, summarised Haydon's painterly career as "ludicrous". He had bad luck but compounded his misfortunes with a bad temper, bad money management, bad choices of projects and antagonism even towards his would-be patrons. Wordsworth, **Lamb** and Keats all admired Haydon's work, which perhaps indicates how far his inspiration and his genius were literary, rather than visual, but **Hazlitt**, on being shown Haydon's *Judgment of Solomon*, commented bitchily "Why did you paint it so large? A small canvas might have concealed your faults."

Benjamin Haydon lived at 46 **Great Marlborough Street** from 1808 to 1817. During this period he began work on an enormous canvas of *Christ's Entry into Jerusalem*. It was to take him six years. When he was finally able to exhibit the finished work at the new Egyptian Hall on Piccadilly in 1820 he charged a shilling a head admission to inspect it, which, with the sale of the accompanying catalogue, brought in £1,760 – a handsome sum but not nearly enough to pay off his debts.

Haydon was to be imprisoned three times for debt and to suffer the deaths of five of his children. Driven to despair by his debts, he ended dismally – cutting his throat *and* shooting himself in the head – thereby abandoning his widow and six surviving children to their fate. Seven years later Haydon's diaries were published – 27 volumes of marvellously observed gossip and anecdote, recorded in sparkling prose, iridescent with delicate barbs – his life's missing masterpiece. Haydon's 1842 portrait of William Wordsworth, whose poetry he passionately admired, can be seen in the **National Portrait Gallery**.

(B R Haydon and John Joliffe *Neglected Genius: The Diaries of Benjamin Robert Haydon 1808-46* Hutchinson 1990)

The new Haymarket Theatre c. 1821, with its predecessor to the left in the process of being demolished.

John Hayls

Portraitist John Hayls (died 1679) lived on **Southampton Street** before moving to **Long Acre** in 1668. **Samuel Pepys** had Hayls paint portraits of himself, his wife and his father. Pepys' own portrait shows him in a hired silk gown, holding a piece of music of his own composition. He complained that the pose gave him a sore neck. The painting cost him £14 and can now be seen in the **National Portrait Gallery.**

Haymarket Theatre, Haymarket

The first, unlicensed, theatre on this site was put up in 1720. Under the management (1735-7) of **Henry Fielding** it staged satires against the government so damaging that a regime of legal censorship was imposed which restricted English theatre until 1968. Reopened briefly in 1744 by **Charles Macklin** and again from 1747, the Haymarket, despite an insecure existence, was rebuilt (1820-1) in its present form to designs by **John Nash**. Following the abolition of the Patent Act in 1843, which had severely limited the presentation of legitimate drama, the Haymarket flourished under the management of J.B. Buckstone (from 1853 to 1878), Sir Squire and Lady Bancroft in the 1880s and, between 1887 and 1896, Herbert Beerbohm Tree, when it staged the first performances of **Oscar Wilde's** *A Woman of No Importance* (1893) and *An Ideal Husband* (1895). In 1914 the first licensed English version of Ibsen's *Ghosts* was staged; dealing with the impact of syphilis, its performance had previously been restricted to private theatre clubs. The interior of the Haymarket was rebuilt in 1904 and a further restoration made in 1994.

William Hazlitt

" *... perhaps the most uninteresting mind of all our distinguished critics"* T S Eliot

William Hazlitt (1778-1830) was probably the first Englishman to make a living as a professional critic, reviewing not only books but also plays and art as well. Hazlitt's career also included spells as a parliamentary reporter and a freelance lecturer, though he is better known as an accomplished essayist on a par with his friends **Lamb** and Coleridge. Both Hazlitt's marriages failed; he once fell in love so obsessively that his sanity was in peril; and he was imprisoned for debt. His unfashionably laudatory biography of Napoleon was a flop, both commercially and critically. In September 1830 Hazlitt found a final refuge a No. 6 **Frith Street**, dying there shortly afterwards, his

Hazlitt portrayed in his book, Table Talk, *and his tombstone in St Anne's churchyard.*

last words supposedly being, "Well, I've had a happy life." He was buried in the churchyard of **St Anne's**, Soho, where a handsome slab with a lengthy inscription of praise marks his resting-place.

No. 6 Frith Street, dating from 1718, is now Hazlitt's Hotel, renowned for the individual décor of its rooms and the discreet centrality of its location. It was from Hazlitt's that the American author Bill Bryson set out on the nationwide jaunt that resulted in his best-selling *Notes from a Small Island* (1995).

(Stanley Jones *William Hazlitt: A Life from Winterslow to Frith Street* Oxford University Press 1989; Duncan Wu *William Hazlitt: The First Modern Man* Oxford University Press 2008)

Thomas Hearne FSA

A native of Malmesbury, Wiltshire, Hearne (1744-1817) came to London young, trained as an engraver and spent six years recording the Leeward Islands. His *magnum opus* includes fifty-two detailed water colours to illustrate *The Antiquities of Britain*. These were doubly significant in reviving interest in Gothic architecture and providing models which were copied by such later eminent water-colourists as Girtin and **Turner**. A plaque on the north side of **Meard Street** records his residence there, although he died while living in **Macclesfield Street**.

William Heinemann

The British-born son of a German immigrant, William Heinemann (1863-1920) intended a career in music but recognised that his greatest talent lay in spotting talent in others. Setting up his own publishing business in **Bedford Street** in 1890, he had an immediate success with *The Gentle Art of Making Enemies* by the American painter and wit James Whistler. Heinemann soon managed to recruit a brilliant stable of writers including R L Stevenson, Rudyard Kipling, H G Wells, Somerset Maugham, **Joseph Conrad**, Max Beerbohm and John Galsworthy. He was also responsible for introducing the British to the works of Dostoyevsky, Turgenev, Tolstoy and Ibsen and initially financing **Foyle's** bookshop..

Henrietta Street

No building remains of the original street laid out in 1631 and named for Charles I's French consort, Henrietta Maria. It was largely rebuilt by 1730. Nos. 9 and 10 are of 1726-7, 5-8 of 1730-31 and 3 and 4 of 1780-81. Most of the current buildings are second rebuildings of the later nineteenth century. A 'trade street' from the beginning, Henrietta Street's earliest residents included four licensed victuallers and two shoemakers. Strype described it in 1720 as inhabited by "Mercers, Lacemen, Drapers etc." But the portraitist Samuel Cooper (1609-72) was also a long-time resident. Specialising in miniatures, he was referred to by **Pepys** as "the great limner in little". Apart from Mrs Pepys, Cooper's subjects included Cromwell, his family and his generals, Monck, Milton, **Charles II**, Catherine of Braganza, Prince Rupert, James II, Thomas Hobbes and **Samuel Butler**.

The self-educated astrologer and quack John Partridge (1644-1715) began life as apprentice to a Covent Garden shoe-maker but switched to publishing an annual almanac from premises in Henrietta Street.

The marine artist Samuel Scott (?1710-72), a close friend of **Hogarth**, lived at No. 2 from 1747 to 1758. Scott's paintings of the Thames earned him the accolade of "the English **Canaletto**". The discriminating Horace Walpole admired and collected Scott's work.

The eminent society physician Dr Richard Mead (1673-1754) habitually used coffee-houses as consulting rooms for meeting patients but Rawthmell's Coffee House was his preferred venue when he wished to socialize. Mead's patients included **George II** and **Sir Isaac Newton**, whom he attended through his last illness. The Society of Arts, later Royal Society of Arts, was founded at Rawthmell's in 1754. Unlike the Royal Society, the Society was concerned with the application of science to practical purposes "to promote the arts, manufactures and commerce of this kingdom".

At the long-vanished Castle Tavern the playwright **Sheridan** fought his third duel with Matthews, his rival for the affections of the angelic soprano Elizabeth Linley. Both men were badly cut about but Sheridan had the last laugh, eloping with Miss Linley from her plush home on Bath's Royal Crescent.

Jane Austen stayed in Henrietta Street twice; Washington Irving (1783-1849) lodged at No. 22 in 1824; and the dying Italian poet and patriot **Ugo Foscolo** found refuge at No. 19 in 1827. In 1819 No. 8 was the home of Fanny Kelly, later proprietor of the ill-fated **Royalty Theatre**. A smitten **Charles Lamb** proposed to her by letter while she was living there and she turned him down by return of post.

No. 3 was the address of Duckworth & Company, publishers of John Galsworthy and D H Lawrence. No. 11 once housed the offices of Chapman & Hall, publishers of **Charles Dickens**. Nos. 12-13 was Ashley's Hotel. No. 18 was built (1891-2) for the publisher **C Arthur Pearson**.

No. 10 Henrietta Street, where Jane Austen stayed twice.

Following Pearson's publication of Robert Baden-Powell's runaway success *Scouting for Boys* (1908), the firm served as the infant Boy Scout movement's first office. No. 14 was the offices of **Victor Gollancz**.

In 1922 T E Lawrence (1888-1935) came to the recruiting office of the Royal Air Force at No. 4 and tried to enlist under the pseudonym of J H Ross. Unable to produce any papers to prove his identity or to provide any satisfactory explanation for the lash-marks on his back (the result of a masochistic session) he was turned down by Captain W E Johns, author of the derring-do 'Biggles' books for boys (which had – no doubt unconscious – homo-erotic undertones of their own). To his amazement 'Ross' returned with a messenger from the Air Ministry and a directive to accept him, now revealed as the legendary hero of the 'Revolt in the Desert', 'Lawrence of Arabia'. Lawrence's subsequent experiences of service life were chronicled unflinchingly in *The Mint* (1936).

Nos. 25-29 once (1882-92) housed St Peter's Hospital for Stone, the first institution in England to specialise in urology. The four ground floor shops were part of the original design, intended to generate income for the hospital.

Hickford's Rooms

The first Hickford's Rooms, John Hickford's Dancing School at **Panton Street,** was used for concerts between 1697 and 1738, the year in which

T E Lawrence (left) as 'Ross' in his air force unit.

The Hippodrome at the corner of Charing Cross Road and Cranbourn Street, c. 1905.

the establishment moved to new-built premises at 63-65 (formerly 41) **Brewer Street,** Soho. This hosted the visiting child prodigy Mozart and his sister Nannerl in 1765. It subsequently became the home of the Philharmonic Society, founded in 1813, and survived as a building until its demolition in 1934 to make way for an extension to the Regent Palace Hotel.

Hippodrome, 1 Cranbourn Street

Opened in 1900, the Hippodrome was designed by Frank Matcham as a setting for "a circus show second to none in the world, combined with elaborate stage spectacles impossible in any other theatre". Reconstructed internally in 1909 it was used to present ballet, music hall, revues and musicals, such as **Ivor Novello's** *Perchance to Dream*. From 1958 to 1982 it was a restaurant and cabaret, The Talk of the Town. At the time of writing there is a plan to convert it into a casino.

William Hogarth

William Hogarth (1697-1764) was the first great native-born British artist, London's certainly. His most durable image, *Gin Lane*, was a visual sermon on the disastrous impact of cheap alcohol on fellow-Londoners. Born in Smithfield, Hogarth aimed at painting until his father's imprisonment for debt forced him to become an engraver. In 1720 he joined the **St Martin's Lane Academy** to further his artistic ambitions and settled on the south-east corner of **Leicester Square**. Having known poverty, Hogarth was determined to avoid it. His first popular success was *A Scene from the Beggar's Opera*, a typically opportunistic take on John Gay's hit musical of 1728. Hogarth's engraving skills enabled him to make art cheap enough for a mass-market, bypassing aristocratic patronage. He confirmed his reputation with a new genre – 'modern moral subjects' – commenting on the foibles of the day. The six engravings of *The Harlot's Progress* (1731) show Moll Hackabout, an innocent rural migrant, enticed into prostitution, dying of the pox. The series received the unwelcome compliment of being

Hogarth's famous depiction of 'Gin Lane' – a comment on the squalid life encouraged by cheap drink. The scene is set in the St Giles area, looking towards the spire of St George's Bloomsbury.

A bust of Hogarth in Leicester Square, yards from the site of his former home and studio.

widely pirated. In 1735 therefore Hogarth promoted a Copyright Act which gave visual artists the protection from piracy writers enjoyed. *The Rake's Progress* (1735) parallels the harlot's saga; empty-headed Tom Rakewell squanders his inheritance, ending insane in Bedlam. *Marriage à la Mode* (1742-4) chronicles the disastrous misalliance of a spendthrift aristocrat with a wealthy merchant's daughter. *The March to Finchley* satirises the army at the time of Bonnie Prince Charlie's Jacobite uprising in 1745.

A fervent patriot, Hogarth despised the craze for Italian and French culture espoused by the Society of Dilettanti and became a founder-member of the oppositional **Beefsteak Society**. His painting of *Calais Gate, or the Roast beef of Old England* mocks the poverty of the priest-ridden French, indirectly recording his sole trip abroad, where compulsive sketching got him arrested as a spy. Hogarth's aspirations to paint in the grand manner, like his father-in-law, Sir James Thornhill, were ultimately unsucessful. His murals at St Bartholomew's Hospital are sociologically interesting but aesthetically weak. Hogarth's attempt at art theory, *The Analysis of Beauty* (1753), was derided by younger contemporaries. Posterity has been more positive. Hogarth's images still inspire the cartoonists of today. Original Hogarth paintings can be see within easy distance of his Leicester Square base – *Marriage à la Mode* in the **National Gallery**, *The Rake's Progress* and the *Election* series in Sir John Soane's House at 12-14 Lincoln's Inn Fields. *The March to Finchley* and the masterly *Captain Coram* are at the Foundling Hospital on Brunswick Square. Hogarth's country house at Chiswick is open to the public. He lies nearby in St Nicholas' churchyard. A self portrait of the artist at his easel can be seen in the **National Portrait Gallery**. Hogarth's bust is in **Leicester Square** gardens.

(Jenny Uglow *Hogarth: A Life and a World* 1997; www.library.northwestern.edu/spec/hogarth/; www.lamp.ac.uk/hogarth/; http://hogarth_scholar.fortunecity.com/)

Homosexuality

Homosexual acts between consenting males were, until 1968 in Britain, deemed to be criminal and punishable by imprisonment, in the past by more severe retribution. In 1811 six men were pelted in the pillory at the Haymarket after being accused of sodomy. But 'Molly houses' for the provision of homosexual services had existed in Covent Garden for a century. Both Soho and Covent Garden have long enjoyed an air of tolerance of varied sexual preferences. Discretion could be purchased, at a price, in apparently respectable establishments – **Oscar Wilde** entertained rent boys in a restaurant in **Rupert Street.** According to the author Thomas Burke the **Café Royal** was a regular haunt of "hard featured ambassadors from Lesbos and Sodom". The theatrical world was notably tolerant in its attitudes to homosexuality, particularly when, like **Noel Coward**, the person concerned behaved with discretion. **Gielgud**, prosecuted for importuning in 1953, was nevertheless knighted that same year and applauded by the audience the next time he went on stage, though the experience kept him clear of Hollywood for decades.

Easy-going Soho, especially such venues as the **Colony Club**, accepted positive flaunting, as in the case of **Francis Bacon** or **Daniel Farson**. At different periods the **Alhambra**, the bar of **Daly's** theatre, the Long Bar of Lyons' Corner House on **Coventry Street** and the Golden Lion public house have all served as regular venues of assignation. At the **Gargoyle Club John Minton** often had a sailor in tow. Quentin Crisp, 'the Naked Civil Servant', by contrast, records spending evenings of endless frustration drinking coffees in Au Chat Noir at No. 72 **Old Compton Street**, now the acknowledged epicentre of gay London. Patrons of the **Admiral Duncan** pub were victims of a homophobic bomb outrage in 1999. Tolerance of homosexuality also attracted predators – serial killer Dennis Nilsen, who worked in **Denmark Street**, picked up several of his fourteen victims in Soho pubs.

One of the earliest British films to deal openly with homosexuality, *Victim* (1961), starred Dirk Bogarde as one of a circle of men being blackmailed. One scene is set among the gay clientele of **The Salisbury** in St Martin's Lane and another in a barbershop next to the **Marquis of Granby** pub at **Cambridge Circus**, where the proprietor keels over with a heart attack after being threatened by sinister blackmailer Derren Nesbitt.
(www.untoldlondon.org.uk)

Hospital for Women

Founded by Dr Protheroe Smith in Red Lion Square in 1842 as the Hospital for Diseases of Women, this was the first institution to deal exclusively with "those maladies which neither rank, wealth nor character can avert from the female sex". In 1845 the named was changed to Hospital for Women to avoid the unwanted implication that it dealt only with venereal diseases. In 1852 the hospital moved to No. 30 **Soho Square** where it expanded to absorb adjoining properties. Independent until 1989, in 2000 the building reopened as the first NHS Walk-In Centre. Other activities include general practice, dentistry and specialist services for the homeless and drug addicts and the local Chinese community.

Hotels

Soho's hotels were invariably built as something else, and were small. **Fauconberg House** was Wright's Hotel and Coffee House for a spell. Imposing **Carlisle House** in Soho Square in 1860 became a boarding-house for 'Clerical Medical and Law Students', then Whittaker's Private Hotel. The Hampshire on **Leicester Square** was, until World War Two, London's leading dental hospital. Hooper's Hotel at 21 Soho Square was briefly (1772-5) the home of the Spanish ambassador before its acquisition (1778) by Thomas Hooper, who managed it as an hotel, while also providing visitors with the opportunity to gratify themselves in chambers variously entitled 'the Painted Chamber', the 'Skeleton Room' and the 'Coal Hole'. Hooper's Hotel is mentioned in a treatise on *The Mysteries of Flagellation*. The home of anatomist **William Hunter** on **Great Windmill Street** had a subsequent incarnation as the Hotel d L'Etoile. Charles Dibdin's **Sans Souci** theatre eventually became the Hotel de Versailles before being demolished to make way for the Hotel de l'Europe, later the Victory Hotel. Most hotels, however, began as private houses, like Morland's on **Dean Street**, run by Henry, brother of the talented but feckless painter **George Morland**, and the modern day **Hazlitt's**.

The Sabloniere Hotel was at 29-31 Leicester Square from 1788 to 1867. It was described as a French house where "a table d'hote affords the lovers of French cookery and French conversation an opportunity for gratification at a comparatively modest charge".

Karl Marx initially settled his family in the German hotel at Nos. 1-2 Leicester Place, where the composer Johann Strauss had also been a guest in 1839. There was another German hotel, Wedde's, at Portland House in Greek Street but this closed down on the outbreak of war in 1914.

The 1908 edition of the celebrated Baedeker's *Handbook to London* referred the area around **Leicester Square** as "much frequented by French visitors" and added an admonitory note that "the stranger is cautioned against going to any unrecommended house near Leicester Square, as there are several houses of doubtful reputation in this locality." Of the establishments on Leicester Square only the Queen's, where dinner was served to the accompaniment of a band, was given a nod of approval; elsewhere the only other to past muster was the Hotel Suisse at 53 Old Compton Street – "unpretending, well spoken of" – where at 2/6d a room cost half what it did at the Queen's.

House of St Barnabas, Greek Street

Also known as the House of Charity this centre for London's homeless at 1 Greek Street is hailed by Pevsner as "one of the best and best preserved mid-18th century houses in London", renowned for the magnificent Rococo plasterwork of its great staircase and three main first-floor rooms and the excellence of its carved wooden doorways, windows and chimneypieces. It is open to visitors on the first Monday of the month.

A house was built on the site in 1679 and occupied by a series of aristocratic tenants until its demolition in 1742. The present building was

The House of St Barnabas at 1 Greek Street, renowned for its Rococo plasterwork.

put up as a shell in 1744-46 but remained empty until bought in 1754 by Richard Beckford, newly-elected MP for Bristol and a fabulously wealthy Jamaica slave and plantation owner. He lavished cash on its completion but scarcely had time to occupy it before dying in France in 1756. As the area lost its appeal to fashionable residents in 1811 the building was taken over by the Westminster Commission for Sewers and was occupied by its successor the Metropolitan Board of Works, from 1855. It was from these premises therefore that the MBW's brilliant chief engineer Sir Joseph Bazalgette (1819-91) designed and began the construction of London's modern sewerage system. In 1861 the Board moved out and the House of Charity acquired the building to use for its work with homeless women, adding the petite French Gothic chapel which can be seen in **Manette Street**. The House of St Barnabas ceased to offer residential accommodation for women in 2006.

(D Avery *The House of St Barnabas-in-Soho* 1999; www.houseofstbarnabas.org.uk)

Huguenots

The tympanum over the entrance to the French Protestant church on the north-west side of **Soho Square** depicts Edward VI (reigned 1547-53) extending a welcome and a charter of privileges to persecuted Huguenots fresh off the boat in 1550. In 1681 Louis XIV stepped up his persecutions of Huguenots and that year **Charles II** offered "all such afflicted Protestants" the prospect of his royal protection and ordered a national collection for their relief. In 1682 newly-arrived Huguenots took over a vacated **Greek church** in Hog Lane, Soho. In 1685 Louis XIV revoked outright the Edict of Nantes, issued by Henri IV in 1598 which confirmed the toleration of Protestantism in France. The trickle of exiles became a flood. In London they settled in Spitalfields, Wandsworth and Soho, all areas outside the boundaries of the City of London and therefore beyond the jurisdiction of City Livery Companies to regulate their trades. The newcomers were industrious, skilled and thrifty, bringing to their new home not only their expertise as silk-weavers, clock-makers, engravers and silver-smiths, but also culinary inventiveness. 'Oxtail soup', that most English of dishes, was a Huguenot innovation, the English having previously discarded that portion of the animal as useless. The spicy saveloy sausage was another delicacy much favoured by Huguenots.

By 1692 Soho's Huguenots could attend not only the Hog Lane chapel but had the choice of another in **Glasshouse Street**, 'La Patente' in **Berwick Street**, 'Le Tabernacle' in Milk Alley (now Bourchier Street) and 'Le Quarre' in the back of **Monmouth House**, Soho Square.

In 1711 the vestry (parish council) of **St Anne's**, Soho reckoned the population of the parish at 8,133,

The bi-lingual trade card of Huguenots, Daniel and Thomas Grignion, watchmakers in Russell Street.

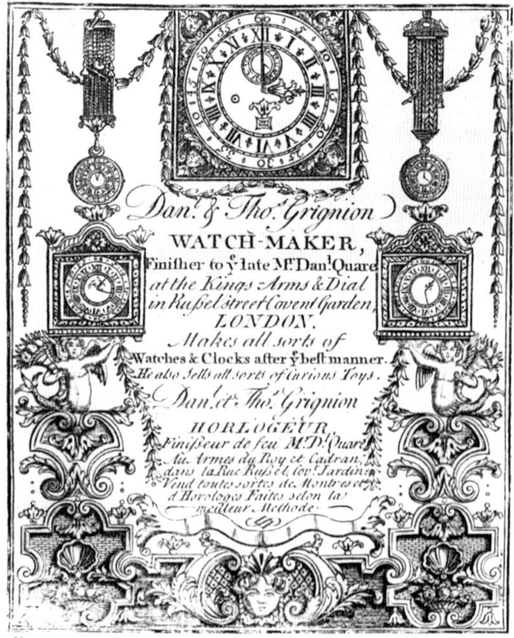

of whom some forty per cent were estimated to be French, the vast majority lodgers, rather than householders. The historian Strype in 1720 described the area as having an "Abundance of French people, many whereof are voluntary Exiles for their Religion... following honest Trades; and some Gentry of the same Nation"; but there is a certain condescension in his dismissal of **Old Compton Street** as being "of no great Account for its inhabitants which are chiefly French." By 1739 William Maitland was striking a note of surprise, rather than disdain –

"it is an easy Matter for a Stranger to imagine himself in France."

Though most Soho Huguenots were craftsmen or designers, such as silversmiths, silk-weavers, wood-carvers and gunsmiths working to the orders of the wealthy inhabitants of nearby St James's, some did achieve social eminence or wealth, or both. One of the earliest was Abraham Meure, who lived in Greek Street from 1691 to 1714 and ran an academy which took in both French and English pupils. It was an elite establishment, offering a curriculum of Latin, French, drawing, dancing and fencing. His pupils included the son of the Earl of Montagu and the future first Earl of Londonderry. Another tutor to the aristocracy was M. Jouneau, the minister of the Huguenot church in **Berwick Street**, who taught the celebrated wit and dilettante, Lord Chesterfield. (Chesterfield also had a Huguenot cook, tailor and doctor.)

Physician Jean Misaubin (1673-1734) was also living in Berwick Street when, in 1709, he married Marthe Angibaud, whose father later became Master of the Society of Apothecaries. Portraitist and art-dealer Philip Mercier (1689-1760), who lived at 40 **Leicester Square**, was appointed Principal Painter and Library Keeper to Frederick, Prince of Wales in 1729. Mercier painted the portrait of the Huguenot Lieutenant General De Jean of the Grenadiers, who also commanded a volunteer militia of London Swiss and became Director of the French Hospital, the leading Huguenot charity. After Mercier's death his widow, Dorothy, opened a shop in Little Windmill Street selling imported prints, artists' supplies, fans and 'Flower Pieces in Water Colours Painted by herself from life.'

Matthew Maty (1718-1776), lived in **Frith Street** from 1752 to 1756, when he was working as an under-librarian at the newly-established British Museum. He was also single-handedly producing a monthly '*Journal Britannique*', intended to acquaint French readers with English literature. A generous benefactor of the Museum, Maty, a Fellow of the Royal Society, was also a regular patron of **Slaughter's Coffee House** in **St Martin's Lane**, a favoured resort of French-speaking intellectuals. Another distinguished Huguenot, the MP Anthony Chamier (1725-80), was a founder-member of Sir Joshua Reynolds' **'Club'**. Reynolds painted Chamier's portrait three times. The most eminent Soho Huguenot of them all was Sir Samuel Romilly (1757-1818). The son of a Frith Street jeweller, he rose far beyond his humble origins to become a leading law-former and, as Solicitor General, abolished the death penalty for mugging, while opposing slavery and supporting Catholic emancipation. Romilly was also influential in promoting the career of his nephew, the physician and polymath Peter Mark Roget (1779-1869). Born in **Broadwick Street**, Roget not only had a successful medical practice but also served as Secretary of the Royal Society and helped to found the University of London. He is chiefly remembered for the *Thesaurus* now synonymous with his name.

By the last quarter of the eighteenth century the Huguenots had been largely assimilated into British society, rather than constituting a separate and distinctive community. In 1800 there were eight French Protestant churches in all of London, by 1900 only three and nowadays only one - in Soho Square. A few of Soho's street-names recall its former character as a French 'quartier'. Sheraton Street was, until 1937, Little Chapel Street, commemorating the chapel known as 'La Petite Patente', where Huguenots worshipped from 1694 until 1784. Foubert's Place was originally Major Foubert's Passage, an alley which ran beside the fashionable riding-school run by the Foubert family until 1778. **Dufour's Court** takes its name from its builder, Paul Dufour, who is possibly the 'Captain Defour' or 'Defaux' who lived at 54 **Poland Street** from 1705 to 1740. D'Arblay Street is taken from the married name of the novelist **Fanny Burney** (1752-1840).

(Tessa Murdoch *The Quiet Conquest: The Huguenots 1685 to 1985* Museum of London 1985)

John Hunter FRS

John Hunter (1728-93) never even tried to qualify as a doctor but was elected a Fellow of the Royal Society and appointed Physician Extraordinary to **George III** and Surgeon-General to the British army. After a derisory formal education and a spell as a

John Hunter – a great man, in his own opinion.

cabinet-maker Hunter learned his trade by preparing dissections for the courses in anatomy taught by his celebrated brother, **William Hunter**. He also worked as a surgeon at St George's Hospital and broadened his experience by serving in the army (1760-63). From 1763 until 1770 Hunter lived at 31 **Golden Square** and from 1783 until his death at 28 **Leicester Square**. Acknowledged as the founding father of pathological anatomy and scientific surgery, Hunter was also an indefatigable and fearless experimenter, whose vast knowledge was based almost entirely on personal investigation rather than books. His interests ranged from the physiology of hibernation to the formation of pearls in oysters. One of Hunter's trials involved injecting himself with syphilis in an attempt to prove that it was a variant form of gonorrhoea. As a result he contracted syphilis, which seems a plausible explanation for the maladies and eccentricities of his later years, when he was renowned for both his apoplectic temper and apparently overweening vanity. Hunter once told Lord Holland that if he had ever wanted to look at a great man his wish had been granted, for he considered himself a far greater man than **Sir Isaac Newton**. As a teacher Hunter was inhibited by a diffident manner radically at odds with his unpredictable rages but his pupils included Edward Jenner, discoverer of vaccination, and the eminent surgeon Astley Cooper. As a practitioner Hunter never charged curates, authors or artists. He eventually earned over £6,000 a year and was able to establish a menagerie of exotic animals at Earl's Court and to build up an unrivalled collection of medical specimens which, after his death, was bought for the Royal College of Surgeons. Hunter's publications include *The Natural History of the Human Teeth* (1771) and *A Treatise on the Venereal Disease* (1786). Hunter's most important work, based on a lifetime's study, was *A Treatise on the Blood, Inflammation and Gunshot Wounds*, which appeared posthumously (1794). The Hunterian Society was established in his honour in 1819. A bust of John Hunter stands in the gardens of Leicester Square.

(www.rseng.ac.uk; www.hunteriansociety.org.uk)

William Hunter FRS FSA

The professional training of William Hunter (1718-83) included travel in Paris and the Netherlands and formal study at the University of Glasgow, so that he was almost forty before he became licensed to practise as a physician in London. There he pioneered the practice of dissection as an essential element of medical training, ably assisted by his brother, **John Hunter**. Hunter's main contribution to medicine in Britain was the development of obstetrics as a specialism, being appointed Physician Extraordinary to the fecund Queen Charlotte in 1764. Unlike his brother, who was obsessively devoted to medical investigation, William Hunter was a man of broad general culture, a Fellow of the Society of Antiquaries, as well as a Fellow of the Royal Society. In 1768 he was appointed first Professor of Anatomy at the newly-established Royal Academy. Like his brother, John, William Hunter built up an extensive collection of anatomical and pathological specimens but he also acquired coins, medals, minerals, shells, corals and an extensive library of Greek and Latin texts.

Hunter's three-storey house in **Great Windmill Street** was built in 1767 by his kinsman Robert Mylne. As the surviving cornice shows it had five bays. At the back was Hunter's museum and anatomy school. Hunter's medical specimens were removed to the University of Glasgow in 1807, although medical lectures continued to be given at the Great Windmill Street premises until 1831. After that the building became a printing works, then an hotel and was finally absorbed into the **Lyric Theatre** in 1887. (www.hunterian.gla.ac.uk)

Mrs Elizabeth Inchbald

Elizabeth Simpson (1753-1821) ran away from home at eighteen to become an actress and succeeded in doing so, despite a speech impediment she never entirely conquered. Following the death of her actor husband, as the widowed Mrs Inchbald, living on **Frith Street**, she turned to writing, churning out revamped versions of French and German dramas. **Jane Austen** was more amused than impressed by her efforts and in *Mansfield Park* has the Bertrams choose Mrs Inchbald's *Lovers' Vows* for their effort at amateur dramatics. From 1798 to 1803 Mrs Inchbald was resident in the same **Leicester Square** hotel as the former **Mrs Thrale**. As a freelance and a widow Mrs Inchbald was sometimes exposed to attempts on her honour. On one occasion she was virtually assaulted by a potential producer but had the presence of mind to grab his hair with one hand while ringing a bell for help with the other. Recounting her narrow escape afterwards she would always conclude the anecdote with the observation " How f-fortunate for me he did NOT W-EAR a W-IG."

(James Boaden *Memoirs of Mrs Inchbald* BiblioBazaar 2008)

Industry has all but departed from Soho in modern times. One of the largest concerns, R W Wilson, manufacturers of tinplate and baths, had a two-acre site between Wardour Street and Dean Street.

Industry

In the course of the eighteenth century Soho changed from being a residential area to an increasingly industrial one, though the industries were mostly small-scale, highly skilled and geared to the luxury end of the market – **silver, tapestry, furniture, leather**, **musical instruments**, guns and clocks.

The manufacture and sale of glass was represented by Goslett & Co. and Hetley and Co., both of **Soho Square** and Ward & Hughes of **Frith Street**. Hetley & Co. supplied Queen Victoria with glass shades for Windsor Castle and Buckingham Palace, while the business founded by Thomas Ward made windows for Westminster Abbey, Guildhall, the Savoy chapel and **St Anne's, Soho**.

Soho Square was also home to Burroughs & Watts, inventors of the slate-bed billiard table, and to their rivals, Orme & Sons. W G Nixey, also of Soho Square, mixed artists'colours. R W Wilson, manufacturers of tinplate and baths, occupied a two acre site between **Wardour Street** and **Dean Street**. Trenchard House on **Broadwick Street** occupies the site of the former (1801-1937) Lion Brewery. In the 1850s there was also a percussion cap factory there. At 33 **Gerrard Street** George Minter manufactured specialised 'campaign furniture' for the Victorian military and wheelchairs for the disabled.

Covent Garden was long dominated by the coach-building industry along Long Acre and its associated trades such as saddlery. The Strand and the streets leading off it were important centres for the making of maps and scientific instruments, represented by craftsmen such as **Rocque** and **Sisson**. Printing, represented by **Odham's**, **Newnes**, **Pearson's** and Hazell, Watson and Viney became the most important business by the later nineteenth century. Long Acre shifted from custom-built coaches to motorised transport, accommodating sales offices for Fiat, Daimler, Mercedes – and Bleriot aeroplanes. Other significant establishments included **Chippendale**'s workshop, a papier-mâché factory in **Bow Street**, Lavers and Barraud's stained-glass factory in **Endell Street** and Lambert and Butler's tobacco factory in Wild Street. Minor trades included the manufacture of market porters' barrows and packing-cases.

(David Barnett *London, Hub of the Industrial Revolution A Revisionary History 1775-1825* Tauris Academic Studies 1998)

First Knight – Henry Irving caricatured in Vanity Fair *in 1874.*

Henry Irving

As Henry Irving, John Henry Brodribb (1838-1905) became the first British actor ever to be knighted. Making his debut at eighteen, Irving served a three year provincial apprenticeship in which he played over four hundred roles. In 1867 he acted for the first time opposite Ellen Terry, in *Katharine and Petruchio*, **Garrick**'s adaptation of *The Taming of the Shrew*. Twenty years later George Bernard Shaw, then working as a dramatic critic, would be mesmerised by their complementarity – " she, all brains and sympathy ... he, all self". In 1878 Irving took over the **Lyceum** theatre to make it what the critic J T Grein hailed as "the embodiment of all that is refined, sumptuous and noble in English histrionic art". Irving, as painstaking a producer as he was passionate an actor, demanded the highest standards in terms of music, set design, lighting and ensemble playing but did nothing to raise the standards of contemporary playwriting, sticking to Shakespeare and well-tried melodramas. Irving was obsessed with acting and his theatre but indifferent to *the* theatre as a national institution.

Knighted in 1895, Irving died a decade later after a provincial performance and became the first major celebrity to be cremated at the newly-established crematorium at Golders Green, subsequently a Valhalla for the British stage. His ashes were interred at Westminster Abbey. With remarkable rapidity a memorial fund was established which raised money on both sides of the Atlantic for the erection of a public statue. Designed by Sir Thomas Brock, the most favoured sculptor of the day, it was unveiled in 1910, in the shadow of the **National Portrait Gallery**. It stands on what may well have been the site of **Dickens**' *Old Curiosity Shop*. Immediately adjacent is Irving Street, which appropriately leads up to the half-price theatre ticket booth in Leicester Square. An archive of Irving's immense correspondence with over two thousand correspondents is accessible at www.henryirving.co.uk.

(Jeffrey Richards *Sir Henry Irving: A Victorian Actor and His World* Hambledon Continuum 2006; www.theirvingsociety.org.uk)

Italians

The association between Soho's Italians and catering has been close and continuous.

The high-profile precursors of Soho's Italian community – Casanova and **Ugo Foscolo** – were followed by fellow-countrymen with more prosaic priorities. Political refugees from failed revolutions were succeeded by economic migrants.

Descendants of Joseph Moretti, a Venetian, claim that he ran an 'Italian Eating House' off **Leicester Square** in 1803-5. The Restaurant d'Italie – note the French name – opened at 35 **Greek Street** in 1854. The Sabloniere Hotel on Leicester Square was also under Italian management. Naturally these establishments attracted the patronage of visiting Italians, like the world famous tenor Enrico Caruso (1873-1921), who favoured Gennaro's at No. 44 **Dean Street**. The eighteenth of twenty children and a fine actor, Caruso made his debut at the **Royal Opera House, Covent Garden** in 1902 and became one of the first classical singers to reach a mass-audience through recordings. At restaurants he would amuse fellow diners with his party trick of swallowing an entire peach whole.

By 1886 Italians were numerous enough to form the *Societa Italiana Cuochi-Camerieri*, based in **Gerrard Street,** which functioned as a benefit and social club for Italian workers in the catering trade. It also served as an informal labour exchange for new arrivals seeking work. Within ten years the club had four hundred and fifty members and was wealthy enough to buy the lease of 27 **Soho Square** and employ a paid secretary and steward. Music, cards and bicycle races round Soho Square appear to have been favourite pastimes. A survey of the 1890s shows that Soho's Italians (652) were still outnumbered by the French (901) and Germans (1,070) and London's 'Little Italy' remained concentrated in Clerkenwell, a couple of miles north-east of Soho.

By the turn of the century Italian restaurants had begun to find favour with showbiz personalities. In 1905 conjurors and illusionists gathered at Pinoli's at 17 **Wardour Street** (see p. 150) to found the prestigious 'Magic Circle'.

The 1908 edition of Baedeker's celebrated guide to London simply notes that "Soho contains a large colony of Italian cooks, couriers, waiters, tailors, restaurant keepers, servants, teachers etc." but it was in fact during the inter-war period that Soho became more Italian than French. Landmark restaurants opened in this period included Leoni's Quo Vadis, Quaglino's and Bianchi's. The Italian Fascist movement had an office at 25 **Noel Street** and ran annual summer camps attended by large numbers of the children of Soho's Italian community. A few streets away, at No. 37 **Old Compton Street**, anti-fascist anarchists met at the King Bomba deli – "the sole macaroni factory in England" – and plotted how to assassinate Mussolini.

World War II represented a serious setback for the community as hundreds of Italians were rounded up as suspect 'enemy aliens'. Included among their number were the five Sabini brothers, feared mobsters who no longer even spoke Italian. Property was confiscated or damaged by mobs as police turned a blind eye.

A post-war renaissance accompanied the emergence of the **coffee bar**. In 1954 a post-war immigrant and former waiter at the Savoy, Otello Schipiori, opened a new sort of establishment offering informal dining but excellent food, Trattoria Toscana. This was followed in 1959 by Mario and Franco's La Terrazza, a trattoria which recognised the regionality of Italian cuisine. (www.italiansinlondon.co.uk)

The Ivy Restaurant, West Street

The Ivy was opened in 1911 by Abel Giandellini. Initially no more than a modest café, it soon became a favourite with the theatrical profession, one of whom gave it its name. When the actress Alice Delysia overheard 'Monsieur Abel' apologising to a customer for the inconvenience caused by building works, she butted in to reassure him that his customers would always remain faithful, quoting a line from a popular song of the day "we'll cling together like the ivy". The Ivy's success was largely the product of its maître d'hotel, Mario Gallati. In 1940 The Ivy was still full of "prosperous-looking people as usual, all eating a whacking good meal, meat, plovers and a delicious creamy pudding." In 1942 it was still able to offer smoked salmon, cold grouse and chocolate mousse but by 1944 it was down to oysters, elderly hens and Algerian wine. At times it was even reduced to serving Spam and tripe and onions – when it could get the onions. Mario Gallati once confessed with a shudder that he had been reduced to serving a 'mayonnaise' concocted out of flour, mustard, powdered egg, vinegar and water. Gallati left in 1947 to found Le Caprice. In 1950 M. Abel sold The Ivy to Wheelers' and it was later owned by Joseph

Corner café to the stars – the Ivy Restaurant.

James II – a better statue than king.

Melatini, Lady Grade and the Forte organisation before it was acquired by Chris Corbin and Jeremy King in 1989 and relaunched in 1990.

(A A Gill, Harriet Logan and Henry Bourne *The Ivy: The Restaurant and Its Recipes* Hodder and Stoughton 1997 www.the-ivy.co.uk)

James II statue, Trafalgar Square

The statue of James II (reigned 1685-88) which now stands outside the **National Gallery** is thought by some to be the handsomest in all London. Produced by the studio of **Grinling Gibbons**, though probably not by Gibbons himself, it presents the king as an imperious victor in Roman armour. The gift of a minor courtier, Tobias Rustat, Page of the Backstairs, "a very simple, ignorant but honestly loyal creature", it cost a modest £300.

James was the younger brother of **Charles II,** who ensured his succession but correctly predicted that his reign would end in exile. As Duke of York and Lord High Admiral of England James proved a competent and popular commander, achieving (1664) the capture of the Dutch colony of New Amsterdam, which was renamed New York in his honour. Ably served by the ambitious and hardworking **Samuel Pepys**, he did much to strengthen the Royal Navy. Following the death of his first wife, however, James converted to Roman Catholicism and married a Catholic princess. James then swiftly alienated both the affections of the public and the loyalty of the political elite by appointing Catholics to key posts in the military, courts and universities, thus creating a general fear that he was determined both to re-impose the Roman religion on a fiercely Protestant nation and to rule as an absolute monarch. Within three years conspirators invited James's Protestant daughter, Mary, and her Dutch husband, William, to assume the throne as joint sovereigns, subject to accepting the supremacy of Parliament over the Crown. James was eventually allowed to flee unmolested to France. His statue stood, also unmolested, in the gardens behind the Banqueting House on Whitehall for almost two hundred years, then was moved onto Whitehall, then into St James's Park and then for safekeeping during the **Blitz**, in Aldwych Underground station, before finding its present resting place in 1948. Though devout and abstemious, James II was an undiscriminating womaniser. He was also an early pioneer of tea-drinking, fox-hunting and playing the guitar. Brave, bigoted and not very bright, he would have made an excellent king of Spain but unfortunately was called upon to occupy the throne of Britain – though not for long.

(John Miller *James II* Yale University Press 2000)

James Street

The north entrance to Covent Garden **Piazza** was built up in 1635-8. The parsonage of **St Paul's** church was originally at No. 27. The portrait painter John Michael Wright (1617-1700) was a resident; his most celebrated commission was a series of portraits of the judges of the court specially convened to sort out property rights after the Great Fire of 1666. The breadth of the street encouraged its use by market traders thus diminishing its attraction for upmarket residents. The present Nos. 27-31 date from ca. 1700. The double-bowed shopfront at No. 29 is from ca. 1800. The florid White Lion pub is of 1888 and the present Nag's Head building from 1900, although a pub is shown on the site in 1673.

Jazz

By the **Fifties** Soho could fairly claim to be the heart of London's contemporary music scene. The first jazz venue, Club 11, was established in 1948 at Mac's Club/ Rehearsal Rooms, a basement on the corner of **Archer Street** and **Great Windmill Street**, by **Ronnie Scott** and John Dankworth. The same premises were later used by Cy Laurie's, which claimed a membership of seven thousand and was the first to offer seven sessions a week. In 1951 **George Melly** and Mick Mulligan organised the first all-night session at the Mandrake, a chess club by day, on **Meard Street**. In the same year Ken Colyer's 'Studio 51' opened at Nos. 11-12 **Great Newport Street** to offer New Orleans jazz. This could also be heard four times a week at No. 44 **Gerrard Street**, Tuesdays being reserved for "the jazz curiosity, Skiffle music." Devotees of the latter could also patronise the Skiffle Cellar at 49 Greek Street. The late Humphrey Lyttelton (1921-2008), an Old Etonian and former Guards officer, played trumpet in 'trad jazz' in a room on **Leicester Square** before establishing the 100 Club ('Humph's) at No. 100 Oxford Street. Modern jazz could be heard in the subterranean Metro in **Old Compton Street**, a venue much favoured by French students.

Ronnie Scott's jazz club at 43 Frith Street.

Jews

Writing in 1840 Flora Tristan, the French radical, noted the existence of impoverished Jewish communities in **Newport Market** and **Seven Dials**. A synagogue existed somewhere along **Dean Street** at that time. The succeeding century tells a story of self-help in which respect for heritage and identity was balanced with successful integration into British society. By the 1850s a Western Jewish Girls' Free School had been established, initially at 21 Dean Street, then 6 **Greek Street**. The Jewish presence was further strengthened by the immigration of Russian and Polish Jews after the pogroms of the 1880s. At the end of that decade, following the initiative of **Maude Stanley**, a West-Central Jewish Girls' Club was founded by Lady Battersea and Miss Emily Harris. By 1898 it had over two hundred members. Classes were offered in musical drill, French, English, Hebrew, basket-weaving, singing, cooking, laundry and first aid. New immigrants were given coaching in reading and writing English. Saturday evenings were given over to less serious pursuits – music, dances and a monthly debate. Sundays meant tea and a lecture, followed by dancing. The supervising ladies came from such areas as Kensington, Bayswater and Maida Vale.

The actual members included domestic servants, stationers and makers of wigs and cigars but the overwhelming number were employed in the garment trade, making caps, waistcoats and dresses. Many Jewish men also found employment as outworkers in the tailoring business, cutting, sewing and pressing for the up-market Savile Row houses on the far side of **Regent Street**. In 1917 the West End Talmud Torah and Bikkur Holim Synagogue took over the old workhouse in **Manette Street**, which served as a synagogue until 1941. By 1944 the congregation had taken over the former St Anne's National School building on Dean Street. This was demolished in 1961 and replaced by a new building incorporating a youth club and the gallery of the Ben Uri Art Society, which promoted the work of Jewish artists.

Dr Samuel Johnson, after the painting by ***Sir Joshua Reynolds****.*

Palladian pioneer – Inigo Jones.

Dr Samuel Johnson

"... a man of most dreadful appearance ...very big ... troubled with sore eyes, the palsy and the king's evil ... very slovenly in his dress and speaks with a most uncouth voice. Yet his great knowledge and strength of expression command vast respect and render him very excellent company ... "

James Boswell

Dr Samuel Johnson (1709-84), celebrated author of the first true dictionary of the English language, had his first London lodgings in Exeter Street at the house of staymaker Richard Norris. The site is now covered by **Wellington Street.** Johnson met his future biographer, James Boswell, in Davies's bookshop at No. 8 **Russell Street** in 1763. Johnson was also a regular patron of **Tom's** and **Old Slaughter's** and a founder member of '**The Club**'. **Fanny Burney** was much flattered to hear his praise of her novel, *Evelina*. **Reynolds**' portrait of Johnson is in the **National Portrait Gallery**.

Johnson is the second most quoted English writer after Shakespeare. A selection of some 1,800 quotes can be viewed at www.samueljohnson.com. His former home at Gough Square, off Fleet Street, is a museum devoted to his life and works; about ten minutes walk from Covent Garden.

(Liza Picard – *Dr. Johnson's London* Weidenfeld & Nicolson 2000; www.drjohnsonhouse.org)

Inigo Jones

Born in Smithfield of Welsh descent, Inigo Jones (1573-1652) was the first British architect to travel to Italy and gain a first-hand understanding of classical architecture.

On returning he gained royal patronage by designing costumes and scenery for court masques and was appointed Surveyor of the King's Works in 1615. Best remembered for designing the Queen's House at Greenwich and the Banqueting House in Whitehall, Jones was also responsible for **St Paul's** and the **Piazza** at Covent Garden.

(Michael Leapman *Inigo: The Troubled Life of Inigo Jones, Architect of the English Renaissance* Review 2003)

Edmund Kean

" ... to see him act is like reading Shakespeare by flashes of lightning" S T Coleridge

Edmund Kean (1790-1833) was the personification of the self-destructive theatrical genius. The illegitimate son of a minor actress who tried to exploit him as an infant prodigy and abandoned him in a doorway in **Frith Street**, he was brought up by an uncle in **Lisle Street**. Kean appeared at both the **Theatre Royal Drury Lane** and the **Sans Souci** while still a child, then subjected himself to a rigorous provincial apprenticeship, becoming an accomplished mime and skilled acrobat. Swarthy

Edmund Kean as Sir Giles Overreach in A New Way to Pay Old Debts*, c. 1820.*

and athletic he looked like a gypsy and sometimes believed himself to be one. Kean finally made his adult London debut at Drury Lane in 1814 as Shylock, when the theatre was overshadowed by the financial crisis of **Sheridan's** last years. Defying tradition, Kean rejected both caricature and pathos to play the Jew as a monster of demonic and dynamic evil. The audience was stunned. Further triumphs with Hamlet, Othello, Iago and Richard III brought the house £20,000 in a single season. Years of struggle, crowned with adulation, metamorphosed into further years of struggle, drenched in alcohol. Having given his all upon the stage, Kean would repair nightly to the Coal Hole on the Strand where his 'Wolves Club' of actor acolytes spun out supper and singing into the small hours. During his last appearance, as Othello, he collapsed on stage, dying within weeks. Alexandre Dumas senior thought Kean's life so extraordinary he wrote a play about it and in 1954 this was adapted by Jean-Paul Sartre as a comedy. Kean figures prominently in the collection of theatrical portraits at the **Garrick Club**. Kean Street at the rear of Drury Lane is named for Kean's less talented but infinitely more respectable son, Charles (1811-68), who enjoyed great success as a manager. Charles Kean took advice from architect **George Godwin** to ensure historical accuracy in building his sets and was a friend of **Dickens.** As thrifty as his father had been reckless, Charles Kean was able to retire with a fortune before he was fifty.

Charles Kemble

"*... a first-rate actor in second-rate parts*"
William Macready

Brought up by a brutal uncle in **Lisle Street**, Charles Kemble (1775-1854) was the younger brother of **John Philip Kemble** and tragedienne **Sarah Siddons**, but unlike his more famous siblings was effective in comedy as well as tragedy. As manager (1822-32) of **Covent Garden** he made a pioneering effort in his production of *King John* to present historically accurate costumes but drifted into such financial straits that he was obliged to summon the talents of his daughter, Fanny (1809-93), to a profession from which he had hoped to spare her. Her debut, as Juliet, was a sensation. When Kemble retired in 1837 the **Garrick Club**, of which he was a founder member, gave him the singular honour of a congratulatory dinner.

John Philip Kemble

"*... the very ... statuary of the stage; a perfect figure of a man; a petrification of sentiment ... an icicle upon the bust of Tragedy*". **William Hazlitt**

Born into a family of strolling players, J P Kemble (1757-1823) made his London debut (1783) at the **Theatre Royal Drury Lane** playing an idiosyncratic Hamlet whose grace and gentleness puzzled, then captivated, his audience. Lawrence painted him in the part. Strikingly handsome, he excelled in tragedy but lacked the lightness of touch for comedy or romance. Kemble managed both Drury Lane and **Covent Garden**, where his attempt to raise prices after the disastrous fire of 1809 caused prolonged riots.

(Linda Kelly *The Kemble era: John Philip Kemble, Sarah Siddons and the London Stage* Random House 1980)

Kettner's

Auguste Kettner, formerly chef to the French emperor Napoleon III, founded his eponymous restaurant at 29 **Romilly Street** in 1867. One evening in 1869 a journalist wandered in, found the food excellent, the service pleasant and the bill surprisingly moderate. Moved to share his good fortune with his compatriots he did what all good Englishmen then did to express an opinion and wrote it up in *The Times*. Kettner's was made and

Kettner's – Oscar Wilde was a regular.

within a decade had become a national institution. Kettner's *Book of the Table* became an iconic work of reference in culinary matters. (Kettner himself supplied the recipes but the book was actually written by a scholarly journalist and gourmand E S Dallas 1828-79). **Oscar Wilde** was a regular, valuing the privacy of the upstairs rooms as much as the cuisine. Edward VII had similarly – and more successfully discreet – liaisons with the actress Lillie Langtry. The restaurant is now owned by Pizza Express but still serves posh nosh and has a famed champagne bar. (www.kettners.com)

Thomas Killigrew

"*a merry droll*" Samuel Pepys

A former child actor and youthful playwright, (Sir) Thomas Killigrew (1612-83) became a courtier to **Charles I** and a companion in exile to **Charles II**. The reward for his loyalty was to be appointed one of two holders of royal Letters Patent, licensed to present legitimate dramas on a London stage. He also benefited from having exclusive rights over the services of dramatist **John Dryden**. In 1663 Killigrew moved his company, the King's Men, from its temporary home in a tennis-court to a converted riding-school at Brydges Street, later to be known as the **Theatre Royal Drury Lane**. Killigrew boasted to **Pepys** that he had greatly raised standards from what had been usual in his youth – wax candles instead of smoky tallow ones, ten violinists instead of two, "now, all things civil, no rudeness anywhere; then as in a bear-garden … the stage is now a thousand times better and more glorious than ever heretofore". Whereas under Charles I "the Queen seldom and the King never would come" to the theatre, under Charles II "not the King only … but all civil people do think they may come". By 1671, however, Killigrew had begun to tire of the business and hand it over to his son Charles, who had assumed complete control by 1677.

King Street

"*The most rewarding street in Covent Garden …*" Pevsner

King Street, leading into Covent Garden on the north-west side, was laid out in 1633-37 and named in compliment to **Charles I**. The more imposing residences, with yards, stables and coach houses to the rear, were built along the north side. No. 43 has had a particularly interesting history (see pp 5-6). Nos. 15, 37 and 38 are of 1773-4.

In contrast to **Henrietta Street**, King Street initially became established as a prestigious residential address, attracting dramatist **Thomas Killigrew**, William Lenthall, Speaker of the House of Commons, the privateer, courtier, theological author, diplomat and scientific dabbler **Sir Kenelm Digby** FRS, and the Shakespeare scholar and Poet Laureate, Nicholas Rowe.

In 1672 there were seven titled occupants, as well as several 'eminent tradesmen'.

Actor James Quin and composer **Thomas Arne** were both born in King Street. **David Garrick** lived there in 1743-45 and Samuel Taylor Coleridge at No. 10 in 1801-2 when he was writing for the ***Morning Post***. The street then became increasingly commercial. The Essex Serpent public house dates from at least 1743. In 1808 the Westminster Fire Office was established there – its royal warrant is still emblazoned on Nos 27-8. Gliddon's Cigar Divan was in business ca. 1820 and the **Garrick Club** had its first premises there. Moss Bros. moved there in 1881. The headquarters of the **Communist Party of Great Britain** were at No. 16 from 1920 until 1980.

Kingly Street

Originally a footpath between Piccadilly and Marylebone this thoroughfare was built up from 1686 onwards and known until 1906 as King Street. The first houses were poorly built and replaced in the 1720s when Strype described it as "a pretty good street, having divers very good Houses fit for Gentry."

Nos. 1, 2, 7-11 and 19 are of this period, though mostly with later frontages. Nos. 12-13 was built (1887) as a vicarage for the church of St Thomas which stood opposite until 1973. A pub (now the Blue Posts) has been at No. 18 since at least 1737 but the present one and The Clachan are flamboyant survivals from the apogee of the pub-building boom of the 1890s. In the interwar period there was a night-club, The Nest, which attracted "all the famous coloured stars" and featured a one-legged tap-dancer.

Sir Godfrey Kneller

Born in Lubeck as Gottfried Kniller, this prolific painter and self-assured socialite successfully anglicised himself to become Sir Godfrey Kneller (1646-1723) Bart. JP, with a London base in Covent Garden and a grand house near Hounslow. Having studied under Rembrandt and in Rome, Naples and Venice, Kneller arrived in England in 1674/5 and soon made himself known at Court. The death of **Sir Peter Lely** enabled Kneller to take his place as the favoured royal portraitist, through five reigns. William and Mary appointed him Principal Painter at their accession and knighted him in 1692 and in 1715 George I created him a baronet. Kneller's home (1682-ca.1702) at Nos. 16/17 the **Piazza** was organised as a miniature factory for the mass-production of society portraiture. Sitters, as many as fourteen a day, were required to pose only for a drawing of their face, the details of setting, costume and accessories being agreed in advance and delegated to specialist assistants, many of them foreigners, like their employer and coordinator. Among Kneller's subjects were the Duke of Monmouth, the family of the Duke of Bedford, **Newton**, Pope and **Dryden**.

The last twenty years of Kneller's life were passed at 57/8 **Great Queen Street**, where from 1711, until it collapsed in 1718, he supervised London's first painting academy. Kneller's less prosaic productions include *The Chinese Convert* (1687, Kensington Palace), which he thought was his best picture, and the cut-down portraits of the KitCat Club (ca. 1702-17, **National Portrait Gallery**).

Kneller enjoyed good health, amassed a great fortune, painted the likeness of no less than ten reigning sovereigns, including Louis XIV and Peter the Great, and was much feted in his day. Dryden wrote a poem in his praise and Pope composed the fulsome epitaph on his monument in Westminster

Sir Godfrey Kneller, self portrait 1683.

Abbey. **Hogarth** and **Reynolds** were also admirers of his work. Although **Hazlitt** dismissed his portraits as "turned in a machine", modern opinion recognises Kneller's great technical facility and a genuine ability to convey character as well as likeness when confronted with a sitter of personal rather than merely social consequence.

Sir Francis Kynaston

A favoured courtier of Charles I, Sir Francis Kynaston (1587-1642) was a talented orator and competent poet, who, with royal approval and support, converted his **Bedford Street** house into a Museum Minervae to provide the sons of the nobility and gentry (only) with the "ornaments of travel" to equip them "before their undertaking long journeys into foreign parts". An elaborate curriculum offered options in antiquities, astronomy, dancing, fencing, heraldry, husbandry, law, music, numismatics, optics, riding, sculpture and seven languages. The full course was intended to last seven years, with an abbreviated version of three years. Students were to undertake not more than two courses at a time, one intellectual, one physical. **Charles I** not only granted the venture a royal licence and a contribution of £100 but also visited it on at least one occasion, during which the students performed a masque.

The academy was dissolved on the death of Kynaston, its founder and 'Regent'. A Kynaston's Alley, a reminder of its former site, was still in existence in 1892.

A caricature of Charles Lamb, by Daniel Maclise, published in 1835.

Charles Lamb

"May my last breath be drawn through a pipe and exhaled in a pun".

Educated at Christ's Hospital and uncongenially employed for life as a clerk for the East India Company, Charles Lamb (1775-1834) was afflicted by an incurable stutter and burdened for life by the care of a sister who, having (accidentally) killed their mother, was subject to periodic bouts of derangement. Yet few men have ever had a wider circle of more varied and loving friends, including Coleridge, Wordsworth, **Haydon** and, crucially, **William Hazlitt**. Supplementing a meagre income by contributing light-hearted pieces to the ***Morning Chronicle***, he also managed in 1805 to have a farce put on at the **Theatre Royal Drury Lane** but this proved a miserable failure. The radical publisher William Godwin commissioned Lamb and his sister to produce for a child readership the *Tales from Shakespeare* with which their names were ever after linked. Lamb subsequently confirmed a growing literary reputation with masterly essays on **Hogarth** and on the Elizabethan dramatists. It was while living (1817-23) at **Russell Street** that Lamb composed the *Essays of Elia* on which his standing as a writer chiefly rests. These were initially written for the newly-established *London Magazine*, whose staff included the invaluable Hazlitt. When finally pensioned off Lamb spent many happy hours working on the **Garrick** collection of plays in the British Museum. Several portraits of Lamb can be seen in the **National Portrait Gallery** including one of him in fancy dress, by Hazlitt.

(David Cecil *Portrait of Charles Lamb* Constable 1983)

The popular but secluded Lamb and Flag in Rose Street.

Lamb and Flag, Rose Street

This public house at No. 33 Rose Street may date from as early as 1623, though Pevsner favours ca. 1688. Although the Georgian exterior was refaced in 1958, it remains one of the few wooden-framed buildings to survive in central London. A plaque records how **John Dryden** was savagely attacked nearby in 1679.

Paul de Lamerie

Born in the Netherlands, **Huguenot** Paul de Lamerie (1688-1751) came to London as a child and by 1713 was established in his own workshop in **(Great) Windmill Street**. In 1738 he moved to No. 40 **Gerrard Street** where a plaque marks the house in

Sir Thomas Lawrence, from the painting by Charles Landseer.

which he remained until his death. De Lamerie's clients included Sir Robert Walpole, **George II** and Catherine the Great of Russia. Examples of his work can be seen in the British Museum. He was buried in **St Anne's, Soho**.

Sir Thomas Lawrence PRA

"His manner was elegant but not high bred ... He had smiled so often and so long that at last his smile wore the appearance of being set in enamel."
Benjamin Haydon

While **William Blake** and **George Morland**, in their different ways, defied convention and paid the price, Thomas Lawrence (1769-1830) was intent on embellishing it and reaping the reward. A self-taught prodigy, Lawrence as a child had already come to the notice of **Garrick, Mrs Siddons, Fanny Burney** and **Sir Joshua Reynolds** himself. Graduating from fashionable Bath, he settled initially at 4 **Leicester Square** and was, thanks to royal favour, irregularly elected to the Royal Academy at twenty-five. From 1798 until 1810 Lawrence lived at No. 60 **Greek Street**. A devoted disciple of Reynolds in his attitude to both painting and patrons, Lawrence succeeded him as the leading society portraitist of his day and, following the death of **Benjamin West**, eventually succeeded his mentor as President of the Royal Academy, eminently suited, both by talent and personality, to serve as figurehead for the profession of painting. Lawrence's brilliant, bravura portrait (ca. 1814) of **George IV** as Prince of Wales can be seen in the **National Portrait Gallery**.
(A Levey *Sir Thomas Lawrence: The Artist* Yale University Press 2005)

Leather Trades

Leather-working was a significant Soho and Covent Garden industry in the nineteenth century. Almgill & Son of **Gerrard Street** supplied bridles to **George IV**. Horton's of **Lisle Street** specialised in the metal fittings for horse's harness. Their next-door neighbour, the appropriately named Mr Leatherby, made the saddle which won first prize at the International Exhibition of 1862. Robson's, at the other end of Lisle Street, were curriers, preparing leather for use by other craftsmen. Joseph George of **Dean Street** specialised in supplying ornamental upholstery and embossed fittings for such prestigious locations as Longleat, Knebworth and the Houses of Parliament. Gamba's of Dean Street, makers of boots and shoes for the theatre, included Fred Astaire among their clients.

Leicester House

Soho's first palatial residence was built by Robert Sidney, 2nd Earl of Leicester, in the 1630s, on the northern side of what is now Leicester Square, then Leicester Fields. With thirty rooms,'for a generation Leicester House was one of the greatest houses in London. **Charles I's** devoted and unpopular minister, Thomas Wentworth, Earl of Strafford convalesced there in the summer of 1640, laid low by dysentery. When the king solicitously came to visit him Stafford deferentially threw off his warm gown and took a chill that nearly killed him. He recovered only to be sacrificed to the king's enemies a year later. When **Charles II's** aunt, Elizabeth of Bohemia, 'the Winter Queen', took up residence at Leicester House in 1662 she died within a week. Lord Leicester recorded ungraciously that "it seems the Fates did not think it fit that I should have the Honour, which indeed I never much desired, to be the Landlord of a Queen." From 1668 to 1670, however, Lord Leicester was landlord to the French ambassador.

The diarist John Evelyn (1620-1706) dined at Leicester House in 1672 and watched a fire-eater as part of the evening's diversions. The 3rd Earl of

Leicester House in Leicester Square, 1748. The sentries and sentry boxes denote a royal residence.

Leicester occupied the house from 1677 until his death in 1698, regularly entertaining the dramatists **Dryden** and Wycherley. In 1712 the Duke of Marlborough's comrade-in-arms, Eugene, Prince of Savoy, lodged at Leicester House during an abortive diplomatic mission; the government treated him uncivilly but the mob adored him.

In 1717 the then Prince of Wales, the future **George II**, moved in after being evicted from St James's Palace by his father, following a font-side quarrel at the baptism of the Prince's son, the future **George III**. The Prince kept a counter-court at Leicester House for the next decade and was proclaimed monarch outside the gates in 1727. Fifteen years later the king's son, Frederick, Prince of Wales, maintained family tradition and provoked his father, less by reckless gambling and indiscriminate womanising ("beauty was not an ingredient") than by entertaining opposition politicians. Foolish, feckless Fred failed to succeed to the throne, dying at Leicester House in 1751, after a sporting accident when a cricket ball hit him in the throat, causing an abscess, which burst with fatal results.

In 1774 Leicester House was taken over by a Lancashire naturalist, Sir Ashton Lever (1729-88) who filled sixteen rooms and numerous passageways with his immense collections of shells, fossils, stuffed birds and "savage costumes and weapons" and opened it to the public as the 'Holophusikon'. In 1781 Lever, an enthusiastic archer, convened at Leicester House a meeting which led to the formation of the Toxophilite Society. Lever's collection of almost 8,000 specimens was valued at £53,000 but the British Museum declined to buy it and, after Lever failed to raffle it off, he was forced to sell it at such a loss that he was obliged to retire to the country. Items from his collection can be seen in the Cuming Museum in south London.

Leicester House was demolished in 1791. Its site is now covered by Leicester Place, **Lisle Street** and the **Empire cinema**.

Leicester Square

"*... the Square itself has little to offer other than hordes of people looking for something to happen.*" Ed Glinert *The London Compendium*

This judgment is uncharacteristic of Glinert's normally cheery take on London and belies the square's long history. **Leicester House** once dominated it on the north side. Former residents of the Square, represented by busts in the gardens, include the anatomist **John Hunter**, **Sir Isaac**

The north and east sides of Leicester Square c. 1926, with the Shakespeare statue in the centre. Note the hotels with Continental names - on the north the Hotel de Paris, and on the east the Sabloniere and Provence and to its right the Hotel Cavour. The low buildings on the left are on the site of today's Empire Cinema.

Newton, **Hogarth** and **Reynolds**. Others have included the architect **James 'Athenian' Stuart**, the American painter **John Singleton Copley** and the engraver **Gardelle** who murdered his landlady.

Long known as Leicester Fields and originally laid out in the 1670s, Leicester Square was initially lined with handsome houses before succumbing to the intrusions of commerce, crafts and, in the nineteenth century, hotels and respectable entertainment in the shape of the **Alhambra** and Wyld's **Great Globe**. There was also a darker side. Writing in 1846 J T Smith commented that "there is a considerable number of gaming-houses in the neighbourhood, so that the bad character of the place is at least two centuries old or ever since it was built upon." Forty years later Baedeker warned readers that "the stranger is cautioned against going to any unrecommended house in Leicester Square.".

The central gardens assumed their present appearance thanks to a much-needed makeover funded by the swindler **Baron Grant**, who also paid for London's only outdoor statue of Shakespeare. The statue of Charlie Chaplin was added in 1981 and the square refurbished in 1992.

Sir Peter Lely

"Th'amaz'd world shall henceforth find
None but my Lilly ever drew a Mind."
Richard Lovelace *To My Worthy Friend Mr. Peter Lilly*

Born Pieter Van Der Faes, Lely (1618-80) arrived in England ca. 1643, rapidly established a thriving portrait practice and successfully managed the transition to the Restoration regime, becoming Principal Painter to **Charles II** from 1660. From 1651 until his death the painter lived at Nos. 10-11 the **Piazza**. Prolific rather than profound, Lely is best remembered for his portrait series of sensuous court lovelies, the 'Windsor Beauties', now at Hampton Court, but also painted a series depicting the admirals victorious at the Battle of Solebay (1665), now to be seen at the National Maritime Museum in Greenwich. Unrivalled until the arrival of **Kneller**, Lely was knighted the year before his death, even as his younger rival eclipsed him convincingly. Despite a prodigious income Lely, who lived extravagantly and was inattentive to business, left a financial mess behind him. Seven years after his death his collection of prints and drawings alone fetched £26,000 at auction. Lely was buried in **St Paul's, Covent Garden**.

Liberty's

Arthur Lasenby Liberty (1843-1917) grew up in the Nottingham lace industry before becoming manager of Farmer and Roger's 'oriental warehouse' on **Regent Street**, England's foremost retail outlet for high quality Asian craft goods. The contemporary craze for *japonisme* attracted an artistic clientele which included Leighton, Burne-Jones, Rossetti, Whistler and William Morris. In 1875 Liberty set up in business for himself at 218a Regent Street, which, despite being only half a shop with just three staff, he grandly christened East India House. Within eighteen months he had acquired the other half of the shop. By 1882 he was able to open further premises at 142-4 Regent Street for the sale of home furnishings and carpets. The original site, which sold fabrics and dresses, expanded to occupy the sites of numbers 216, 218 and 222 Regent Street. An enlightened employer and pioneer of early closing, Liberty was also a learned and discriminating connoisseur, able to attract the services (at the not inconsiderable fee of one guinea an hour) of such talented designers as the architect E W Godwin (1833-86), a founder member of the Costume Society. One of his buyers was Charles Holme (1848-1923) who became the founding editor of *The Studio* magazine. Archibald Knox (1864-1933) supplied designs in silver and pewter for Liberty's famous Cymric and Tudric range of decorative homewares, as well as designs for carpets and pottery – and for his employer's tombstone. Liberty's policy of maintaining his designers' anonymity ensured that Knox's fame was to be almost entirely posthumous. Legendary couturier Jean Muir (1928-95) started her fashion career in Liberty's stockroom before graduating, via scarves and lingerie, to designing for the Young Liberty department.

In 1881 Liberty supplied fabrics for costumes for Gilbert and Sullivan's *Patience* and in 1884 authentic Japanese kimono for the first production of *The Mikado*. In 1888-89 Liberty visited Japan to study its craft industries at first hand and on returning home became a founding member of the Japan Society of London. In 1913 he was knighted for his services to the applied and decorative arts.

In 1922-23 Edwin T Hall and his son Edwin S Hall rebuilt Liberty's main store with a **mock-Tudor** frontage on **Great Marlborough Street** incorporating timbers from the Royal Navy's last two wooden warships, *HMS Impregnable* (launched 1865), once the largest wooden ship afloat and *HMS Hindustan* (launched 1824). Half a century later this famous fabrication could still move Professor Pevsner to incandescent denunciation:

"The timbers are the real article; they come from genuine men-of-war; they are not stuck on. The roofing-tiles are hand-made, the windows leaded. So technically there is nothing wrong – but functionally and intellectually everything. The scale is wrong, the symmetry is wrong, the proximity to a classical façade ... is wrong, and the goings-on of a store behind such a façade (and below those twisted Tudor chimneys) are wrongest of all."

Liberty's Regent Street frontage incorporates a 115 foot panoramic sculptured frieze by Doman and Clapperton portraying the wealth of distant countries, borne by a camel, an elephant and a ship sailing towards a statue of Britannia. Well worth a look.

(Alison Adburgham *Liberty's: A Biography of a Shop* Allen & Unwin 1975 www.liberty.co.uk)

Lisle Street

Now dominated by Chinese restaurants, the western part of the street was laid out (1682-3) in the grounds of **Leicester House** (the Earls of Leicester were also Viscounts Lisle) and in the 1790s extended eastwards to join Little Newport Street. Nos. 14-27, a complete block on the north side, are of this period. The bowed shopfronts of Nos. 34-5 (ca. 1791) are original. The site of the Prince Charles cinema was (1867-89) occupied by the French Hospital and Dispensary before it moved to Shaftesbury Avenue. No. 5 (1897), which features a dramatic stepped gable, inspired by the Meat Hall in Haarlem, was designed by Frank T. Verity. Originally occupied by the French Club, it became the headquarters for the French cinema company, Pathé, then the St John's Hospital for Diseases of the Skin (1935-90) and is currently a pub. No. 9 was the boyhood home of actor **Edmund Kean**.

Litchfield Street

Laid out 1684-91 by **Nicholas Barbon**, Litchfield Street was home to anatomist **William Hunter** in 1763-7 and was the birthplace of singer **Elizabeth Billington** in 1768. Nos. 25, 26 and 27 are original.

A Liberty dress advertised c. 1905 – note the 'Arts and crafts' decor of the setting.

The London Coliseum at night, c. 1920. St Martin-in-the-Fields is to the right.

The London Palladium in the 1970s.

London Coliseum

Built (1902-4) to the designs of Frank Matcham, London's largest theatre (2,358 seats) incorporated England's first revolving stage (about a century and a half after they existed in Japan) and was also the first in Europe to have lifts. Intended for variety, the Coliseum hosted seasons of Diaghilev's Ballet Russe (1918, 1924, 1925) and was also a cinema (1961-8). In 1968 the theatre became the home of the Sadler's Wells Opera Company which in 1974 became English National Opera, presenting opera in English. The theatre's most recent make-over installed a roof-top bar giving spectacular views over the area. (www.eno.org)

London Palladium, Argyll Street

"*a big theatre with a strange history*" Pevsner

Wine cellars were built here (1865-6) on **Argyll Street**, the building above becoming the Corinthian Bazaar and Exhibition Rooms. In 1871 this was converted into Hengler's Circus, a permanent London home for circus and, periodically, ice skating. In 1909-10 £250,000 was spent on refurbishing as a variety theatre to designs by Frank Matcham.

Revue soon replaced variety. In the 1930s the (from 1934 London) Palladium became the home of the Crazy Gang, a comic troupe of stage-hardened middle-aged males, and staged an annual Christmas production of *Peter Pan*. As the setting for the long-running (1955-75) TV variety show *Sunday Night at the London Palladium* the theatre became a national institution. A further restoration was carried out in 1996-8.

The London Palladium has also been used more times than any other to stage the annual fund-raising Royal Variety Show. In Alfred Hitchcock's film (1935) of John Buchan's spy thriller *The 39 Steps* Richard Hannay (Robert Donat) sees the luckless Mr Memory shot on stage at the Palladium. (www.london-palladium-co-uk)

London Pavilion, Piccadilly Circus

Originally the site of the Black Horse Inn, which became a music hall in 1861, this was the birthplace of 'jingoism', the aggressive nationalism inspired by an ultra-patriotic anthem sung here when Britain

Piccadilly Circus c. 1896 when the London Pavilion was a music hall. The Pavilion is the pedimented building to the right of the central group of buildings. The facade remains today but internally it is connected to the Trocadero – the other pedimented premises to the left. The Pavilion is now used by 'Ripley's Believe It or Not' dedicated to weird and unusual exhibits.

seemed to be about to intervene in the Russo-Turkish war of 1877-78:

> "*We don't want to fight*
> *But, by Jingo, if we do,*
> *We've got the ships,*
> *We've got the men and got the money, too.*"

The present building dates from 1885 as part of the making of Shaftesbury Avenue. The lease was acquired by somewhat shady means and the construction completed in four months and three days as the builders used the new miracle of electric light to work round the clock. In 1918 it became a theatre, where C B Cochran staged lavish revues and in 1934 was converted to a cinema which closed in 1982. In 2000 the building became part of the **Trocadero** entertainment complex.

London Transport Museum, Covent Garden Piazza

Located since 1980 in the former Flower Market, the collections which now form the London Transport Museum were previously located at Chiswick, Reigate, Clapham and Syon House. Much remains in store at a depot at Acton Town. The museum covers all aspects of public transport in London since 1800, with an emphasis that is as much social as technological. Its collections are therefore not limited in their appeal to small boys or railway and bus buffs but contain thousands of exhibits, documents, maps and images of appeal to visitors or researchers with an interest in architecture, photography, costume history, graphic design, typography and poster art, of which it has an outstanding archive. A Heritage Lottery Fund Grant of £9,500,000 in 2003 has helped to fund an extensive upgrading of facilities and displays, many of which are now interactive.
(www.ltmuseum.co.uk)

The London Transport Museum, which occupies the old Covent Garden Flower market.

Long Acre

A descriptive place name if ever there was one, but misleading. Although the area in question was lengthy and narrow, it stretched over seven acres and 'acre' might in ancient usage mean simply field or strip in a field. Once part of Westminster Abbey's kitchen garden, Long Acre was cultivated by the monks and their servants until 1407, then leased out. In 1552 the land was acquired by the first Earl of Bedford, who established a pathway to mark the northern boundary of his holding. The area to the north of this came into the possession of the Mercers, the richest of the hundred or so Livery Companies which controlled the economic life of the City of London and have continued to play a philanthropic role – hence Mercer Street, with its superior artisan houses at Nos. 3-5 (ca. 1905) and 6-8 (1909) and the several buildings which bear the mark of the Virgin Mary, denoting them as Mercers' property.

The boundary path between the Bedford and Mercers' holdings had by 1615 become part of King James I's regular route from Westminster to his favourite hunting ground at Theobald's in Hertfordshire and was therefore kept in good repair, attracting prestigious residents. The foremost sculptor of his time, the appropriately named Nicholas Stone (1583-1647), lived on Long Acre from 1615 to 1645.

Perhaps in consequence of this, and its proximity to the fashionable **Piazza,** Long Acre by the mid-seventeenth century became a centre of the coach-building and **furniture** trades, though these would, in the nineteenth century, be joined by printing works, fruit warehouses, a brewery and

Long gone – the Bird in Hand pub in Conduit Court, off Long Acre, c. 1920.

showrooms for imported motor cars. A plaque records the site of the workshop where in 1819 Dennis Johnson (?1760-1833) built and sold the first 'hobby horse' bicycle.

Significant institutions associated with Long Acre have included **St Martin's Hall**, later the **Queen's Theatre**, **Odham's Press** and **Stanford's**, the world's largest map shop. There are also three Victorian pubs – the **Kemble**'s Head (1836), the Sun Tavern (1856-7) and the Freemason's Arms (1896).

In September 1929 **John Logie Baird** (1888-1946) broadcast the first television programme in Britain from the site of Nos. 132-5. The Royal Ballet School has been at Nos. 53-4 since 2003.

Lyceum Theatre

Built on the **Strand** in 1771 to the designs of James Payne, the future Lyceum was originally intended to be a concert and exhibition hall. In 1794 Dr. Samuel Arnold converted it into the English Opera House, although it actually survived by presenting a potpourri of lectures, freak shows, concerts and, in 1802, the first permanent display of Madame

The Lyceum in Wellington Street. Today, the 1834 portico shown here survives, but the remainder of the theatre was rebuilt as a music hall in 1904.

Tussaud's waxworks. From 1809 to 1812 the Lyceum was the temporary home of the displaced **Drury Lane** theatre company and also served as the home of the **Beefsteak Society** from 1809 to 1830 and again from 1838 until the club's demise in 1867. Rebuilt in 1815-16 to the designs of **Samuel Beazley**, in 1817 the Lyceum became the first British theatre to be lit permanently by gas and in that season saw Fanny Kelly make her reputation. Destroyed by fire in 1830, the theatre was rebuilt in four months, again to Beazley's designs, on a site to the west of its original location, now covered by **Wellington Street**. Under the management of Madame Vestris (1797-1856) and her husband, the comedic actor Charles Mathews (1803-78), the Lyceum enjoyed considerable popular success but the extravagance of their productions led to Mathews' imprisonment for debt. In 1878 the Lyceum was taken over by **Henry Irving** who made it virtually a national theatre. Rebuilt in 1904 as a music hall, the Lyceum failed to last six months in that incarnation but survived as a home of melodrama and pantomime before serving as a dance hall in World War Two. On 18th July 1975 the Lyceum staged a memorable session by Bob Marley and the Wailers, recorded as 'Live at the Lyceum'. After a prolonged period of dereliction and uncertainty the Lyceum was finally restored in 1996, reopening with Andrew Lloyd Webber's *Jesus Christ, Superstar.* (www.lyceum-theatre-co-uk)

Charles Macklin

"This is the Jew, That Shakespeare drew."
Alexander Pope

The Shylock performed by Charles Macklin (1699-1797) in 1741 was the inspiration which brought **Garrick,** eighteen years his junior, to the stage, yet Macklin would outlive his disciple by a further eighteen years. A touring apprenticeship laid the groundwork for the massive repertory of roles he would eventually accumulate and established a reputation for wild living and ready fists. Macklin's first major success came in a 1736 production of *The Beggar's Opera*. In 1739 he quarrelled fatally with a fellow actor over a wig and was fortunate to get away with manslaughter. By 1753 Macklin's reputation as a teacher encouraged him to retire to run a drama academy and coffee house in **Floral Street** but bankruptcy forced him back to the boards. Macklin had his first success as a dramatist with *Love A-lá-Mode*, an unsubtle exploitation of English prejudices against Scots, Jews and the Irish – of whom Macklin was one, born in Co. Donegal as Cathal MacLochlainn. He continued playing and writing until a failing memory induced his retirement at ninety. Macklin lived for some years at Nos. 10-11 the **Piazza**, the former home of **Sir Peter Lely**, and lastly at Tavistock Row; he was buried in **St Paul's**, Covent Garden. A laudatory verse epitaph gives his age at death as 107. There is an annual summer school, named after him, held near his birthplace. (www.charlesmacklin.com)

Garrick's mentor – Charles Macklin.

A Royal coat-of-arms by the stage door of the Adelphi Theatre in Maiden Lane.

The Chapel of St Barnabas in Manette Street.

Maiden Lane

Part of an ancient track between **St Martin's Lane** and **Drury Lane**, running behind the houses facing onto the **Strand**, this street was built up from ca. 1631 and is first referred to in 1636. The name may refer to a statue of the Virgin Mary or may simply be a corruption of 'midden' i.e. rubbish heap. Nos. 16-17 date from ca. 1635 behind a refacing of ca. 1806-7. The eminent Dutch engineer Sir Cornelius Vermuyden (?1595-?1683) lodged at No. 28 in 1647 when he was advising the Earl of Bedford on his ambitious scheme to drain the fens of Cambridgeshire. The poet **Andrew Marvell** lived on the site of No. 9 in 1677. A plaque at No. 10 marks where **Voltaire** stayed in 1727-8. The artist **J M W Turner** was born here. Notable places of refreshment have included the **Cider Cellars**, **Rule's restaurant** and the former Bedford Head public house, now the Maple Leaf Canadian bar. Corpus Christi Roman Catholic chapel dates from 1874.

Manette Street

Originally Rose Street and built up in the 1690s, this was by the 1720s largely "taken up for coach houses and stables". When the floral artist Mrs Delany lived here in 1721-2 she thought it "a very unpleasant part of the town". No. 14 was designed in 1770-1 by James Paine to serve as the parish workhouse for **St Anne's, Soho**. Heightened in 1804, it remained in use as such until 1837. Between 1917 and 1941 the building was used by the West End Talmud Torah and Bikkur Holim Synagogue. Later in the century there was a Social Democrats club on the street, a favoured meeting-place of East European anarchists. The organ builders **Bevington & Sons** began business here around 1794.

In 1895 the street was renamed for the character of Dr Manette, in **Dickens**' *A Tale of Two Cities*, whose house is supposed to have been here with a courtyard and a shady plane tree. On the south side above the door of Goldbeater's House is a replica of the Golden Arm mentioned in Chapter 6 of Book 2 of the novel. The original is to be seen at the Dickens House Museum at 48 Doughty Street. Manette Street was traditionally pronounced Manetti by the Soho-born.

Andrew Marvell

Best known to modern readers for his accomplished erotic paean *To His Coy Mistress*, in his own day Andrew Marvell (1621-78) was celebrated as a pamphleteer and satirist. His *Horatian Ode upon Cromwell's Return from Ireland* has been hailed as "perhaps the greatest political poem in English". A protégé of Milton and Cromwell, fluent in six languages, a conscientious MP for Hull and probably a spy, Marvell was in **Maiden Lane** in 1677 and also lived for a period in **St Martin's Lane**. He was buried in **St Giles-in-the-Fields**, where there is a memorial to him. **Charles Lamb** initiated the rediscovery of Marvell as a lyric poet.

(Nicholas Murray – *World Enough and Time: The Life of Andrew Marvell* St Martin's Press 2000)

Andrew Marvell.

Karl Marx lived with his family in poverty above 28 Dean Street, pictured below. The premises are now Quo Vadis restaurant. Note the plaque at 2nd floor level.

Karl Marx

Marx (1818-83) first visited London in 1847 when he addressed the German Workers' Education Society at its club room at 20 **(Great) Windmill Street**. When the German liberal revolution of 1848 failed, Marx and his family fled, finding refuge in the German Hotel (now Manzi's) in **Lisle Street**, until having never paid a bill, "we were forced to look for other lodgings." For five years home would be two rooms at the top of No. 28 **Dean Street**. Here they lived through cholera and lost three children. Despite their confinement Marx also fathered another child with his long-suffering wife, Jenny – and a boy with family servant, Lenchen, its paternity attributed to Marx's equally long-suffering benefactor Friedrich Engels (1820-95).

Marx lectured on 'What is bourgeois property?' at the German Society. He was a good teacher, defining terms clearly, avoiding jargon and illustrating arguments from his own wide reading. He attempted to make Windmill Street a base for a Communist organisation but this was aborted amid the usual mutual recrimination. He also held court to visiting revolutionaries and fenced, ferociously, at a gymnasium in Rathbone Street. The Prussian government kept tabs on him but failed to persuade the British he was dangerous. Thanks to their surveillance reports Dean Street's squalor was recorded in detail:

"Marx lives in one of the worst ... cheapest, quarters ... In the whole apartment there is not one clean and solid piece of furniture ... Everything is dirty and covered with dust ...". Marx himself was "an extremely disorderly, cynical human being", smoking incessantly, washing rarely, frequently drunk but also a loving father, idolised by his children and capable of bouts of intense effort ... "often idle for days on end, he will work day and night with tireless endurance ... He has no fixed times for going to sleep ... often stays up all night and then lies down fully clothed." Having renounced Prussian citizenship, Marx could be indifferent to Prussian opinions; but he remained stateless, being refused British nationality. During the Soho sojourn Marx was sometimes unable to pay for meat or even medicines. The death of a daughter at two obliged him to borrow two pounds for her tiny coffin. Marx's adored and ebullient Edgar died at eight, bringing him to utter misery. Much must be blamed on Marx himself. For a world-class economist he was rotten with money. His vitriolic pen served the *New York Daily Tribune*, the world's biggest-selling newspaper. He found "newspaper muck" a chore but it brought up to £150 a year. A Swiss journal paid another £50. Engels fiddled expenses at his family's textile business in Manchester to subsidise his feckless friend. Marx meanwhile devoted himself to the Reading Room of the British Museum, ten minutes from Dean Street, composing *Das Kapital*.

Dean Street cost only £22 a year, leaving plenty to live on. Marx's poverty was caused by his own pretensions. Acutely conscious of the German exile community Marx, in funds, was generous with handouts. He kept both a servant and a secretary, a useless syphilitic youth – until his disgrace. He insisted his three girls have country and seaside holidays and lessons in drawing, piano, French and Italian. Jenny, a Prussian aristocrat, must have name-cards proclaiming her status. (The Prussian Interior Minister responsible for Marx's surveillance was Marx's own brother-in-law.) Relief – and release – for the family came from the deaths and legacies of Jenny's uncle and mother. These modest windfalls enabled the family to move to Kentish Town near Hampstead Heath. Leaving their "evil, frightful rooms" Jenny got her silver and crockery out of storage. The children had a garden. Years later Marx would confess that "the region round Soho Square still sends a shiver down my spine if I happen to be anywhere near there." The blue plaque on Dean Street remains the only official acknowledgment of the thirty-four years Karl Marx passed in his adopted country.

(Asa Briggs *Karl Marx in London: An Illustrated Guide* BBC 1982; Francis Wheen *Karl Marx* Fourth Estate 1999)

Jessie Matthews

"All my life I had been frightened."

One of the eleven surviving children of a **Berwick Street** market trader, Margaret – 'Jessie' – Matthews (1907-81), gifted as both dancer and singer, made her stage debut at twelve and was appearing in New York at sixteen. Graduating from revue to musical comedy, she introduced such famous 'standards' as **Noel Coward's** *A Room With a View* and Cole Porter's *Let's Do It.* As Britain's highest paid actress, she then became Britain's first international movie star, making fourteen films in the 1930s. Professional triumph was dogged by private tragedies and personal insecurity - the rapid failure of her first marriage, hostile publicity when she was blamed for the divorce of co-star Sonnie Hale, who became her second husband, the death of her first baby, two nervous breakdowns and financial disaster when the outbreak of war torpedoed a successful musical scheduled for the **London Coliseum**. Ironically, it was entitled *I Can Take It*.

The magnetic Jessie Matthews who later on became the BBC's dutiful 'Mrs Dale'.

A Broadway offer seemed a lifeline but illness meant the play flopped while, in her absence, Sonnie began an affair with the nurse of their adopted daughter. Divorce followed. Jessie threw herself into entertaining the troops with ENSA, met a lieutenant twelve years her junior and married him in 1945. Their son was stillborn and she was told another pregnancy could kill her. A third divorce finally issued in 1958. By then Jessie had re-established herself on stage and screen, though as a versatile professional actress rather than a musical star. A new incarnation, as Mrs. Dale (1963-9), the endlessly supportive wife of a country doctor in the BBC radio series, *Mrs Dale's Diary*, brought her a new generation of fans. Jessie Matthews was appointed OBE in 1970 and published an autobiography *Over My Shoulder* in 1974. In 1978 she appeared on stage again as the Duchess of Berwick in **Wilde**'s *Lady Windermere's Fan*. Given her birthplace, the name of this role doubtless had a special appeal for her. In 1979 her one-woman show *Miss Jessie Matthews in Concert* won the US Drama Critics Award.

John Meard

John Meard was a carpenter who became a builder and a speculative developer. Despite becoming a Soho vestryman he was not above evading his obligations as a ratepayer by shifting "from one House to another of different Rent, so that they never knew how to charge him". No. 68 **Dean Street** became the Meard family home; with No. 67 it is reckoned among the best early Georgian houses to survive in London. Apart from the street named for him Meard's other Soho ventures include 48-58 **Broadwick Street** and the original spire of the parish church of **St Anne**

Meard Street

Early Georgian terraces are rare survivals in London. Meard Street is also representative of the process by which many were built – in stages and ranging in size, quite grand at the **Dean Street** end but diminishing from four storeys to three going westwards. It was built between 1722 and 1732 over two previous courts built up in the 17th century on differing freeholds. Meard acquired the western one, facing towards **Wardour Street** first and built two facing terraces, of which Nos. 13-21 survive on the south side. Acquiring the eastern court enabled him to then break through to complete the street and add four superior houses facing onto Dean Street. As befitted houses made by a carpenter they had good wooden staircases and panelling from floor to ceiling. Early tenants included Bernhard Tschudi, a noted maker of harpsichords and J C Schmidt, who was Handel's amanuensis. Batty Langley (1696-1751), the prolific author of more than twenty books on design, gardening and surveying lived in the street from ca. 1740 until his death. With his engraver brother, Thomas, he ran evening classes to teach architectural drawing.

Diminutive but distinctive – Meard Street.

Perhaps the most distinguished resident was François Philidor (1726-95), who had been a child prodigy as a musician, a composer and a chess-player, capable of playing three simultaneous games – blindfold. As a chess-master Philidor stood first in Europe; his analytical treatise, which stressed the need to value pawns and build a strong middle game, was still being reprinted half a century after his death.

By 1758 the tone had been notably lowered by the tenant of a single room at No. 9, Elizabeth Flint, 'generally slut and drunkard; occasionally whore and thief". Even **Dr Johnson**, however, conceded that she had a certain style having "a spinet on which she played and a boy that walked before her chair." In 1951 **George Melly** and Mick Mulligan organised the first all-night **jazz** session at No.4, the Mandrake, by daytime a chess club. A Meard Street property for sale at Christmas 2007 offered almost 4,000 square feet over five floors, including three reception rooms, two kitchens, four bedrooms, study, dining room, basement and roof terrace – price £4,500,000.

George Melly

An exuberant bisexual Bohemian, jazz singer George Melly (1926-2007) was also variously a sailor, film critic and cartoon caption-writer. A lifelong devotee of fly-fishing, he was also an acknowledged expert on Surrealism. A stalwart of the **Colony Club**, Melly was a characteristic archetype of Soho in the **Fifties**. The author of more than a dozen books, he recounted passages of his colourful life, characteristically in reverse order, in three volumes of autobiography *Owning Up* (1965) (jazz singing), *Rum, Bum and Concertina* (1977) (the Royal Navy) and *Scouse Mouse* (childhood).

(www.georgemelly.com)

Military Ground

In 1615 a 'Military Company' was formed in Westminster and, encouraged by the Crown via the Privy Council, acquired three and a half acres in the north-west part of 'St Martin's Field' as an exercise ground. In 1616 the area was surrounded by a brick wall nine feet high, which protected a two-storey brick Armoury House with a tile roof. Over a hundred feet long and about a third as wide, this housed a large hall – to serve as a gymnasium, fencing *salle* and occasional banquet-house – complemented by a library, a kitchen and a meeting-cum-dining-room. The furnishings included tables, four dozen leather chairs, a carved and gilded royal coat of arms, a chained Bible, a large iron grate which ran on wheels, painted candle-holders and several 'Statues of Emperors' heads, as well as quantities of arms, armour and ammunition.

What the Military Company did during the civil wars of the 1640s is unknown, if, indeed, it functioned as a unit. By 1656 it is certain, however, that the Company as a corporate body was indisputably in debt, doubtless because its erstwhile members had long been otherwise distracted and dispersed, and the rates on its house and grounds were being paid by a cook and a gardener, presumably employees who had been charged with their safekeeping. In 1661 the cook and a number of surviving members of the Company were paid £500 for their interests in the premises by the ferocious Col. Gerard, who built **Gerrard Street** on it.

John Minton

Trained at the St John's Wood School of Art and in France, John Minton (1917-57) taught at Camberwell, the Central School and the Royal College of Art, turned out a steady flow of paintings, drawings and illustrations and was a prolific designer of bookjackets, wallpapers and theatre sets. A fine draughtsman with a distinctive romantic style, Minton also had seven one-man shows at the Lefevre Gallery. Unlike many of his fellow patrons of the **Colony**, the **French** and the **Gargoyle**, Minton was well-off and could afford to travel in Spain, the West Indies and Morocco, which provided much inspiration for his work. Open-handed with his cash, in Soho Minton was invariably encouraged by an entourage of adoring students or compliant sailors. He died of an overdose of drugs – possibly accidental – and left his Chelsea home to **Henrietta Moraes**.

(Frances Spalding *John Minton: Dance till the stars come down* Lund Humphries 2005)

Mock Tudor

'Stockbroker's Tudor' was one of several styles characteristic of London's inter-war building boom, usually associated with suburban residential avenues and vast 'road house' pubs ranged along

Tudor run riot – the newly-built Liberty store on Great Marlborough Street in the 1920s.

the new arterial roads leading out of them. The presence of several examples in inner-city Soho is therefore all the more striking. Perhaps it was the unrestrained example of **Liberty's** Great Marlborough Street frontage (1922-23) that provided the impetus. The Shakespeare's Head (1928) stands in close proximity at the northern end of **Carnaby Street**. Other examples include The Three Greyhounds (1924), the **Golden Lion** (1929), the **Pillars of Hercules** (1935) and the whimsical arbour (1925-6) in **Soho Square** which has excited the curiosity of generations of visitors and has become something of a minor icon for the whole locality.

Model Housing

The provision of 'model housing' was one embodiment of a belated mid-Victorian response to the environmental and moral threat represented by 'rookeries' like **Seven Dials** and **St Giles**. Built to house skilled workers and petty tradespeople - not the very poor – these often fortress-like blocks were usually robust in construction with especial attention to drains, hygiene etc. and were rigorously managed to ensure adequate maintenance, regular payment of rents and the prompt suppression of drunkenness and anti-social behaviour. Model housing was intended to provide a secure setting for family life which would prevent respectable residents from being dragged down into London's ever-growing underclass. The providers included charities, City Livery Companies, housing reform bodies, private companies and local government. All their efforts added together over the course of the nineteenth century would prove inadequate to house what by the 1880s was even one year's increase in the population of the capital. Examples of model housing in the areas covered by this book can be seen at Wild Street and **Bedfordbury** (Peabody Trust), Drury Lane (Metropolitan Board of Works), Ingestre Place (Metropolitan Association for Improving the Dwellings of the Industrious Classes), Sandringham Buildings, **Charing Cross Road** (Improved Industrial Dwellings Co.) and Mercer Street (Mercers' Company).

(Susannah Morris – *Private profit and public interest: Model Dwellings Companies and the housing of the working classes in London 1840-1914* Oxford University Press 1998;
www.victorianlondon.org/houses/modelhousing.htm)

Monmouth House, c. 1720.

Monmouth House, Soho Square

Around 1682 James Scott, Duke of Monmouth (1649-85), bastard son of **Charles II**, began to build himself a fine mansion on the south side of **Soho Square**. Although in occupation before it was completed, he did not enjoy it long. In 1685, following the death of Charles II, Monmouth attempted to thwart the succession of his Catholic uncle, **James II**, by raising a Protestant rising in the West Country. Backed by a credulous but ill-armed peasantry, who allegedly adopted 'Soho' as their battle-cry, Monmouth was easily crushed at Sedgemoor, the last battle fought on English soil. Monmouth had ventured far out of his depth but he was handsome and popular and when his executioner at Tower Hill took five strokes to sever his head the clumsy butcher needed an armed escort to protect him from the enraged crowd.

Despite Monmouth's downfall, an interest in the Soho residence was transferred to his widow but the house was still uncompleted and both this task and the question of ownership became the subject of legal proceedings so complex and protracted that Monmouth House remained virtually uninhabitable for thirty years. Meanwhile, between 1689 and 1694, a converted back-room served as a chapel, known as L'Eglise du Quarre, for recently-arrived **Huguenots**.

Monmouth House was finally sold in 1717 to Sir James Bateman, Lord Mayor of London, who had the front remodelled, possibly to the designs of his relative, Thomas Archer, then building St John's, Smith Square.

Monmouth House, however, was demolished in 1773. The sculptor Joseph Nollekens visited while this was being done, accompanied by his friend and biographer J T Smith, later Keeper of Prints at the British Museum. Even half-ruined, Monmouth House was evidently still impressive, with massive iron gates, mounted on stone piers, and a spacious courtyard for carriages. The ground floor had eight rooms, with carved and gilded panelling and ornamental plaster ceilings – "The principal room on the first floor was lined with blue satin, which was superbly decorated with pheasants and other birds in gold." What the uppermost floors were originally like could not be recorded as they had already been wrecked.

Two substantial houses, Nos. 28 and 29 Soho Square were erected on the site, with behind them a double row of very modest dwellings, Bateman's Buildings.

The first occupant of No. 28 was the dramatist and manager of the Haymarket Theatre, George Colman the Younger (1762-1836). He was followed by the Radical MP Joseph Hume (1777-1855). Tireless and incorruptible, Hume waged an endless war on government waste and peculation and served on more committees than any other MP in the House. From 1834 to 1860 No. 28 served as the recruiting office for the armed forces of the East India Company and after that as a parsonage house for the Rectors of **St Anne's, Soho**.

No. 29 was occupied by the Shakespearean actor **Charles Kemble** in 1822-5; during this period he took over the management of **Covent Garden Theatre**. No. 29 was demolished in 1875 to make way for extensions to The **Hospital for Women**.

Lady Mary Wortley Montagu

The forceful Lady Mary Wortley Montagu (1689-1762) was baptised at **St Paul's, Covent Garden** and lived for some time in a house at the north-west corner of the **Piazza**. Largely self-educated, she wrote poems sufficiently accomplished to be published in a pirated edition by **Curll**. Marrying in defiance of her father, she accompanied her husband to Istanbul (1716-18) when he was appointed ambassador there and learned the practice, common among Turks, of inoculation against smallpox. On her return she was successful in promoting its acceptance in England.

Lady Mary Wortley Montagu.

Active in social and literary circles, she won the warm admiration of Alexander Pope, who had **Kneller** paint a portrait of her, but Pope subsequently became her bitterest enemy, attacking her viciously in print. The cause of their quarrel is disputed but may have been a declaration of love to which she is said to have responded with incredulous laughter. In 1739 Lady Mary left her miser husband to spend most of her later life on the Continent. Her waspish, witty letters were published posthumously and won the admiration of both **Johnson** and **Voltaire**. She once remarked that the main consolation in being a woman was that she didn't have to be married to one.

Her last words were "It's all been very interesting".

(Isobel Grundy *Lady Mary Wortley Montagu: Comet of the Enlightenment* Oxford University Press 2001; www.montaguemillennium.com)

Henrietta Moraes

Born in Simla, India, deserted by her father, beaten by her granny, Audrey Abbott (1931-99) was working as a model in London art schools when in

1950 she met first husband, film-maker Michael Law, who rebranded her as Henrietta. Setting up home in a **Dean Street** attic, she became a regular at **The French House**, the **Colony**, the **Gargoyle** and the **Gay Hussar**. After marrying body-builder Norman Bowler, she ran a coffee-bar in David Archer's **Greek Street** bookshop, where she met the elfin teenage Indian poet Dom Moraes, eventually her third husband. Inheriting a Chelsea home from painter **John Minton**, she sat many times for Lucian Freud and **Francis Bacon** and posed for pornographic shots for **John Deakin**. Variously described as warm, witty and lovable, foul-mouthed, amoral, a drunk, a drug addict and a thief, Henrietta lost her Chelsea home in the '60s, took to the hippy trail and became a PA to singer Marianne Faithfull before serving a fortnight in Holloway after an unsuccessful essay into burglary. In later years she devoted herself to her dachshund, Max, and sat for the artist Maggi Hambling. She is buried in Brompton cemetery. A selective memoir *Henrietta* appeared in 1994.

George Morland

Born on Haymarket, the son of a bankrupted painter/engraver/dealer, George Morland (1763-1804) was exhibiting sketches at the Royal Academy by the age of ten and endured a rigorous seven-year apprenticeship under his father, who saw the boy's prodigious talent as a remedy for the family's fallen fortunes. Morland reacted to the ending of his servitude by embarking on a life of dissolution, financed by a prolific output ranging from soft-porn 'galanteries' to fake Dutch landscapes, sentimental prints of young romance and, ironically, moralising narratives à la **Hogarth**. From 1790 onwards he shifted to rural genre subjects such as higglers, gypsies and fisherfolk. Morland's nomadic existence included intermittent residence with John Harris, publisher of his sketch-books, at 29 **Gerrard Street** and with his brother, Henry, proprietor of Morland's Hotel on **Dean Street**, who probably accommodated him less from fraternal duty than from the opportunity to deal in his works. Although he produced perhaps a thousand paintings and had over 250 engravings of his work published, Morland was permanently in debt and usually on the run from creditors. He did, however receive the testimony of his artistic contemporaries of being consistently plagiarised. Four posthumous biographies appeared in quick succession after his alcohol-hastened death at the early age of forty-one. Examples of Morland's portraits and self-portraits are in the **National Portrait Gallery** and his genre paintings are in Tate Britain, though rarely displayed.

The artist George Morland at work.

Morley's Hotel in Trafalgar Square.

Morley's Hotel, Trafalgar Square

Originally built as apartments by George Ledwell Taylor (1788-1873), this neo-Classical block dominating the east side of **Trafalgar Square** was soon converted to become a reasonably priced hotel, popular with foreign, especially American, visitors.

In 1921 it was taken over by the South African High Commission and demolished in 1923 to make way for **South Africa House**.

Morning Chronicle

Founded in 1769, the *Morning Chronicle* survived until 1862 and numbered among its contributors, **Sheridan, Lamb** and **Dickens**. Its offices were in **Catherine Street**.

Morning Post

Founded in 1772, the *Morning Post* survived until 1937, when it was amalgamated with the *Daily*

The longest-running theatrical show in the world – The Mousetrap *is still playing at the St Martin's Theatre. It opened in 1952.*

Telegraph. Early contributors included the poets S T Coleridge, William Wordsworth and Robert Southey. The newspaper's offices were in **Catherine Street**.

The Mousetrap

This murder mystery is a phenomenon of theatrical history. *The Mousetrap,* by Agatha Christie, ran from 1952 at the **New Ambassador's** Theatre in **West Street**, and since 1974 has been nearby at the **St Martin's Theatre**. By 1958 it had already become the longest run in British theatrical history and is the longest running show of any kind in the world. At the time of writing it has been performed over 23,000 times. The original set was replaced for the first time in 2000. www.the-mousetrap.co.uk

Mozart

"Those Ladies and Gentlemen who will honour him with their Company from Twelve to Three in the afternoon, any Day in the Week ... may ... gratify their Curiosity, and not only hear this young Music Master and his Sister perform ... but likewise try his surprising Musical Capacity, by giving him anything to play at Sight..."
The Public Advertiser March 1765

Child prodigy Johann Chrysostom Wolfgang Amadeus Mozart (1756-91) came to London in 1764-5 as part of an extended European tour in company with his father, Leopold, and sister Nannerl, with whom he performed duets. They stayed initially at No. 19 **Cecil Court,** then at 20 **Frith Street**, the home of a corset maker. The Mozarts performed at Caldwell's Assembly Rooms at No. 21 Dean Street and at **Hickford's Rooms.** They also met **J C Bach** and performed three times before **George III**.

One of the concerts was adroitly timed by Leopold to coincide with the king's birthday and netted 100 guineas in three hours. Leopold, however, then fell perilously ill and the family moved out to Ebury Street, Chelsea, where the child Mozart whiled away his father's convalescence by dictating his first symphony to his sister.

(Ruth Halliwell *The Mozart Family: Four Lives in a Social Context* OUP 1998; www.mozartproject.org)

Musical Instruments

By the mid-eighteenth century at least four violin-makers were active in Soho, which thus became the capital's chief centre for the manufacture and sale of stringed instruments, under the dominant leadership of the Hill, Hart, Lott, Tubbs and Panormo families. As late as the 1890s there were no fewer than eight Soho firms making or dealing in violins, from one which imported fine Stradivarius instruments to another which yearly exported hundreds of 'dilapidated fiddles' to Chicago for refurbishment and an unknown fate in the Wild West.

The harpsichord maker, Jacob Kirkman, was established at 17 **Great Pulteney Street** from 1739-50, when he moved to 54 **Broadwick Street**, where the business continued until 1832. Burckhardt Tschudi (*aka* Burkat Shudi) and his son-in-law **John Broadwood**, and then their successors, ran the same business at No. 32 Great Pulteney Street from 1743 to 1904. A family portrait of Burckhardt Tschudi, his wife and two young sons, can be seen in the **National Portrait Gallery**. Painted by Tuscher ca. 1742, it shows Tschudi tuning a magnificent harpsichord; also included in the picture are a Chinese tea-service to emphasise their fashionable lifestyle and a portrait of Frederick, Prince of Wales, to indicate royal patronage.

In the 1790s the Italian composer Domenico Corri and his son-in-law, the Czech J L Dussek, ran a combined music-publishing and musical instrument business at 90 **Dean Street**. Organ-builders **Bevington & Sons** were in **Manette Street**. Instruments for the rock 'n' roll industry are now sold in **Denmark Street**.

Musical Visitors

In August 1839 Richard Wagner (1813-83), then an obscure conductor with a dismal employment record, stayed for a week on **Old Compton Street** to recuperate from a horrendous voyage across the Baltic, the memories of which were to inspire *The Flying Dutchman.*

In 1839 Johann Strauss (1804-49) made his first triumphant visit to London, putting up in style at the German Hotel in Leicester Place which, as Manzi's, still provides convenient accommodation for music technicians working in nearby session and dubbing studios.

The composer and piano virtuoso Franz Liszt (1811-86) stayed at No. 18 **Great Marlborough Street** in 1840-41.

(Lewis Foreman and Susan Foreman *London: A Musical Gazetteer* Yale University Press 2005)

My Fair Lady

Ovid's *Metamorphoses* recounts the story of the sculptor Pygmalion falling in love with his own work, an ivory statue of a woman. Venus answered his prayers and brought it to life. In 1734 at **Covent Garden Theatre** two French dancers presented what is claimed to be the first ballet ever staged – *Pygmalion.* In 1823 **Hazlitt** wrote an account of his disastrously unrequited passion for his landlord's daughter, entitling it, *Liber Amoris; or, The New Pygmalion.* George Bernard Shaw (1856-1950) used the legend as the basis of his wittiest play, *Pygmalion* (1913) in which a professor of linguistics, Henry Higgins, sets out to transform the appearance, manners and, above all, the speech, of Cockney flower-girl Eliza Doolittle, whom he encounters under the portico of **St Paul's, Covent Garden**.

The part of Eliza was tailored by Shaw for his friend, actor Mrs Patrick Campbell (1865-1940). The musical of Shaw's play, *My Fair Lady* (1956), by English-educated Alan Jay Lerner (1918-86) and German-born Frederick Loewe (1901-88), set new records for the longest-running original musical in both New York and London, where it was staged at the **Theatre Royal Drury Lane**. Five million copies of the Broadway cast recording were sold in the USA alone. Translated into eleven languages, the musical played in twenty countries. The film version (1964), costumed by Cecil Beaton, was awarded seven Oscars, including Best Actor for Rex Harrison (1908-90), who famously could not sing a note.

Flower girls and customers beneath a colonnade at Covent Garden Piazza.

John Nash

Having trained under Sir Robert Taylor, the architect John Nash (1752-1835) lost severely on his first building speculation, retired to Wales and was past forty before he was persuaded to return to London and resume his professional practice. In 1798 he married Mary Bradley, a cast-off mistress of the Prince of Wales (later **George IV**), whose favourite architect he became. In 1806 Nash was appointed architect to the Chief Commissioner of His Majesty's Woods, Forests and Land Revenues, which put him in line to tender for important public contracts. Now best remembered for laying out Regent's Park and building its terraces and grand houses, **Regent Street**, Carlton House Terrace and Clarence House, Nash was also responsible for the **Argyll Rooms**, a Gallery of British Artists in Suffolk Street, the Italian Opera House and the **Haymarket Theatre**. As early as 1812 Nash sketched out proposals for the redevelopment of Charing Cross and demolishing the Royal Mews to create a square. In 1826 he revised these plans to include a new Royal Academy building on the north side. The death of George IV in 1830 deprived Nash of his patron and protector and was followed by his disgrace over the delays and cost-overruns associated with his unfinished efforts to upgrade Buckingham Palace. It was, therefore, left to others to realise Nash's scheme for what became **Trafalgar Square**. (Micharl Mansbridge – *John Nash: A Complete Catalogue* Phaidon 2004)

The National Gallery, Trafalgar Square

"*... its doors must always be open, without fee or reward, to every decently dressed person ... It must be situated in the very gang-way of London.*"

George Agar Ellis MP

Unlike the Louvre or the Prado, the establishment of the National Gallery was not the outcome of royal initiative, although **George IV**, himself a considerable connoisseur, did give the project his endorsement and support – but got Parliament to pay for it. The core collection of thirty-eight paintings was made, with the advice of **Benjamin West** and **Sir Thomas Lawrence**, by John Julius Angerstein (1735-1823), a Russian-born merchant who was, in effect, the founder of Lloyd's insurance market. Initially the collection, purchased for £60,000 after Angerstein's death, remained in his modest former home at 100 Pall Mall. But, as further works were presented, notably by Sir George Beaumont (1753-1827), the prime mover in the gallery scheme, it became clear that a purpose-built gallery on a much larger scale would be required for them to be displayed adequately.

The present National Gallery building, completed in 1838, occupies the site of former royal stables. The architect was William Wilkins (1778-1839) who recycled much of the portico of George IV's recently demolished nearby residence, Carlton House, into his design. Initially the painting collection occupied the west wing only, while the Royal Academy was accommodated in the east wing. The building has been extended several times, by **E M Barry** in 1876, by Sir John Taylor in 1887, in 1911 and most recently in 1991 when the Sainsbury Wing was added, to the designs of American architect Robert Venturi. The **Orange Street** extension, added in 1975, was redesigned in 1999. The pedestrianised terrace linking the gallery to **Trafalgar Square** was made in 2003.

The early collection was strongly biased towards the work of a relatively limited range of artists, a dozen of whom accounted for nearly two-fifths of the gallery's paintings by the 1840s. Prominent among these were Correggio, Titian, Rubens, Rembrandt, Claude, Poussin, **Hogarth**, **Reynolds** and **Lawrence**. Initially under the management of a Keeper, in 1855 the gallery acquired its first Director, the influential Charles Eastlake, who was appointed specifically to broaden its range of acquisitions, particularly of early Italian art and managed to acquire some 139 canvases. His successor Sir William Boxall bought the collection of the late Prime Minister, Sir Robert Peel, including one of the most celebrated Dutch landscapes, Hobbema's *Avenue, Middelharnis*. Sir Frederick Burton acquired Botticelli's *Venus and*

The National Gallery in Trafalgar Square, with the church of St Martin-in-the-Fields to the right.

Mars and the works of then unfamiliar artists, such as Vermeer's *A Young Woman standing at a Virginal*. When the Tate Gallery was opened in 1897 many works by British artists were transferred from the National to its collection. At that time the National's collection still reflected little interest in Italian or French painting after the seventeenth century, deficiencies partly remedied by acquisitions and bequests in the twentieth century.

In 1914 the gallery was the scene of an 'outrage' when a suffragette, campaigning for votes for women, slashed the Velazquez nude known as 'the *Rokeby Venus*'. The damage was skilfully repaired but the stitch-marks are visible when caught at the right angle to the light (Room 29). During World War II the gallery's treasures were secreted in Wales, but it was still thronged by visitors attending the free lunch-time piano recitals given by Dame Myra Hess or visiting the fund-raising displays of current work by contemporary war artists. By 2005 the National Gallery owned some 2,300 pictures, two-thirds of which had been acquired through gifts and bequests from private individuals.

More than a thousand paintings are on display in the main galleries. These include only single paintings by Hieronymous Bosch (*Christ Mocked*) and Michelangelo (*Entombment*) and the only two paintings by David in Britain, two self-portraits by Rembrandt, painted thirty years apart and no fewer than nine by Raphael. Of the artists mentioned elsewhere in this book there are examples of work by **Hogarth** (*Marriage à la Mode*), **Canaletto** (*Venice: The Basin of San Marco on Ascension Day; Stonemason's Yard*), **Reynolds** (*Sir Banastre Tarleton, Captain Robert Orme, Anne, Countess of Albemarle*), **Lawrence** (*Queen Charlotte, The 2nd Earl of Liverpool*) and **Turner** (*The Fighting Temeraire* and *Rain, Steam and Speed*).

The author's personal choice of 'must see' from across the centuries would be:

1. The Wilton Diptych – an anonymously painted fourteenth-century portable altar-piece showing the boy-king Richard II being presented to the Virgin and Child, supported by assorted angels. (Acquired in 1929) (*Room 53*)

2. The Battle of San Romano – a stylised exercise in perspective by Paulo Uccello, celebrating the Florentines' victory over their arch-enemy, Siena. (Bought by Eastlake) (*Room 55*)

3. The Arnolfini Marriage – a marvel of detail and reflection by Jan van Eyck, the first master of painting in oils. (Acquired 1843) (*Room 56*)

4. Doge Leonardo Loredan – a study of personal dignity and restrained luxury, masterfully lit, by Giovanni Bellini (Acquired 1844) (*Room 61*)

5. The Ambassadors – an enigmatic double portrait by Hans Holbein, packed with symbolic accessories (*Room 5*)

6. A Woman and her Maid in a Courtyard – time suspended by Pieter de Hooch (*Room 16*)

7. Whistlejacket – simply stunning stallion by the doyen of equine painters, George Stubbs (*Room 34*)

8. The Duke of Wellington – a haunting insight by Franciso de Goya into the solitary nature of England's greatest hero (*Room 41*)

9. The Hay Wain – quite simply Britain's favourite picture, by John Constable (*Room 34*)

10. Lord Ribblesdale – by the supremely accomplished American society portraitist John Singer Sargent; the subject, a Trustee of the National Gallery, gave the picture in memory of two sons killed in the Great War.

One of the unexpected pleasures of the National Gallery – quite often literally overlooked – are the floor mosaics designed by the delightfully dotty Russian artist Boris Anrep (1883-1969). *The Awakening of the Muses*, on the halfway landing of the staircase leading to the Central Hall, features the novelist Virginia Woolf as Clio, the muse of History, and film star Greta Garbo as Melpomene, Muse of Tragedy. The mosaic on the landing closest to the Central Hall, illustrating *Modern Virtues*, features philosopher Bertrand Russell and the poet and eccentric Edith Sitwell and has poet T S Eliot contemplating the Loch Ness Monster and Churchill standing on the cliffs of Dover giving a V-for-Victory sign to a swastika-shaped monster. (National Gallery Companion Guide NGC 2006 www.nationalgallery.org.uk)

The National Portrait Gallery, St Martin's Place

The National Portrait Gallery was established by Act of Parliament in 1856 at the suggestion of Philip, 5th Earl of Stanhope, with the strong support of Prince Albert. It first opened in Great George Street, Westminster in 1859 with fifty-seven pictures but as the collection rapidly expanded it was moved to South Kensington (1869) and then to Bethnal Green (1885). The present building was funded by the generosity of W H Alexander and built (1890-5) to the designs of Ewan Christian. The **Orange Street** wing was added (1931-3) at the expense of

The National Portrait Gallery in 2009, advertising an exhibition featuring ***Mary Seacole****, a Soho resident.*

the art dealer Lord Duveen and the Ondaatje wing (1998-2000) thanks to Sir Christopher Ondaatje, a philanthropist of many such projects.

The original intention of the National Portrait Gallery was to perpetuate the memory of the 'great and the good' as a source of moral inspiration for succeeding generations, thus endorsing the assertion of historian Thomas Carlyle that history was essentially "the biography of great men". The grave statesmen and imperial proconsuls of Victoria's empire were subsequently joined by poets and composers, then engineers and entrepreneurs, academics,anti-establishment intellectuals, heroes of populat culture and latterly rock stars, footballers, models and media 'personalities'. Subjects were not considered for inclusion until a decade after their death. Both these criteria have since been amended. Although the collection contains many works by artists of the first rank, the significance of the person has always been considered a more important criterion for their inclusion than the quality of their portrait as art.

Works by artists mentioned in this book include **John Hayls'** portrait of **Samuel Pepys**; **Kneller**'s Duke of Marlborough, Sir Christopher Wren and series of the staunchly Whig Kit-Kat Club; a self-portrait by **Hogarth**; **Reynolds**' self-portrait and portraits of **Garrick**, Sterne, **Dr Johnson** and **Sir Joseph Banks**; **Lawrence**'s **George IV** and William Wilberforce; and **Haydon**'s Wordsworth. Portraits of personalities mentioned include a miniature of **Sir Kenelm Digby** by Peter Oliver and van Dyck's flamboyant rendering of Digby's wife, Venetia Stanley; an exhausted **Charles II** by Edward Hawker, a follower of **Lely**; a pert **Nell Gwyn** by Simon Verelst; **George II** by Thomas Hudson; **Sarah Siddons** by John Downman; a naïve sketch of **Jane Austen** by her sister Cassandra, the only contemporary rendering of the novelist in existence; **William Blake** skilfully captured by Thomas Phillips, who got his subject animated by encouraging him to talk about his conversations with angels; a youthful, dandified **Dickens** by his friend Daniel Maclise; **Ellen Terry** as an idealised, sensuous nymphette by G F Watts, to whom she was briefly and disastrously married; and a caricature of **Sir Henry Irving** by 'Ape'.

Other highlights of the collection include the weird, anamorphic portrait of Edward VI, which must be viewed sideways through a squint-hole; what is almost certainly the only contemporary portrait of Shakespeare, 'Jack the Lad' with an earring, rather than the staid businessman of the First Folio; a Bonnie Prince Charlie so effeminate you can only wonder how the Highlanders were induced to follow him once they had seen him; haunting photographs by the pioneer of soft focus, Julia Margaret Cameron; a characteristically brilliant pencil sketch of 'Lawrence of Arabia', captured in half a dozen lines by Augustus John; a stone effigy of the same troubled hero, dressed in Arab tribal robes; (Sir) William Orpen's portrait of Augustus John – an insouciantly scruffy student, whose drawings John Singer Sargent thought the finest since the Renaissance; Graham Sutherland's oil sketch of Churchill, who ordered the destruction of the portrait based on it, commissioned by Parliament for his eightieth birthday; representations of the current Royal Family ranging from the obsequious to the eccentric; and finally the merciless cartoon caricatures by Gerald Scarfe – but in the National Portrait Gallery there is no finally... Fortunately, while the visitor gathers strength for another bout on behalf of posterity there is a stylish basement café and bookshop, another shop selling postcards and a rooftop restaurant famed for its view over **Trafalgar Square** toward's **Nelson's Column** and the Houses of Parliament.

(David Cannadine *The National Portrait Gallery: A Brief*

History NPGC 2007; John Cooper *The National Portrait Gallery: A Visitor's Guide* NPGC; www.npg.org.uk)

Neal Street

Developed by Thomas Neale, this thoroughfare had become a slum by the nineteenth century when it was dominated by a brewery. The opening of The Punjab at No. 80 – now the UK's oldest Punjabi restaurant – in 1951 proved to be an early indicator of Neal Street's subsequent reinvention but it retained an artisan aspect into the 1960s when it still accommodated a coppersmith, makers of porter's barrows and **musical instruments** and a precision engineering works.

In 1971 a 'progressive rock bar', Chaguaramas, opened at Nos. 41-43. By 1974 it had become a gay disco. In 1976 it was taken over by Andy Czezowski and Barry Jones who made it the London centre for the embryonic 'punk' movement, changing the name to the Roxy. Performers include Generation X, the Heartbreakers and, on New Year's Eve 1977, the Clash. The Roxy lasted only until April 1978, forced out of business by two robberies, a huge rent rise and the rapid gentrification of the area following the exodus of the fruit and veg market premises. This led to the building's conversion to retail use.

In 1971 designer Terence Conran opened the Neal Street Restaurant, which was taken over in 1989 by TV chef Antonio Carluccio but forced to close by developers in 2008. Sam Mendes' film and theatre production company, Neal Street Productions, has been at No. 28 since 2003. Neal Street is now lined with retailers of footwear and fashion clothing and specialist outlets for products as varied as filofaxes, Japanese tabi (split-toed socks) and astrological supplies.

Neal's Yard

Described by a *New York Times* correspondent as "a tiny world unto itself", this square of former flower market warehouses, between Monmouth Street and Shorts Gardens, began its reinvention in 1978 with the opening of a bakery. This was followed by a dairy (1979), a shop selling 'natural remedies' (1981) and a vegetarian salad bar (1982). Given the existence of such outlets it was appropriate that the attractions of Neal's Yard should have been spread by 'word of mouth' to become a 'brand' variously incarnated in outstations as distant as Valencia and Dubai and Central St Martin's School of Art where there is a Neal's Yard doctoral studentship for research in textiles. Seekers of 'frankincense nourishing cream' can also choose among 200+ British and Irish farmhouse cheeses, savour a 'sensual jasmine collection', reinvigorate themselves with a 'Walk in Backrub' or book a 'yoga retreat'. They should, however, beware that what the *Washington Post* has flagged as a focal point of "clean-cut, English style New Age hoo-ha" is also a "Mecca for skateboarders" and that a locally-promoted organic preventative against malaria was forced off the shelves by the wrath of the medical authorities.

Thomas Neale

Commemorated in the name of Neal Street and Neal's Yard, Thomas Neale (died 1699) was a chancer at the court of **Charles II**. Nominally Master of the Mint, he also served as Groom-Porter to three monarchs, his chief duty being to supply cards and dice for gaming and to adjudicate disputes at the tables or on the bowling-green. Neale did also oversee the administration of three national lotteries. Neale began laying out **Seven Dials** around 1694 and took an option on a substantial plot in Mayfair where Clarges Street was later built but lacked the resources to develop it, dying insolvent.

Nelson's Column, Trafalgar Square

"He brought heroism into the line of duty"

JosephConrad

Horatio (he preferred to be called Horace), Admiral Viscount Nelson (1758-1805) entered the Royal Navy at twelve and by twenty had been to the Caribbean, the East Indies and the Arctic and was already a captain. A petite five feet four inches, with girlish good looks, variously afflicted by malaria, dysentery and lifelong seasickness, he lost the sight of his right eye and half his right arm in battle. Nelson's smashing victories at Cape St Vincent (1797), the Nile (1798), Copenhagen (1801) and Trafalgar (1805) made him the nation's darling. Never content with mere victory, he aimed at annihilation. Characteristically his last command was "Engage the enemy more closely". As vain as he was brave, at Trafalgar he insisted on wearing the stars of four orders of chivalry, marking him as an irresistible target. Fatally shot by a French sniper, in the hour of triumph, Nelson was buried in St Paul's Cathedral under the very centre of the dome.

A Nelson Memorial Committee was finally

Neal's Yard in 2009.

established in 1838 and a hundred and forty plans submitted for its consideration. First prize was awarded to William Railton (1804-74), second to E H Baily (1788-1867) and third to **Charles Fowler**. Oddly, Railton was commissioned to build the monument in **Trafalgar Square** while the statue was awarded to Baily, who had trained under **Flaxman**. The column was finished in 1842 and the statue hoisted into position in 1843. The bronze bas-reliefs (1849) depicting the battles of Cape St Vincent, the Nile and Copenhagen and Nelson's death, were cast from captured cannon. The lions, designed by animal painter Sir Edwin Landseer (1802-73), were only completed in 1867. The National Portrait Gallery has a dashing portrait of Nelson by Sir William Beechey.

(Roger Knight *The Pursuit of Victory: The Life and Achievement of Horatio Nelson* Penguin 2006; Colin White *Nelson the Admiral* The History Press 2005;
Colin White *The Nelson Encyclopaedia: People, Places, Battles, Ships, Myths, Mistresses, Memorials and Memorabilia* Chatham Publishing 2005; www.nelson.co.uk; www.nmm.ac.uk/collections/nelson)

New Ambassador's Theatre, West Street

The Ambassador's (until 1999) was built in 1913 to the designs of W G R Sprague. **Ivor Novello** made his debut there in 1921 and Vivien Leigh her West

Horatio Nelson, from a painting by J. Hoppner. Note the absence of an eye-patch.

A view of the Column by S Dennant Moss.

The completion of Nelson's Column in 1843.

End debut in 1935. C B Cochran's revues were the staple fare. During World War Two the Ballet Rambert gave daytime performances. From 1952 to 1974 ***The Mousetrap*** played before transferring along the street to the **St Martin's**. From 1996 to 1999 this was the temporary home of the Royal Court Theatre. (www.new-ambassadors.co.uk)

New Row

Now a pleasant street accommodating small shops and residential premises, this short thoroughfare was built up between 1635 and 1644. It was originally home to aristocratic residents like the Countess of Chesterfield. Sculptor **John Flaxman** was born and grew up here. The gas lights add a note of character. Also here is a branch of the bookshop Waterstone's, whose staff inspired the publication of this book.

George Newnes

The son of a Congregational minister, Sir George Newnes (1851-1910) pioneered a form of popular publication which earned him a baronetcy. Starting with ***Tit-Bits***, he went on to establish ***The Strand Magazine*** and ***Country Life***.

Newport Market

Newport Place now centres on a pagoda representing **Chinatown** but for two centuries was the site of a market of mixed fortunes. Before that it was the site of Newport House. Built ca. 1627, its gardens stretched over a patch of land formerly known as Scavenger's Close. After the death in 1666 of its owner, Mountjoy Blount, Earl of Newport (in the Isle of Wight), the property became the subject of a protracted legal dispute until 1682 when it was bought by the notorious property speculator **Nicholas Barbon** for £9,500. With characteristic insouciance Barbon used the property as security for loans of £30,000 and then rapidly demolished it, letting its site on building leases which brought him another £1,000 a year. The remains of the mansion were recycled to bodge up a Market House, the putative profits of which were auctioned off.

Instituted in 1686, Newport Market was held on Tuesdays, Thursdays and Saturdays. Defoe described it in 1725 as one of the capital's main meat markets. Rooms over the Market House were occupied by a congregation of **Huguenots** (who referred to it as the Eglise de la Boucherie) and then by Baptists. The streets leading into the market area were predominantly occupied by goldsmiths, jewellers and clockmakers. Only the upper storeys of 21-24a Newport Court bear much resemblance to their original eighteenth-century state.

Although the Market House was rebuilt in the 1830s, the surrounding area became one of the capital's most reviled slums. A well-meaning committee of do-gooders established a 'Newport Market Refuge' to provide 'nightly shelter and sustenance to the really destitute and houseless', and also ran an 'industrial school' for lads who would otherwise be starving – and thieving – on the streets. An attempt to recapitalise and revive the market in 1872 came to nothing. A decade later the area accounted for two-thirds of arrests recorded in the entire parish of St Anne's and a police report to the Home Secretary noted that "it would be an act of true philanthropy to break up this reeking home of filthy vice … and remove this festering sore from the centre of London life." Building **Charing Cross Road** and **Shaftesbury Avenue** did just that.

Sir Isaac Newton

"Nature and Nature's Laws lay hid in night
God Said 'Let Newton be' and all was light"
Alexander Pope

Sir Isaac Newton (1642-1727) lived at 35 St Martin's Street (now demolished), off the south side of **Leicester Square**, from 1710 until his death. Most of his scientific career was by then behind him but he was working on a third edition of his *magnum opus*, a mathematical description of the universe, the *Philosophiae Naturalis Principia Mathematica*. He remained active in the affairs of the Royal Society, of which he had been elected President in 1703. Much of his time was, however, taken up with his duties as Master of the Mint and in conducting a vindictive feud against the German mathematician Leibniz over which of them had invented calculus. When Newton was buried in Westminster Abbey. **Voltaire** attended the funeral and subsequently promoted a popular understanding of Newton's thought throughout Europe.

Gale E. Christianson *Isaac Newton and the Scientific Revolution* Oxford University Press 1996; www.newtonproject.sussex.ac.uk)

Sir Isaac Newton, an oil attributed to ***Sir James Thornhill.***

Elizabeth Nihell

Trained in Paris, midwife Elizabeth Nihell (1723-post 1772) established herself in **Panton Square**, where her husband, Edward, practised as a surgeon. She opposed male intrusion into birthing, arguing in *A Treatise on the Art of Midwifery* (1760) that men lacked patience and sensitivity and were too ready to resort to metal instruments, thereby causing avoidable infant deaths. Nihell's book was translated into French and Smollett, who ridiculed it, at least paid her the backhanded compliment of saying that it must have been written by her husband.

Nonesuch Press

Established in the basement of a bookshop at 17 **Gerrard Street** in 1923, this publishing firm aimed to produce books of high quality and excellent content at a moderate price. This was achieved by making a prototype on a small hand press and using it as template for reproduction by commercial printers. The founders were Francis Meynell, the son of **Francis Thompson's** rescuer, **David Garnett** and Vera Mendel.

More than 140 titles were produced before its demise in the 1960s. These included editions of **Dickens** and the collected works of Congreve and Wycherley.

Frank Norman

An illegitimate child, abandoned by his mother, Frank Norman (1930-80) was brought up in a succession of care homes, drifted into petty crime and served two years in prison before embarking on a literary career with a memoir of prison life *Bang to Rights* (1958), followed by the smash hit musical *Fings Ain't Wot They Used T'be*. Norman's other works included *Stand on Me* (1960), an autobiographical account of Soho in the **Fifties**, *Soho Night and Day* (1966), written in collaboration with **Jeffrey Bernard**, a further memoir of Soho, *Down and Out in High Society* (1975) and three novels featuring Ed Nelson, an under-employed Soho private detective.

James Northcote

Artist James Northcote (1746-1831) lived with his sister at 39 **Argyll Street** (1789-1822) and at 8 Argyll Place from then until his death. The son of a Plymouth watchmaker, he was taken on as an apprentice for five years by fellow-Devonian **Sir Joshua Reynolds**. After travelling to Italy where he lived in Reynolds' old rooms and met Fuseli, Batoni and David, Northcote established himself as a history painter at the age of forty, was elected

The relief above the entrance to the Notre Dame de France church in Leicester Place.

RA in 1787 and painted numerous scenes for Boydell's Shakespeare Gallery. Portraits and animal subjects provided an income and from 1807 he embarked on a parallel literary career. A bodged memoir of Reynolds proved less successful than a series of 'conversations' orchestrated and published by **Hazlitt**, who also helped him with a life of Titian. Gnomic in stature, skeletal in aspect, vituperative in speech and never losing his deep Devon burr, Northcote struck one of his late subjects, Sir Walter Scott, as like "an animated mummy". Northcote lived in miserly squalor but left £25,000 at his death.

Notre Dame de France

This unexpected gem, on dismal Leicester Place, gives little external clue to the treasures within. It was Cardinal Wiseman who first saw the need for a centrally situated church for French Roman Catholics in London and deputed the Marist Fathers to realise such a project. Funds were raised principally in France and a lease acquired in 1865 on the site of **Burford's Panorama** and an area adjoining it. The former entrance to the Panorama was initially used as a chapel.

An orphanage (transferred to Norwood in 1870) and a school (transferred to **Lisle Street** in 1890) were added in 1866. The conversion of the Panorama building into a church was entrusted to the French architect Louis-Auguste Boileau (1812-96). He made daring use of iron columns, arches and ribs to create a cruciform worship area within a circular shell. The first mass was celebrated by Archbishop (later Cardinal) Manning in June 1868.

Notre Dame de France was severely damaged by bombing in 1940 and redesigned by Professor Hector O Corfiato of the Ecole des Beaux Arts in Paris. A new foundation stone, brought from Chartres Cathedral, was laid in 1953 by the distinguished Europeanist M. Maurice Schumann. The restored church was reopened in 1955.

The statue of the Virgin over the main entrance was carved by Georges Saupique, also of the Ecole des Beaux Arts. The tapestry above the altar was woven at Aubusson to the design of Dom Robert de Chaumac (1907-97) of Buckfast Abbey, Devon, a former student of the Ecole des Beaux Arts. The mosaics of the side altar are by Boris Anrep (1883-1959). The font is of sandstone from the Vosges region. The wall paintings (1960) in the side chapel are by the poet, novelist and film-maker Jean Cocteau (1889-1963). The statue of Our Lady of Victories in the gallery was made by Henri Vallette in Nazi-occupied Paris between 1942 and 1944 and incorporates the head from the original (1865) bomb-damaged version in this church which was dropped into France by parachute to be passed on to the sculptor by the Resistance. The restored statue is considered to be the first export to Britain from liberated France.

Nowadays Notre Dame has a special association with francophone speakers from Mauritius and Africa and a special commitment to the needs of refugees and the homeless.

(www.notredamechurch.co.uk)

Ivor Novello

Born into a musical Welsh household, David Ivor Davies (1893-1951) became a stage-struck habitué of **Daly's Theatre** and, by the outbreak of World War One, was living in the roof-top flat over the **Strand Theatre** at No. 11 Aldwych, which was to be his home for the rest of his life. In 1914 his patriotic anthem *Keep the Home Fires Burning* brought him instant fame and a fortune. By the 1920s, under the name of Ivor Novello, he had become a star of both stage and screen. His first straight play, *The Rat*, in which he himself starred, proved a hit at the **Prince of Wales' Theatre** in 1924. Between 1936 and 1939 the **Theatre Royal Drury Lane** was revived by a succession of his musical plays – *Glamorous Night, Careless Rapture, Crest of the Wave* and *The Dancing Years,*

Matinee idol – Ivor Novello.

which was revived at the **Adelphi** in 1942 to become the greatest stage success of World War Two. Critic Ivor Brown congratulated him on being able to "wade through tosh with the straightest face ... both as actor and author he can pursue adventures far too preposterous for the films." A bust of Novello, by his friend and sometime collaborator, **Clemence Dane**, is in the foyer at Drury Lane. The Ivor Novello Awards were instituted in 1955 to recognise achievement in songwriting and composing.

(Paul Webb *Ivor Novello* Haus Publishing 2005; www.theivors.org)

Novello's

In 1811 Vincent Novello, organist at the Portuguese Embassy chapel, published a *Collection of Sacred Music*. In 1813 he became a founder member of the Philharmonic Society which had its headquarters at **Hickford's Rooms**. In 1829 Vincent's son, Alfred Novello, set up a music publishing business at No. 67 **Frith Street**. Mendelssohn and **Charles Lamb** became frequent guests at the Novello family's convivial musical evenings and by 1834 the business had moved to No. 69 **Dean Street**. In 1845 there was a branch in the City and by 1852 another on Broadway in New York. Novello's prospered by using new printing technology to cut the price of sheet music and by encouraging the formation and activities of choral societies through a monthly publication, the *Musical Times*. In 1860 the company issued *Hymns Ancient and Modern,* a mainstay of Protestant worship for the next century. In the 1890s the company moved its printing and book-binding activities to a purpose-built block on the east side of **Wardour Street**. In 1905-6 an imposing new head office, modelled on the Town Hall of Bremen, was built at 152-60 Wardour Street to the designs of Frank Loughborough Pearson. The main staircase was adorned with **Roubiliac**'s statue of Handel, now on display in the Victoria and Albert Museum. Novello's left here in 1965 but kept an office at No. 27 **Soho Square**.

(www.chesternovello.com)

Odeon, Leicester Square

Built on the site of the **Alhambra** music hall, on the east side of the Square, the Odeon was designed by Mather and Weedon. Its austere façade is of black granite; the flanking tower is 120 feet high. The cinema opened in 1937 with the *Prisoner of Zenda*, starring Ronald Colman. *Gone With The Wind* ran from 1939 to 1943 to become the longest-running film of World War Two. A misguided 'modernisation' in 1967 robbed the interior of much of its Art Deco grandeur but this has been (1989-90) partially restored. The Odeon is the UK's largest cinema and was the first to install a wide screen (1953) and a digital projector (1999). Standing in a Leicester Square phone booth the young actor Maurice Micklewhite was told by his agent that he had landed a plum film part but would need a new stage name. Glancing up to see that the Odeon was screening *The Caine Mutiny* he chose to become Michael Caine.

(www.odeonleicestersquare.co.uk)

Odham's

The printing firm of Odham's began in small premises in **Floral Street** and remained a humdrum business until it was joined by Julius Elias (1873-1946), initially as an office boy. His managerial flair made it the largest printing firm in England and made him Viscount Southwood. In 1890 Odham's

Above, the Odeon Leicester Square, temporarily clothed in red in 2009 over its usual black granite. Below a mural in the former foyer of Odhams, Long Acre, by Frank Brangwyn, bore the optimistic claim that 'The printed word makes the peoples of the world one'.

took over the former **Queen's Theatre** on **Long Acre**, converting it into a printing works which eventually occupied the whole of the north side from **Arne Street** to **Neal Street**. The premises were rebuilt in 1938.

Odham's printed *Sporting Life*, *Woman*, the *Daily Herald*, *Debrett*'s, most of the Labour Party's publicity material and, from 1916 to 1934, Britain's most popular magazine, *John Bull*. Odham's eventually sited their main printing works at Watford but the Long Acre plant continued until closed by Robert Maxwell in 1969. Odham's and George **Newnes** became parts of the International Publishing Corporation.

Old Compton Street

"*... the epitome of hard-core hedonism*"

Ed Glinert *West End Chronicles*

The street was named for Henry Compton (1631-1732) the bishop of London who became a popular Protestant hero in helping to oust Catholic **James II** from the throne in 1688. When being built up (1677-83) by **Richard Frith** and William Pym, Compton was also fund-raising for the projected Soho parish church, which he dedicated as **St Anne's** in 1686. The street's earliest residents included a royal physician and four ladies of title. A generation later about a third were French or of

French descent, including Nicholas Sprimont (1715-71), goldsmith and manager of the Chelsea porcelain factory. Sprimont's silver tableware is in royal collections at Windsor Castle and Buckingham Palace and on display at the Victoria & Albert Museum. Sprimont's friend and near neighbour, engraver Matthew Liart (?1736-?1782) was a life-long resident. Nos. 13-17 may date from the late 17th century. No. 27 and Nos. 27-33 are of the 1720s, while No. 63 and No. 68 date from the 1730s, although refaced. A Swiss hotel once occupied Nos.51-53. By the 1790s the street was primarily commercial; of its seventy-eight houses only seven or eight did not have shop-fronts. In the 1860s Charles Henry Harrod, later founder of the Knightsbridge emporium, (1799-1885) was running a grocery at No. 40. At least nineteen artists or engravers have lived on Old Compton Street, as well as the dealer Panton Betew, who sold Gainsborough's work. Other residents have included the novelist John Cleland, author of *Fanny Hill*, the scientist **Friedrich Accum**, the showman George Wombwell and Edward Inwood, co-architect of St Pancras New Church. Wagner lodged here for a week and the French poets Rimbaud and Verlaine were regular patrons of one of its pubs. In 1894 the publication of the first number of *The Yellow Book* was marked by a celebratory dinner in Old Compton Street. By the 1950s the street was noted for its **coffee-bars**.

Old Slaughter's, St Martin's Lane

Established in 1692 by Thomas Slaughter (died ca. 1740), this coffee house at 74-75 **St Martin's Lane** became a notable haunt of the artists of the **St Martin's Lane Academy**, of **Huguenot** craftsmen and of addicts of chess, draughts, whist and other games of chance. The pioneer art historian and engraver George Vertue (1684-1756) called it "a rendezvous of persons of all languages & Nations, Gentry, artists and others". Regular patrons included **Hogarth**, **Fielding**, **Roubiliac**, **Gardelle**, Goldsmith and **Johnson**. Generations later, as a chop-house, it was much used by **Haydon**. In 1824 what was to become the Royal Society for the Prevention of Cruelty to Animals held its inaugural meeting at Old Slaughter's. It was demolished in 1842-3 to make way for **Cranbourn Street**. Young Slaughter's, a nearby, rival establishment which attracted a coterie of scientists, presided over by **John Hunter**, also disappeared in 1842-3.

Arthur Onslow

Elected Speaker of the House of Commons no fewer than five successive times, Onslow (1691-1768) served in that office for thirty-three years, a period which exactly coincided with his residence in Soho Square, from 1753 at **Fauconberg House**. Onslow's famous squint made "catching the Speaker's eye" problematic but was offset by his iron integrity and encyclopaedic knowledge of the constitution. On his retirement the Commons begged that he be given a special mark of royal favour for the scrupulous conduct of his office. This turned out to be an annual pension of £3,000 for life, to be continued for the benefit of his son and heir George, also for life. The **National Portrait Gallery** has a portrait of him by **Kneller**. Onslow also featured prominently in a group portrait of the House of Commons collaboratively painted by **Hogarth** and **Thornhill**.

Orange Street

Developed by **Thomas Panton** ca. 1673, what Pevsner characterises as "... a wavering composite of three older streets", passes over the site of a former royal (i.e, *real*, not lawn) tennis court – hence the Hand and Racquet pub (1865). **Charles II** once played a two-hour match, had himself weighed before and afterwards, and found that he had lost over four pounds. The bijou Orange Street chapel was established ca. 1693 for **Huguenot** worship; the present building dates from 1927-9. One of its ministers, Augustus Toplady (1740-78), a fierce Calvinist, wrote *Rock of Ages*. Another, Andrew Mearns, wrote a pamphlet, *The Bitter Cry of Outcast*

Orange Street Chapel.

London (1883), which so moved public opinion by its exposé of contemporary destitution that it led to the appointment of a Royal Commission on the Housing of the Working Classes. The former public baths of 1847-9, one of the earliest to be established under the terms of the Public Baths and Washhouses Act of 1846, was displaced by Ciro's exclusive dining club of 1914-15, then became an extension of the dental hospital and now houses the archives of the **National Portrait Gallery**.

Our Friends in the North

Gripping, strongly-cast, award-winning nine-episode TV drama series by Peter Flannery tracing the interlocking lives of four friends from Tyneside between 1964 and 1995. Corruption and criminality in the world of Soho vice contribute to the degradation of 'Geordie Peacock', a youthful Daniel Craig.

Our Lady of the Assumption

Established in Warwick Street ca. 1730 as a chapel for the Portuguese embassy, it came under Bavarian control in 1747, was sacked during the **Gordon riots** of 1780, rebuilt 1789-90 to the designs of Joseph Bonomi and, as a surviving example of an eighteenth-century Roman Catholic chapel, is unique in London. (www.rcdow.org.uk)

Palace Theatre, Cambridge Circus

The imposing Palace Theatre was built by impresario Richard D'Oyly Carte (1844-1901) at the immense cost of £150,000. The interior featured Italian marble and Mexican onyx. There was an independent generator to power the building's 2,000 lamps. There was even a 'royal retiring room'. The elaborate elevation was the work of T E Collcutt (1840-1924). Originally styled the 'Royal English Opera House', it opened in 1891 with the premiere of Sir Arthur Sullivan's *Ivanhoe*. This was replaced by a French opera and then a short season of plays featuring French stage legend Sarah Bernhardt. These pretensions to high culture proved commercially disastrous and by December 1892 the new venture had been sold on to **Sir Augustus Harris** and metamorphosed into the 'Palace Theatre of Varieties'. In 1898 a nineteen-year-old former clerk from Harrod's, Alfred Butt (1878-1962), was appointed company secretary of Palace Theatre Ltd. When managing director (1906-20) he

The Palace Theatre, Cambridge Circus, at the beginning of the 20th century.

An inscription over the Stage Door of the Palace Theatre reads: 'THE WORLD'S GREATEST ARTISTS HAVE PASSED AND WILL PASS THROUGH THESE DOORS'.

turned the Palace into one of London's most prestigious and profitable variety theatres by following a formula of lavish production values and imported foreign talent, from a steady stream of American vaudeville stars to Russian ballerina Anna Pavlova, who made her London debut at the Palace in 1910. In 1912 the theatre hosted the first ever Royal Command variety performance, with a bill including comedians Wilkie Bard (1874-1944) and Harry Champion (1865-1942) and juggler Paul Cinquevalli (1859-1918) who performed his celebrated 'human billiard table' stunt which involved catching four balls and a wineglass in the pockets of a specially-tailored jacket. The Palace has enjoyed its greatest successes as a home to long-running musicals such as *No, No Nanette* (655 performances 1925-6), *Song of Norway* (526 performances 1946), *Finian's Rainbow* (1947), *King's Rhapsody* (839 performances 1949-50), *The Sound of Music* (2,385 performances 1961-7), *Jesus Christ, Superstar* (3,358 performances 1972-80) *Les Miserables* (1985-2004) and, at the time of writing, *Spamalot*.

The Palace was bought by Andrew Lloyd-Webber in 1983 and underwent a major restoration in 2004. (www.palace-theatre.co.uk)

The Pantheon, Oxford Street

On the site of the Marks & Spencer store at 173 Oxford Street, once stood the celebrated Pantheon. Designed by James Wyatt (1746-1813) it was opened in January 1772. The building was inspired by the majestic rotunda of the Church of the Holy Wisdom – Hagia Sophia – in Istanbul and was intended to serve as a winter rival to Ranelagh pleasure gardens in Chelsea. The main concourse was therefore complemented by rooms for tea, supper and cards. Even the hypercritical aesthete Horace Walpole was impressed by "the most beautiful edifice in England". To the musicologist **Charles Burney**, it was "the most elegant structure in Europe, if not on the globe". The well-organised entertainments on offer included concerts, masquerades and assemblies but could not sustain their initial popularity. In February 1791 the Pantheon became a theatre and in 1792 it was gutted by fire. Rebuilt and reopened in 1795, it failed to prosper, failed again as the home of the 'National Institution for Improving Manufactures' and again as an unlicensed Opera House. In 1814 the building was stripped out and abandoned. In the 1830s it became a bazaar and in 1867 a warehouse for Gilbey's, the wine merchants. It 1937 it was sold to Marks & Spencer who demolished it to build a store on its site.

Thomas Panton

Colonel Panton (died 1685) has achieved the historical distinction of being both colourful and shadowy – i.e. little is known for certain about him but that little suggests a character in keeping with the roistering nature of **Charles II's** court. Panton came of a Leicestershire gentry family and may have shared the king's exile. When Britain's first regular army was formed out of the formerly opposing units of the civil war period Panton secured a commission in the Life Guards *and* a captaincy in the Foot Guards, drawing pay from both regiments until 1667. He then became a Roman Catholic. This was not permitted for army officers and as a result he publicly resigned his commission before the king at a review in St James's Park. Like the king Panton appears to have been a compulsive womaniser, of such notoriety that he figured in street-ballads. His real talent, however, lay in gambling. One night he won so much at 'hazard' that he was able to invest it to yield £1,500 a year – at a time when the annual rent on a house in London's most fashionable district was £50. Panton never gambled again, got married, bought estates in two counties and a gaming establishment known as Piccadilly Hall. He also dabbled in property development, building up Panton Street and **Panton Square**, as well as the western part of **Orange Street**, probably. When he died Panton was sufficiently prominent to merit burial in Westminster Abbey, Catholicism notwithstanding.

In Panton Street Nos. 5 and 6, houses of ca. 1673 still survive, though heightened and with

A masquerade at the Pantheon; by Rowlandson and Pugin.The building was gutted by fire in 1792.

nineteenth-century embellishments. The name of Stone's Chop House recalls the hotel established on the site by Mr Stone ca. 1778.

Panton Square

In 1762 a Moroccan envoy living on the square beheaded one of his servants and had his house sacked by a mob in retaliation. Other residents have included American painter **Benjamin West** and French poet Stephane Mallarmé (1842-98), who lodged in one of the square's hotels in 1863.

Panton Square was demolished in 1919 to make way for the extension of Lyon's Corner House in Coventry Street

Cyril Arthur Pearson

Sir Cyril Pearson (1866-1921) owed his start in business to winning a competition in ***Tit-bits***, of which he became the manager at nineteen. At twenty-four he brought out his own rival, **Pearson's Weekly**, which followed the same formula of trivia, undemanding fiction and competitions which boosted circulation to the point where he could afford to launch the *Daily Express* and to acquire the *Standard*, the *Evening Standard* and various provincial titles. Pearson's simple patriotism and philanthropic impulses found an early outlet in his support for Baden-Powell's embryonic Boy Scout movement. Stricken by glaucoma in 1908, Pearson disposed of his newspaper interests by 1912. In the lofty opinion of his obituarist in the *Dictionary of National Biography* this was probably all to the good – "His opinions were the caprice of uncriticized intuitions ... Happily for his readers, whom he sought to stampede, rather than inform, his tastes were harmless and his nature wholesome."

Appalled at the prospect of becoming a blind man, Pearson, with characteristic energy, determined to become *the* blind man. Taking over the National Institute for the Blind, he raised its income forty-fold. The thousands of blinded young men created by the Great War presented an unprecedented challenge which led Pearson to establish specialised hostels for their rehabilitation which evolved into the St Dunstan's organisation.

Created a baronet in 1916 in recognition of his services, Pearson died tragically five years later as a result of a fall in his bath. The holiday fund for disadvantaged children has been renamed in his honour. (www.pearsonsholidayfund.org)

Samuel Pepys

Although the diarist and naval administrator Samuel Pepys (1633-1703) lived in the City, he was thoroughly familiar with the Covent Garden area. In 1662 he records having seen a Punch and Judy puppet show for the first time, in the portico of **St Paul's church**. A keen theatre-goer, he admired **Joseph Haines'** dancing and in 1664 saw an all-female cast perform *The Parson's Wedding* at the **Theatre Royal** and thought the boxes were too far from the stage. Pepys had his family portraits painted by **John Hayls** and visited the studio of **Sir Peter Lely**. When he could afford to buy a coach he came to **Long Acre** and watched in person while he had it repainted yellow. In 1665 Pepys noted with dismay that houses in **Drury Lane** were marked with red crosses to signify that they were stricken with plague. Two years later he recorded that in the same street he saw **Nell Gwyn** at the door of her lodgings *en deshabille* – "she seemed a mighty pretty creature".

(Claire Tomalin *Pepys: The Unequalled Self* Penguin 2003)

A man with a secret diary – Samuel Pepys.

The Phoenix Theatre, Charing Cross Road

Built (1930) on the site of the Alcazar, an undistinguished music hall, the Phoenix was designed by (Sir) Giles Gilbert Scott, an architect best remembered for such London icons as Battersea and Bankside power stations, Waterloo Bridge and the red telephone box. The interior was the work of the Russian producer/set designer Theodore Komisarjevsky (1882-1954). With C B Cochran as manager the first production was **Noel Coward's** *Private Lives*, starring Coward himself, his lifelong co-star Gertrude Lawrence and a youthful Laurence Olivier (1907-89). Coward retained a close association with the Phoenix and in 1969 presided over the opening of the theatre bar named in his honour. A musical version of four of Chaucer's *Canterbury Tales* ran from 1968 to 1973. (www.phoenix-theatre.co.uk)

The Photographer's Gallery

Founded in Great Newport Street in 1971 by Sue Davies the Photographer's Gallery was the first independent gallery in Britain devoted to photography and is still the largest such in London, attracting half a million visitors a year to its new premises at 16-18 Ramillies Street, just off **Great Marlborough Street**. (www.photonet.org.uk)

The Piazza

Covent Garden's central feature, the Piazza, was laid out as an open space between 1633 and 1637 by **Inigo Jones** but is now largely covered by the former market buildings. It was London's first square, modelled either on the Place des Vosges in Paris or the piazza of Livorno (Leghorn), both of which Jones had seen. Originally the south side was defined by the rear wall of **Bedford House**. Following that house's demolition in 1706, fourteen houses were built on the south side of the Piazza as Tavistock Row. The west was dominated by **St Paul's church**, with flanking houses. The north and east side consisted of seventeen superior residences fronted by an arcade. Each house consisted of a basement, ground floor, mezzanine, two brick upper storeys and a dormer. Some on the south-east collapsed in 1670, were rebuilt and rebuilt again in 1769 without the arcade. The north-east corner went in 1858-68 to make way for the Floral Hall (see **Royal Opera House**) and the Tavistock Hotel. The last old houses went ca. 1933. Present day Bedford Chambers, at the north-west corner of the square, were designed by Henry

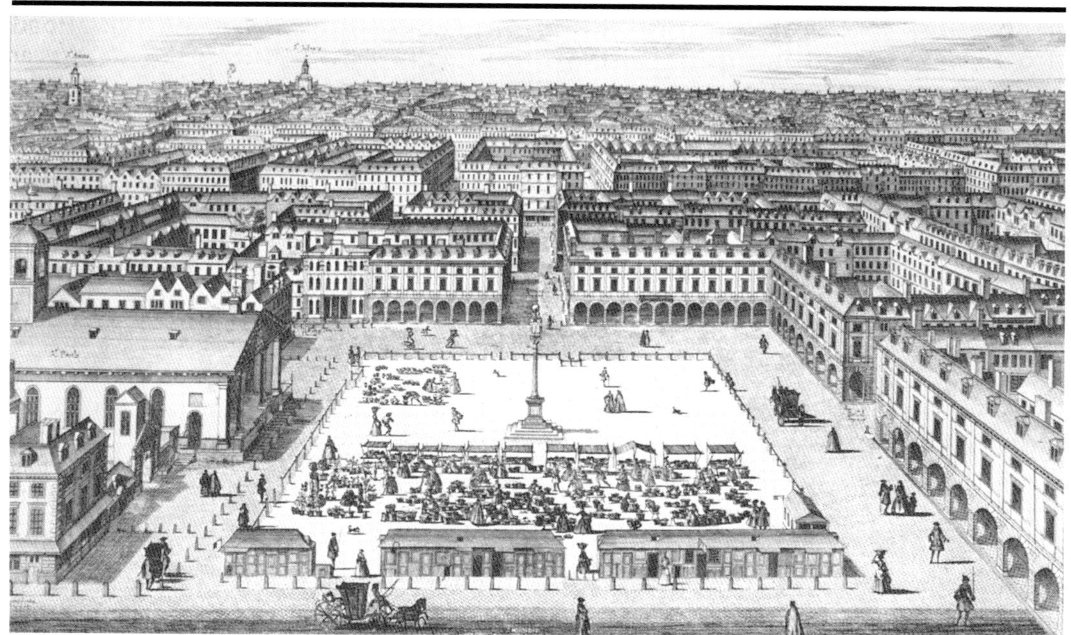

The Piazza, Covent Garden c. 1720, looking north. The early formation of the market is on the south side, but the presence of carriages and a sedan chair denote its prestigious residential status.

Clutton in 1879 as a pastiche of the original seventeenth-century houses.

Intended for 'Persons of the Greatest Distinction', the Piazza initially attracted at least three earls and the king's own personal standard-bearer, Sir Edmund Verney (1590-1642), who fell at Edgehill, the first great battle of the Civil Wars. When the standard was recovered from the field Verney's severed hand still grasped it; his body was never found.

After the social disruption of the Civil Wars, the Piazza re-established itself as a desirable residential location, although the fashionable portraitist **Sir Peter Lely** had remained there from 1651 right through until 1680. Occupants in the 1660s included **Thomas Killigrew** and Pepys's boss, William Brouncker. Later came the painters **Sir Godfrey Kneller** and **Sir James Thornhill,** theatre manager John Rich, surgeon **William Hunter** and actor **Charles Macklin**. During the eighteenth century the 'tone' was lowered by the development of the market and the emergence of **coffee-houses**, taverns and **bagnios** which led a writer in 1776 to characterise it as "the great square of Venus". The erection of hustings outside St. Paul's at election times brought an episodic rowdiness.

Piccadilly Circus

"A distorted isochromal triangle ... an impossible site on which to place any outcome of the human brain except possibly an underground lavatory". Sir Alfred Gilbert

Contrary to the apparent instinct of tourists, Piccadilly Circus is not the centre of London. Nor is this "ill-shaped vortex" (Pevsner) properly a circus. It was created in 1819 as a crossroads where Piccadilly met the new **Regent Street** laid out by **Nash** and acquired its present dimensions when **Shaftesbury Avenue** was made (1884-5). Dominated by the statue of **Eros**, it is famous for its electric signs, among the first of their kind in London, the earliest of which advertised Bovril (a hot drink based on beef extract) and **Schweppe**'s tonic water. The large Underground station (1925-8) was the first to be built entirely underground, accessible only by subways from street level.

Pillars of Hercules pub, Greek Street

There has been a pub on this site since at least 1733 but the present **mock-Tudor** building dates from 1935. Dickens mentions its predecessor in *A Tale of Two Cities.*

Poet **Francis Thompson**, drunken and destitute, was rescued from here in 1888, collapsed in the

Eager customers queue for paella in the Market buildings.

A complete standstill – one of the many street entertainers in the Piazza area.

doorway. The Pillars of Hercules is a traditional name for the Straits of Gibraltar.

Players' Theatre

The first home of the Players' Theatre, in 1927, was at No. 6 New Compton Street, where Peggy Ashcroft made her debut in *One Day More*, based on a story by **Conrad**. In 1934 it moved to the top floor of 43 **King Street,** where from 1937 it began to present Victorian-style music hall. By 1946 the company had relocated to Villiers Street, in part of the premises once occupied by Gatti's-under-the-Arches restaurant beneath Charing Cross station. In 1953 the theatre enjoyed a major hit with the first production of Sandy Wilson's *The Boy Friend.*

(www.players-theatre.co.uk)

Poland Street

Originally a long, narrow field called Little Gelding's Close, Poland Street was built up from 1689 and especially between 1705 and 1707, when the surviving Nos. 11, 15, 24, 48 and 54 were put up. No. 7 was built in 1707 for the Countess of Sandwich. The street took its name from the King of Poland (later Wheatsheaf) public house, which was bombed out in 1940. This in turn took its name from John Sobieski whose brilliant cavalry intervention saved Vienna from capture by the Ottomans in 1683. There has been a tavern at No. 23, the site of the King's Arms, since 1718. A plaque asserts that in 1781 the Ancient Order of Druids was revived here. The Star and Garter of ca. 1705-7 has been a public house since 1825.

Residents have included the architect Giacomo Leoni (1686-1746), from 1744 until his death and from 1767 to 1772 the topographical painter, water-colourist Paul Sandby (1726-1809). (Sir) **William Chambers** (1723-96) lived on Poland Street from 1758 to 1766, being appointed Architect to the King on **George III's** accession in 1760. During this period he completed the famous pagoda at Kew Gardens and published a *Treatise on Civil Architecture,* which became a standard work. The singer **Elizabeth Billington**, resident from 1788 to 1792, was known as "the Poland Street man trap". Musicologist **Dr Charles Burney** lived (1760-70) at No. 50, **Blake** (1785-91) at No. 28 and **Shelley** briefly at No. 15 in 1811.

Poland Street lost its residential demeanour in the nineteenth century when it was taken over by craftsmen, especially jewellers and engravers, and acquired a workhouse and a factory at Nos 1-5, built in 1902-3 for the manufacture of motorized delivery tricycles. London's first ramped multi-storey car park was opened on Poland Street in 1934.

At Nos 1-5 from 1914-88 were the renowned firm of bookbinders Sangorski & Sutcliffe, founded in Holborn in 1901. They were masters of decorative binding, especially in the incorporation of precious stones. Their binding of the *Ruba'iyat of Omar Khayyam* with over 1000 precious and non-precious stones was probably the most expensive example of bookbinding ever produced. Unfortunately it sank with the *Titanic* in 1912. From 1939 the firm, under new management, became leaders in modern bookbinding. They are now owned by Shepherd's and the bindery is in Rochester Row.

Dr John William Polidori

Polidori (1795-1821) was an incarnation of the doomed Romantic hero – prodigiously clever, strikingly good-looking and compulsively self-destructive. After graduating as a doctor at nineteen, he accompanied Byron to the continent as his personal physician. Byron's publisher, John Murray, offered him £500 to keep a journal. (It finally appeared in 1911, the original having been transcribed, censored and destroyed by Polidori's sister in 1869.) Thanks to this we know about the scary story competition at the Villa Doriati which led Mary Shelley to write *Frankenstein*. Polidori's effort, *The Vampyre*, appeared in 1819, after Byron had sacked him. Polidori's vampire, a suave, aristocractic seducer, clearly modelled on Byron, established the archetype for posterity. His publisher passed it off as Byron's work, selling five editions in a year – no help to Polidori, who had taken an outright fee. Having given up medicine and writing for the law, Polidori went on a gambling spree which brought him from debt to despair. He was found dead in his father's house at 38 **Great Pulteney Street**, where he had been born. Polidori probably died in agony by swallowing prussic acid but the coroner, to spare his family, recorded death from natural causes A brooding portrait painted ca. 1816, is in the **National Portrait Gallery**.

Marquis de Pombal

A blue plaque marks the site of the former Portuguese embassy at No. 24 **Golden Square**, where Sebastiao Jose de Carvalho e Melo (1699-1782), future Marquis of Pombal, served from 1738-1744. Son of an army officer and minor landowner, Pombal trained as a lawyer and historian before his first public appointment, as ambassador to Britain. Profoundly impressed by the country's progress and prosperity during his six years of residence, he was to take Britain as his model when he served as Portugal's first minister, and virtual dictator, from 1750 to1777. Today Pombal is best remembered as the man who rebuilt Lisbon after the catastrophic earthquake of 1755 which left 30,000 dead and 9,000 buildings in ruins. Undaunted by the destruction of two-thirds of Portugal's capital, he ordered his countrymen to bury the dead and feed the living and within twenty-four hours had begun to organise the task of reconstruction. While Lisbon was being transformed Pombal turned to the task of modernising the nation, breaking the Jesuits' stranglehold on education, fostering industry and colonial trade and curbing the power of the aristocracy.

(Kenneth Maxwell *Pombal: Paradox of the Enlightenment* Cambridge University Press 1995)

Portland House, Greek Street

What is now 12-13 Greek Street (see illustration on p. 7) was originally a single building, the largest dwelling in the street, known as Portland House. It has been variously a gentlemen's academy, the residence of a Sicilian ambassador, the showroom of **Josiah Wedgwood**, the premises of an upholsterer, a coachmaker and a timber merchant, and a German hotel, Wedde's. In 1837 the occupant was the prolific portraitist John Lucas (1807-74).

Prince Edward Theatre, Old Compton Street

Built in 1929-30, this theatre opened with a musical comedy, *Rio Rita* but then passed through varying incarnations as a cabaret restaurant, the London Casino, the Queensberry All-Services Club in wartime and a wide-screen cinema featuring Cinerama before finally finding success with *Evita*, which ran from 1978 to 1986. Another Lloyd Webber production, *Chess,* also enjoyed a long run but *Martin Guerre* failed in 1996-7, to be succeeded by a successful revival of *Showboat*. The Abba tribute show *Mamma Mia!* then settled in for another long run.

(www.prince-edward-theatre.co.uk)

Prince of Wales Theatre, Coventry Street

Opened in 1884 as the Prince's, the theatre changed its name to the Prince of Wales in 1886 and enjoyed its first real success in 1891 with a mime play *L'Enfant Prodigue*. In 1892 George Edwardes presented the first English musical comedy, *In*

Town, followed by the equally successful *A Gaiety Girl*. In 1900 Marie Tempest starred in the name role in *English Nell,* based on a novel about **Nell Gwyn** and followed it with ***Peg Woffington***. Musicals and then revues became the staple fare until the house was rebuilt in 1937. Subsequent successes have included *Funny Girl,* with Barbra Streisand, *Sweet Charity* and a revival of Brecht's *Threepenny Opera.*

(www.delfontmackintosh.co.uk/Theatres/prince_of_wales.shtml)

Private Eye

The offices of Britain's premier satirical magazine, founded in 1961, occupy No. 6 Carlisle Street, the former home of the musician **J C Smith**. A fortnightly staff lunch is held upstairs at the **Coach and Horses**.

The magazine, once also famous for the libel actions directed at it, was first edited by Christopher Booker and then by Richard Ingrams. Initially successful, though rather juvenile in its content, reminiscent of the school magazine from which it sprang, *Private Eye* turned to a larger field of coverage which now embraces comment on the media, politics, publishing, the City and 'rotten boroughs'.Prominent contributors have been Gerald Scarfe, **Peter Cook**, Barry Fantoni, Willie Rushton, Christopher Logue and Auberon Waugh. Since 1986 *Private Eye* has been edited by Ian Hislop. (www.private-eye.co.uk)

Prostitution

The memory of **Nell Gwyn** casts a certain glow of style, if not respectability, over the prevalence of prostitution in the West End's two premier pleasure districts. By the eighteenth century the **Piazza** was renowned as "the great square of Venus", the obvious resort for out-of-town visitors like **James Boswell**. There was even a guide book. First appearing in 1757 Harris's List of *Covent Garden Ladies* became an annual publication with a print-run of eight thousand. Initially detailing the appearance, sexual skills and scale of charges of some eighty prostitutes, it was purportedly the work of Jack Harris, head waiter at the Shakespeare's Head tavern but was actually written by Samuel Derrick, an Irish poet. In the 1960s Frederick Charles Shaw of **Greek Street**, having sought in vain for police guidance regarding the legality of his proposed venture, decided to issue an updated version of Harris's List under the title of *The Ladies' Directory* and got two years for it.

In 1869 James Greenwood, author of *The Seven Curses of London*, reckoned that there were 152 brothels in Soho. In Covent Garden **Floral Street** and **Wellington Street** were notable for 'disorderly houses'. Soliciting was notorious along the Haymarket and in the foyer of the **Empire Theatre**. In 1885 W T Stead (1849-1912), crusading editor of the *Pall Mall Gazette,* bought thirteen year old Eliza Armstrong from her mother for £5 in a brothel in **Poland Street** and shocked his readers with his account of *The Maiden Tribute of Modern Babylon.* Stead got three months for his exploit and Parliament finally fixed the legal age of consent at sixteen.

Soho's association with commercialised sex in all its forms – prostitution, pornography and strip clubs – peaked in the 1960s, an era brilliantly captured in the TV mini-series, ***Our Friends in the North***. At Murray's Club in **Beak Street**, claimed to be the first venue in London to feature nude 'entertainment', the hostesses included Christine Keeler and Mandy Rice-Davies, who later figured prominently in the disgrace and downfall of War Minister John Profumo. (Giles Emerson *City of Sin: London in pursuit of pleasure* Carlton Books 2003)

Queen's Theatre, Long Acre

Converted from **St Martin's Hall** in 1867, the Queen's Theatre was at that time the second largest theatre in London. **Ellen Terry** and **Henry Irving** appeared together for the first time on stage at the Queen's in January 1868 in *Katharine and Petruchio*, an adaptation of *The Taming of the Shrew* by **Garrick**. In 1873 Ellen Terry made her

The Queen's Theatre, Long Acre, subsequently occupied by the printers, ***Odhams****.*

comeback appearance at the Queen's but thereafter the house enjoyed little success, despite changing its name to the National in 1877. The Queen's closed in 1879 to become a co-operative store, a gymnasium for the YMCA, offices and warehouses and eventually part of **Odham's Press**.

Queen's Theatre, Shaftesbury Avenue

The Queen's was built as a twin to the **Gielgud theatre** and opened in 1907. In 1930 **John Gielgud** reprised his Old Vic triumph in *Hamlet* here and in 1937-8 starred in *The School for Scandal, The Three Sisters, Richard II* and the *Merchant of Venice*, himself directing the two Shakespeare plays. Playing with him were Peggy Ashcroft, Michael Redgrave, Alec Guinness, Anthony Quayle, Glen Byam Shaw, Angela Baddeley and Rachel Kempson. Badly bombed in 1940, the Queen's did not reopen until 1959, the first production being Gielgud's one man Shakespeare recital *The Ages of Man*. In 1966 **Noel Coward** made his last stage appearance in *Suite in Three Keys*. In 1972 Maggie Smith starred in a revival, directed by Gielgud, of Coward's *Private Lives* which was still running when Coward died the following year.

John Radcliffe

Quick-witted rather than scholarly, in 1684 Dr John Radcliffe (1650-1714) abandoned an academic career at Oxford, to settle in **Bow Street**. By the death of Dr Lower of nearby **King Street** in 1685, Radcliffe fortuitously gained a large clientele whom he charmed to such effect that he was soon earning twenty guineas a day. Radcliffe became London's most sought-after physician and a *bête-noire* of the medical establishment, which regarded him as a slick empiric with a long streak of luck. From William III, whose life he saved during an asthma attack in 1690, the doctor earned 600 guineas a year for eleven years. By 1701 Radcliffe was worth £80,000. His posthumous generosity endowed the University of Oxford with three of its most eminent institutions – the Radcliffe Camera (Library), Radcliffe Infirmary and Radcliffe Observatory. Inevitably he was painted by **Kneller**.

(C R Hone *The Life of Dr John Radcliffe: Benefactor of the University of Oxford* Faber & Faber 1950)

Rainbow Club, Shaftesbury Avenue

London's largest American Red Cross Club, with over four hundred staff, stood at the corner of **Shaftesbury Avenue** and Denman Street. American servicemen could drop in to write letters, ask for information, have clothes mended, watch cartoons, play records and revel in delights not normally available in the average English wartime pub – doughnuts, hamburgers, pinball and pool. The club attracted five million visits in its first year alone. A Red Cross Eagle Club was at 28 **Charing Cross Road**.

(David Reynolds *Rich Relations: The American Occupation of Britain 1942-45* HarperCollins 1996)

Regent Street

"... *one of the rare examples in London of the Crown using its power and influence to accomplish an urban transformation.*"

Ann Saunders

Regent Street was laid out (1816-24) as part of an ambitious and only partially realised scheme by **John Nash** to provide a grand triumphal way from Regent's Park to Pall Mall. Seven hundred properties were demolished to give the capital a sweeping boulevard 120 feet wide. Nash consciously intended its line to establish a social frontier between the glitterati of Mayfair and the literati – and other less glamorous inhabitants of Soho – "The whole communication from Charing Cross to Oxford Street will be a boundary and a complete separation between the Streets occupied by the Nobility and Gentry, and the narrower Streets and meaner houses occupied by mechanics and the trading part of the community". Nash designed his new street to "cross the eastern entrance to all the streets occupied by the higher classes and to leave out to the east all the bad streets". Soho may be grateful for Nash's solicitude for the higher orders of society. He established a boundary so unambiguous that it has helped to preserve Soho's identity ever since. Little of Nash's Regent Street, however, survived a comprehensive rebuilding of the 1920s. Commercial landmarks include **Liberty's** and the **Café Royal**.

(Hermione Hobhouse *Regent Street: A Mile of Style* Phillimore 2007; www.regentstreetonline.com)

Restaurants

The Restaurant d'Italie opened at 35 **Greek Street** in 1854 as an Italian establishment serving French food – but cheaper. It later became Au Petit Savoyard. Baedeker's 1886 guide book to London assured readers "there are many cheap and good foreign restaurants in Soho" and recommended ten, including Chiale's at 20 **Leicester Square** ('French

Regent Street c. 1896, looking north towards Oxford Circus. On the eve of the motor age, all traffic is still horse-drawn.

cuisine and attendance, moderate charges'; **Blanchard's** at 5 **Beak Street** ('ladies not after 5pm. Good wines'); Maison Dorée in **Glasshouse Street** ('elegantly fitted up') and – of course – **Kettner's** in **Romilly Street**.

According to the 1908 edition of the guide **Coventry Street** was especially favoured, with Appenrodt's Vienna Café at No. 1, the Globe at No. 3 and Scott's, the fish specialist at No. 18. In adjacent **Rupert Street** was an Italian establishment with a French name, the Hôtel de Florence, at No. 57 and at No. 14 the Blue Posts ('American specialities, clams etc; also grill'). Leicester Square offered the Queen's Hotel, Grand Hotel de l'Europe ('with café and brasserie on the ground floor') and Monte Carlo Restaurant while Chiale's had become the Cavour. Vegetarians could patronise the St George's Café at 37 **St Martin's Lane**.

Even allowing for twentieth-century inflation restaurant prices seem staggeringly cheap. As late as 1912 the European at 44 **Dean Street** offered rumpsteak and frites for sixpence and lobster mayonnaise for tenpence. An abortive attempt to move Soho gastronomically up-market was made in 1889 when the purpose-built Pelican Club opened at 34/35 **Gerrard Street**; it foundered within three years, replaced by a telephone exchange. It was in the brightly-lit environs of Leicester Square, rather than the dowdy back-streets of Soho that grand dining flourished in such establishments as Scott's, the **Trocadero** and Lyons' Corner House. In 1915 Ciro's of Deauville opened a luxurious new dining-club in **Orange Street**; an ironic fate decreed it subsequently housed the University of London's School of Dental Surgery.

The Edwardian theatre-building boom brought Soho an additional market among theatregoers. Stars of stage, screen and radio themselves became regulars at many Soho eateries, appreciating both their varied cuisines and their informality, discretion and long opening hours. A 1940s Soho habitué noted the presence of Peggy Ashcroft, Flora Robson, Paul Robeson, Tommy Handley and Nervo and Knox of the Crazy Gang.

The Mont Blanc at 16 Gerrard Street offered continental cooking and a congenial meeting-place for a literary clique including **Joseph Conrad**. G K Chesterton and Hilaire Belloc met there for the first time in 1900. In the 1920s T S Eliot met would-be collaborators at the Commercio in **Frith Street** to launch his influential critical journal *Criterion*.

As early as the 1890s Sherlock Holmes himself was supposed to patronise an imaginary Soho establishment called 'Marcini's'. By the inter-war period Soho dining had a secure place in popular fiction. Agatha Christie's fastidious Belgian sleuth,

The Lyons Corner House at Piccadilly Circus in 1917. Note the uniformed clientele.

Hercule Poirot and his bumbling English sidekick Captain Hastings were regular devotees of {unspecified) small Soho establishments. Dorothy L Sayers, a regular patron of the Moulin d'Or at 27 **Romilly Street** made it the model for 'Au Bon Bourgeois' in *Unnatural Death*. Sayers' fictional hero, Lord Peter Wimsey, dines (dreadfully) at a mythical Soviet Club on Gerrard Street, based on the **Detection Club**, which did meet at No. 31 and of which Sayers was a luminary.

A 1924 London guide-book listed more than two dozen Soho restaurants, though noting sniffily that "of late years the inexpensive restaurants of Soho have enjoyed an extraordinary vogue, and this fact seems to have somewhat modified the previously exclusive foreign air of the district."

Isola Bella opened at 15 Frith Street in 1923. Apart from the expected ravioli and risotto it also offered a house special consisting of breast of chicken stuffed with a purée of goose and chicken livers, truffles and brandy, breadcrumbed, fried in butter and garnished with asparagus tips and pimentos. In 1926 Quo Vadis took over the former Dean Street building where **Marx** once lived. Au Jardin des Gourmets opened at No. 5 Greek Street in 1931. Bijou and pricey, it attracted a dazzling clientele ranging from Jacob Epstein and Somerset Maugham to Dame Laura Knight and Wimbledon star Suzanne Lenglen.

Even bearing in mind that three pounds a week was a reasonable wage inter-war restaurant prices still seem astonishingly cheap - two shillings for a five course dinner! (Mind you, they did rack up the bill with the extras – coffee sixpence and half a crown – more than the cost of the entire mini-banquet – for a bottle of something a bit special, like Barsac.) At Au Petit Savoyard lunch was 1/6d and a seven course supper 2/6d – with a rose or a carnation, fresh from the Riviera, thrown in for lady diners.

The war brought about the wholesale internment of luckless Italian proprietors who had never bothered to acquire British citizenship. The unluckiest ones were packed on board the *Arandora Star* bound for Canada – only to be torpedoed and sunk four hours out of Liverpool. All of them had their businesses confiscated as enemy property. Soho's remaining restaurants struggled on as best they could. Younger staff were conscripted. Victor Silvy of Au Jardin des Gourmets dutifully went off to serve as a *poilu*. The son of the Spanish proprietor of the Majorca became a Desert Rat. Several of Ley On's Chinese waiters served in the Merchant Navy.

The **Blitz** so disrupted transport that many employees slept on the premises for days at a time. Government regulations imposed a five shilling maximum for any meal, although a modest 'cover charge' could be added for 'extras' like cloakroom attendance, live music, hailing a taxi etc.

Restaurants with a good cellar could boost turnover with hefty charges for the better class of booze – 7/6d for a brandy or 18/- for a bottle of Medoc, with champagne coming in at a whopping 70/-. Kettner's charged 5/- for a meal – and another 5/ for a glass of port. Shortages of ingredients were chronic, especially items normally imported such as pasta, olive oil, charcuterie, bananas, almonds and wine. Wheeler's could not obtain adequate supplies of native oysters, let alone imported varieties. Many establishments were limited in their opening hours, closing on Sundays or opening only in the evenings or until nine o'clock.

Despite the continuation of rationing until 1954 Soho restaurants enjoyed a real boom as the war ended. Staff shortages eased. Diners were, in the words of one contemporary, "desperate for subtle

Pinoli's restaurant at 17 Wardour Street. It boasted the 'best 2/- dinner in London'.

variations on the austerity theme." Soho had chefs who could do something interesting with unrationed items, such as trout, tripe and, rather surprisingly, game. It was, moreover, quite possibly the only area of London where one could find bouillabaisse, moussaka, shish kebab, goulash or zabaglione, quite possibly all on the same street. Unusually for the 1940s Soho had not only multiple Chinese, Jewish and Spanish restaurants but a Russian, a Danish and a Turkish one as well.

A 1956 guide listed over three dozen Soho restaurants including eight Italian, five French, four Chinese, three 'French and Italian', three Hungarian, two Indian, two Spanish and two fish specialists – one accommodating hard-core carnivores by serving meat dishes in a side-room. There were also one each of Swedish, Austrian, Portuguese and Turkish, the last claiming – tentatively – to be "the only purely Turkish restaurant, we believe in England". **L'Escargot**, **The Gay Hussar** and the Versailles all unashamedly described their menus as 'Expensive', while Kettner's acknowledged itself to be 'Far from cheap". Gennaro's offered the doubtless superfluous warning that it was "Not recommended for those on a reducing diet", while the Hong Kong reassured the querulous that they could safely "Leave the choice to the waiter if you're in doubt." Au Petit Savoyard congratulated inself on its "lounge bar décor and murals by Maurice Rickards". Casa Pepe offered instruction in the shirt-threatening technique of drinking wine from a 'porron', an earthen pitcher held at arms length. Tyrol offered the less testing challenge of zither music. At Tre Kronor customers could place themselves with confidence in the hands of "M. André, a restaurateur who served Scandinavian royalty, while at Ley On's Chop Suey they could revel in the ebullience of the proprietor, a "part time film actor and an enthusiastic race-horse owner." Chez Vatel claimed the self-evidently discerning patronage of "TV and French clientele", only to be up-staged by Isow's "large visiting Hollywood clientele."

Wheeler's offered the discerning palate thirty-two different ways of serving sole and lobster and had its own tarnished superstar in the boisterous artist **Francis Bacon**. Owner Bernard Walsh would allow Bacon to run up mountainous tabs until the sale of a painting enabled him to clear it, when congratulatory champagne from the patron would kick-start the process over again.

A decade later the *New London Spy: A Discreet Guide to the City's Pleasures* could assert without qualification that"-

"Soho is the traditional restaurant centre in London ... Traditional restaurants which ... still serve decent meals with professional waiters, clean table-cloths and cutlery, are no longer fashionable but still provide the most consistent value for money!" Indeed, the *Spy* recommended any Soho establishment "where a chasseur can be seen in a brightly-coloured soup-stained uniform looking around helplessly for taxis."

In November 1968 the *Sunday Times*, noting that Soho had 165 restaurants and 78 pubs, conducted a survey of who was lunching there on a single Friday. Jonathan Miller was with the editor of *Vogue* at the Trattoria Terrazza; publisher André Deutsch and veteran journalist James Cameron were at the Gay Hussar; poet Cecil Day Lewis was at L'Epicure, burly, bearded film-star James Robertson Justice was at Wheeler's, newspaper tycoon Cecil King at Quo Vadis and the film making Boulting brothers at Au Jardin des Gourmets.

Forty years later *Eat London: All about food* (2007) made no mention of such Soho stalwarts as L'Escargot, the Gay Hussar, Kettner's orWheeler's although the patisserie of old-established Maison Bertaux did rate inclusion. *Eat London*'s favoured gastronomic thoroughfares were Frith Street – Bar Shu (Sichuan) at 28, Arbutus ('bistro moderne') at 63-4; and Wardour Street – Hummus Bros. (Middle Eastern) at 88; Floridita ('Cuban') at 100 and Imli (Indian) at 167-9. Of the district's many Chinese outlets Ping Pong (45 Great Marlborough Street) and Yauatcha (15-17 Broadwick Street) were singled out. Special mention was given to Irish chef Richard Corrigan's establishment, Lindsay House at 231 **Romilly Street**.

Covent Garden's gastronomic pedigree stretches back to the coffee-houses of the seventeenth and eighteenth centuries, like **Will's** or **Button's**, which served snacks as well as liquid refreshment. **Rule's** in Maiden Lane claims to be London's oldest restaurant in the modern sense of the word. During the early nineteenth century a celebrated steak and chop house, Offley's was in business at No. 23 **Henrietta Street**. In the inter-war period the eponymous proprietor of **Boulestin's** exerted an influence over the British palate far beyond his own establishment. Its contemporary **The Ivy** became a favoured haunt of the theatrical world almost from its beginnings and remains so.

(Edwina Ehrman, Hazel Forsyth, Lucy Peltz, Cathy Ross *London Eats Out: 500 Years of Capital Dining* Philip Wilson 1999; Richard Tames *Feeding London* Historical Publications 2003)

Sir Joshua Reynolds

"*Damn him, how various he is* !" Thomas Gainsborough

If **Hogarth** affirmed the independence of the artist as craftsman, Sir Joshua Reynolds (1723-92) sought to raise his gentility. He certainly succeeded in his own case, being knighted and becoming founding President of the Royal Academy. A Devonian by birth, Reynolds, after studying in Italy, settled in lodgings at 104 **St Martin's Lane** but soon moved to a "commodious house" at 5 **Great Newport Street** and in 1760 took a "superior mansion" at 47 **Leicester Square** where he spent £1,500 adding a detached exhibition gallery, an octagonal painting room twenty feet across and an elegant reception room. Reynolds was not only the foremost painter of his day but also a figure of consequence in society, until failing eyesight and hearing clouded his final years. Reynolds' Royal Academy lectures, published as the *Discourses*, became a classic statement of the orthodox notion of good taste, epitomised in the notion that "the whole beauty and grandeur of art consists in being able to get above all singular forms, local customs, particularities and details of every kind". **Blake** loathed it all and Sir Joshua in particular. **Hazlitt** thought Reynolds' career represented a triumph of taste, rather than talent.

After Reynolds' death his house passed to his niece, formerly his housekeeper. She married a sixty-six-year-old earl, who drank six bottles a day. The house later served as a tailor's and then (1828-52) as home to the Western Literary and Scientific Institution, which aimed to impart "Useful Knowledge among Persons engaged in Commercial and Professional Pursuits". Charles Goodyear, inventor of vulcanised rubber occupied the premises from 1856 to 1859 and they then passed to auctioneers Puttick and Simpson until 1937, when they were demolished to allow for the extension of the A A's headquarters, Fanum House.

The National Portrait Gallery holds the superb

Sir Joshua Reynolds. An engraving after a self-portrait.

self-portrait of the artist in his early twenties, artfully shading his eyes against the light. The Gallery also has his portraits of **Samuel Johnson**, **Garrick** with his wife and of **Sir Joseph Banks**.

(Richard Wendorf *Sir Joshua Reynolds: The Painter in Society* Harvard University Press 1998 Elbert Hubbard *Sir Joshua Reynolds* Kessenger Publishng 2006)

John Rocque

Born in France of **Huguenot** stock, Jean Rocque came to England as a child and initially worked as a garden-designer and surveyor. While living in **Great Windmill Street**, he began publishing maps of the royal parks and gardens, followed by atlases and plans of European capitals and British provincial cities. Rocque's masterpiece, an outstanding map of London in twenty-four sheets, was published in 1746. Thirteen feet across and half that in height, this was the first new map of the capital for half a century and involved measuring ten thousand acres on foot and verifying five thousand place and street names. Thanks to royal engraver John Pine, a friend of **Hogarth**, London's houses and varieties of land use were distinguished by finely graded shades of grey. From 1751 until his death Rocque was at three successive addresses in the **Strand**. Rocque's map has been republished by the London Topographical Society as *The A-Z of Georgian London* and can also be accessed online at www.motco.com.

Romano's 'The Home of Bohemia', Strand

Romano's was opened in 1885 at No. 399 **Strand** by Nicolino Alfonso Romano (died 1901) a former waiter from the **Café Royal** and stood between the **Adelphi** and **Vaudeville** theatres, which provided much of its clientele. The building had formerly been a shooting-gallery and was very narrow. Enlarged by taking in an adjacent shop, it burned down in 1891 but was reopened with a fanciful Moorish décor. George Edwardes, the enterprising theatre manager, arranged for the famous 'Gaiety Girls' to dine there at half price. Much favoured by writers and sportsmen as well as theatricals, the

The reception room at Romano's restaurant in the Strand.

business was rebuilt again in 1911 and finally closed in 1948. The site is now occupied by the world-famous stamp dealer Stanley Gibbons Ltd.

Romilly Street

Originally Church Street, this street, built up from 1678, was renamed in 1937 in honour of Sir Samuel Romilly (1757-1818), who was born at No. 18 **Frith Street**. The son of a **Huguenot** jeweller, Romilly as Solicitor-General achieved many reforms in criminal law, procedure and punishment. His family motto – 'Persevere' – failed to prevent him from slashing his throat in despair three days after the death of his wife. The building housing **Kettner's** restaurant probably dates from ca. 1730.

Louis-François Roubiliac

"... the greatest eighteenth century sculptor of all those working at the Abbey". Pevsner

Louis-François Roubiliac (1695-1762) lived at St Martin's Court, off **St Martin's Lane**, and was an habitué of **Old Slaughter's**. He established his reputation with a statue of a casually-dressed Handel, commissioned for Vauxhall Gardens, now in the British Galleries of the Victoria and Albert Museum. He went on to make busts of his friends, **Hogarth** and **Garrick**. Garrick in turn commissioned a Shakespeare for the temple at his country house, erected in honour of the Bard. The first of Roubiliac's eight monuments for Westminster Abbey was for the Duke of Argyll in 1743. The most dramatic are praised by Pevsner as "spectacular allegorical machines ... heavy in weight, ingenious in conceit and brilliant in execution". Lady Elizabeth Nightingale died in 1731 after a bolt of lightning left her so shocked that she miscarried fatally. Her sorrowing husband survived another twenty years, leaving a posthumous commission to Roubiliac to memorialise her memory. The result – "one of Roubiliac's most famous, masterly and immediate works" – shows Nightingale tenderly embracing his dying spouse while vainly trying to fend off Death in the form of a menacing, malevolent skeleton.

Despite his genius, his industry and his highly-placed patronage, Roubiliac died poor and in debt, if highly regarded. **Hogarth, Reynolds** and other stars of the **St Martin's Lane Academy** turned out in force at his funeral.

(D Bindman and M Baker *Roubiliac and the Eighteenth Century Monument: Sculpture as Theatre* Yale University Press 1995)

Master modeller – Louis-François Roubiliac.

Royal Opera House, Bow Street

The present building, designed by **E M Barry**, incorporates, under the portico, reliefs by **Flaxman,** from the previous **Covent Garden Theatre** and is itself often referred to simply as 'Covent Garden', although until 1892 it was known as the Royal Italian Opera. It opened in 1858 with Meyerbeer's *Les Huguenots*. The house found its first superstar in soprano Adelina Patti (1843-1919) who, after making her debut in 1861, came back every year until 1885. Although attempts to put on opera in English foundered in the 1860s, *Don Carlos* (1867), *Lohengrin* (1875) and *Aida* (1876) all had their first English performances at Covent Garden. As manager (1888-96) **Augustus Harris** installed electric lighting and staged the first complete performance of Wagner's *The Ring* (1892), conducted by Mahler. Puccini's *Tosca* received its English premiere in 1900 and *Madame Butterfly* in 1905, Richard Strauss's *Elektra* and *Salome* in 1910 and *Der Rosenkavalier* in 1913.

Patrons were drawn from the highest ranks of society. In 1900 box-holders included a dozen titled persons, two members of the Rothschild family, the diamond millionaire Alfred Beit and the financiers Sir Ernest Cassel, W W Astor and J P

The Royal Opera House in Bow Street, with on the left the old Floral Hall, now an integral part of the opera house. Both buildings were designed by E M Barry.

Morgan. During World War One the theatre was requisitioned for use as a storage depot for furniture.

The entrepreneurial and flamboyant conductor Sir Thomas Beecham (1879-1961) successfully introduced opera in English in the 1920s but finances remained precarious and recourse was had to circus performances, pantomime, cabaret and film shows. With the expiry of the lease in 1929 demolition was threatened. The granting of a new lease in 1932 and the appointment of Beecham as artistic director (1933-39) fended off extinction but during World War II the theatre was relegated to serve as a dance-hall. Re-established after the war as the officially recognised home of the national opera company, it also became the home of the Sadler's Wells Ballet (from 1956 Royal Ballet). New operas included Benjamin Britten's *Peter Grimes, Billy Budd* and *Gloriana,* William Walton's *Troilus and Cressida* and Michael Tippett's *Midsummer Marriage*.

An architectural renewal, completed in 1992 at a cost of almost £10,000,000, extended the building to the corner of **Floral Street**. A further massive makeover was undertaken in 1997-99. At this time, the Floral Hall, also built by Barry in 1860 utilising the iron and glass technology made popular by Paxton at the Great Exhibition in 1851, was made an integral public part of the opera house complex. Originally a flower and then a foreign fruit market, it had for many years been used for storage by the opera house. It boasts one of the longest bars in London. The cost of all this reconstruction was in excess of £200,000,000. The Royal Opera House is the most highly subsidised cultural facility in Britain. Tours are available at 10.30, 12.30 and 2.30 Monday to Saturday.

(Kate Mosse *The House: Inside the Royal Opera House* BBC 1995; *Royal Opera House retrospective 1732-1982 250 years of actors, singers, dancers, managers and musicians of Covent Garden seen through the eyes of the artist* Royal Opera House 1982; www.roh.org.uk)

Royalty Theatre, Dean Street

Dean Street was, for over a century, the site of a theatre whose significance in the history of drama was to be out of all proportion to its size. It was also, in the discouraging words of the *Survey of London*, "small, obscurely sited, perilously combustible and rarely prosperous for long." The theatre was built in 1834-37 at the rear of Nos. 73-74 by **Samuel Beazley**. The sponsor was Frances 'Fanny' Kelly (1790-1882), an aging actress, who aimed at a new incarnation as director of a drama school. The opening of the school was, however, delayed until 1840 for the installation of some newfangled, prize-winning stage machinery which was so disastrous when public performances began that the theatre closed in a week. Broken by ill-health and public ridicule, Miss Kelly allowed the theatre to be used by amateurs, including **Charles Dickens**. The luckless Miss Kelly, having sunk £16,000 into her dream, was evicted in 1849. Re-launched in 1850 as the Royal Soho Theatre the establishment staggered on for another decade with a combination of amateur productions and French plays aimed at London's French-speaking population and French-speaking visitors. Despite being occasionally served by such prodigious talents as Dion Boucicault, **Ellen Terry** and Charles Wyndham, the theatre enjoyed only indifferent success. In 1875 Richard D'Oyly Carte put on his first ever Gilbert and Sullivan opera *Trial by Jury*. It was an instant hit – and transferred to the **Globe** within a fortnight. Rebuilt in 1882 by Thomas Verity, the Royalty found a lifeline in twice-yearly seasons of plays in French. The 1890s were to prove momentous. In 1891 the first ever British production of an Ibsen play, *Ghosts*, was staged. In 1892 the first ever premiere of a George Bernard Shaw play, *Widower's Houses*, was rapidly overshadowed by the runaway success of Brandon Thomas's hilarious farce *Charley's Aunt*. In 1893 William Poel staged an experimental production of *Measure for Measure* according to his understanding of the acting conventions of Shakespeare's day, set within a reproduction of the Fortune Theatre. In 1894 there was a production of Ibsen's *The Wild Duck* and in 1899 of Shaw's *You Never Can Tell*. The Irish National Theatre Society made its first London appearance in 1904, performing works by Yeats and Synge. Later milestones included **Noel Coward's** first play *The Vortex* (1924) and Sean O'Casey's *Juno and the Paycock* (1925). By 1936 the risk of fire from stores of celluloid film in adjacent properties brought the threat of final closure, which came in 1937. A neo-Georgian office-block, Royalty House, was built on the site in 1955-59.

Fanny Kelly, founder of the Royalty Theatre.

Rule's Restaurant, Maiden Lane

Rule's at 35 **Maiden Lane** claims to be London's oldest restaurant, founded by Thomas Rule in 1798 and initially famed for oysters, pies and porter. Manly fare, notably beef in various modes, has continued a staple of the house. Rule's was a regular place of assignation for Edward VII, when Prince of Wales, and the actress Lily Langtry. Other regular diners have included **Dickens**, Thackeray, H G Wells and Graham Greene, who set key scenes of his novel *The End of the Affair* in Rule's. The present building dates from 1873.

Rupert Street

Built up after 1680, partly by **Nicholas Barbon**, this street takes its name from the dashing Royalist cavalry commander of the civil wars, Prince Rupert of the Rhine (1619-82). It was cut through by **Shaftesbury Avenue** in the 1880s. The west side of the southern part is taken up by the **Trocadero** block. Nos. 14-16 was built as the Gambarinus **restaurant**. There has been a White Horse pub at No. 45 since at least 1739. The Blue Posts at No. 28

A spectacular dining room at Rule's Restaurant.

is of a similar antiquity. In the 1870s there was a club in one of Rupert Street's pubs for veterans of the Paris Commune.

Russell Street

Laid out in the 1630s, Russell Street was notable for its celebrated coffee-houses, **Will's**, **Tom's** and **Button's**. The diarist John Evelyn lodged here in 1659. Actor **Thomas Betterton** died here in 1710. **James Boswell** met **Dr Samuel Johnson** for the first time in Davies's bookshop at No. 8 in 1763. It is now a coffee shop. From 1817 to 1823 **Charles Lamb** lived with his sister, Mary, above No. 20, which had become "a brazier's shop ... a place all alive with noise and bustle ... where we are morally sure of the earliest peas and 'sparagus'". The **Fortune Theatre** is on one side of the street, the **Theatre Royal**, Drury Lane on the other.

St Anne's, Soho

The parish church of Soho was designed by Sir Christopher Wren (1632-1723) but finished by William Talman (1650-1719). Fund-raising difficulties led to construction being stretched out over a decade (1677-86). The spire, by local carpenter **John Meard**, was not completed until 1718. The tower and steeple still stand, but the body of the church was destroyed by bombing in 1940.

St Anne's was finally consecrated by Henry Compton, Bishop of London, in 1686. As the Catholic convert, **James II**, had just ascended the throne its dedication may well have been a veiled

St Anne's church, built by Wren. Only the tower and steeple survived bombing in the last war.

compliment to his staunchly Protestant daughter, the future Queen Anne, who had been Compton's pupil. **George II** worshipped at St Anne's when he was Prince of Wales.

The church organ was acquired as a gift from the Queen's Chapel at St James's Palace, a donation which proved auspicious of a distinguished musical tradition. The first organist, Dr Croft, was the composer of a much-used hymn tune which he appropriately called *St Anne's*. St Anne's musical fame reached its apogee under **Joseph Barnby**.

Over the course of the eighteenth century much was expended on maintenance and decoration, including the acquisition of paintings of Aaron and Moses by **Benjamin West.** Nevertheless a major reconstruction was considered essential in 1802 and it was in the course of this work that Meard's steeple was replaced by the distinctive tower designed by Samuel Pepys Cockerell (1753-1827). Its peculiar clock-mounting has been likened to a Russian-style 'onion dome' and, less flatteringly, a beer barrel, but Pevsner praises it as "so remarkable a piece of intransigent early nineteenth century architecture that it must not be allowed to disappear." In addition to a new tower the church also acquired a new watch-house, from which a guard could view the churchyard to deter grave-robbers, a room for the vestry to meet in and another for storing the parish fire-engine. Further rebuilding was undertaken in 1830-31, 1866, 1887 and 1895-7.

St Anne's was deconsecrated in 1953. Its reconstruction as a community centre was completed in 1993 and includes a chapel, a rectory, premises for the Soho Society, twenty flats for the Soho Housing Association and commercial offices. In 1969 the Vicar, Ken Leech, opened the basement of the church as a night shelter for the homeless, especially the young; out of this initiative grew the charity Centrepoint, now nationwide.

St Anne's churchyard became a garden in 1891-2. There are notable monuments to **Theodore, King of Corsica**, **William Hazlitt** and the crime novelist Dorothy L. Sayers.

(www.stannes-soho.org.uk; www.centrepoint.org.uk)

St Giles area

In *London: The Biogaphy* Peter Ackroyd devotes an entire chapter to St Giles (Ch 12, The Crossroads). He emphasises that St Giles has been quintessentially "the haunt of the poor and the outcast". Initially associated with the leper hospital of St Giles-in-the-Fields, it received an influx of "poore plundered Irish', Protestant refugees from the Catholic uprising of 1641-2. The Great Plague which devastated London in 1665 first broke out here in the last weeks of 1664. By then the locality was notorious for the squalor of its tenements and the prevalence of cellar dwelling. **Henry Fielding** observed in *An Enquiry into the Causes of the Late Increase of Robbers* (1751) that St Giles was notable for its "great number of houses set apart for the reception of idle persons and vagabonds". That same year **Hogarth** chose the area as the setting for his most famous engraving, *Gin Lane*. The charity boy Tom Nero, who ends on the gallows in *The Four Stages of Cruelty* is also from St Giles. Another peculiarity of the parish was its concentration of black residents, known as 'St Giles blackbirds'. While many of the local inhabitants were beggars, **prostitutes** and petty criminals, others gained a more or less honest living as street musicians, fortune-tellers. sellers of ballads and printers of pornography. The worst of the 'rookery' was demolished by the creation of New Oxford Street in 1842-7.

What remained, however, received in that very same decade a further influx of Irish, this time economic refugees from the potato famine. By 1851 they accounted for more than 10% of the local population, the highest concentration in London. It was to meet their spiritual needs that **St Patrick's**, Soho Square was rebuilt. Commercial redevelopment of the area for offices, shops and light industrial premises squeezed out many. By 1891 the population of the parish was less than half what it had been in 1821. Since then the area has been so comprehensively redeveloped that many of the original street-lines can only be retraced on old maps.

Part of the St Giles Rookery in 1850.

St Giles-in-the-Fields Church

The former chapel of St Giles Leper Hospital was handsomely rebuilt in 1624-30 but undermined by the excessive number of burials the church attracted. It was rebuilt in 1731-3 by Henry Flitcroft (1697-1769), the son of William III's gardener and a protégé of Lord Burlington, who won the competition at the expense of **Gibbs** and Hawksmoor. Flitcroft, Master Mason and Deputy Surveyor to the Office of Works, was strongly influenced in his design – especially of the steeple and the interior – by the recently completed **St Martin-in-the-Fields**. The architect's name can be

St Giles-in-the-Fields church, with Centre Point in the background.

seen prominently above the west doorway. Inside is a memorial to George Chapman (died 1634) whose translation of Homer inspired a celebrated poem by Keats ("*Oft have I travelled in the realms of gold* ...") and whose monument is attributed to **Inigo Jones.** Richard Penderell (died 1671) "preserver and conductor" of **Charles II**, was one of five brothers who helped the defeated monarch hide and escape into exile after the battle of Worcester in 1651. A 'Peter de Val' is mentioned in the parish register although the memorial stone to **Claude Duval** is in **St Paul's, Covent Garden**, where there is no record of him in the register. Other memorials honour **Calvert**, **Marvell** and **Flaxman**. Burials include those of Luke Hansard, the printer whose name has become synonymous with the debates of the House of Commons, and of the architect Sir John Soane. Marriages at St Giles include those of the prolific Bohemian engraver Wenceslaus Hollar, of actor **David Garrick** and actress Fanny Kemble.

In the northern aisle is part of a pulpit from which John Wesley once preached.

(www.stgilesonline.org)

St Giles' Leper Hospital

The hospital for lepers at St Giles was one of ten such, established on the roads leading out of London. The founder, in 1101, was Matilda, wife of Henry I. Its chapel was where the parish church now stands. The four 'spital' houses accommodated forty patients, who worked the surrounding land. The institution was suppressed in 1539. **Andrew Boorde** occupied the former master's house at some time.

St Martin-in-the-Fields

"... *as grand an eighteenth century church as any in London*" Pevsner

Probably originating as a twelfth-century chapel, in 1222 St Martin-in-the-Fields was assigned to the jurisdiction of the Abbot of Westminster, rather than the Bishop of London. Rebuilt by Henry VIII in 1543-4, it was rebuilt again in 1722-6 by **James Gibbs** for the considerable sum of £33,000, twice as much as the most expensive of Wren's City churches. St Martin's claims to have established London's first free lending library and in 1924, under the Revd **Dick Sheppard**, was responsible for the BBC's first religious outside broadcast. Ever since then the two institutions have combined to organise an annual Christmas appeal for the destitute and the distressed which currently raises some £500,000. For over sixty years the church has been working with London's homeless through a unit now known as The Connection at St Martin's. While serving local communities with services in English and Chinese, the church has also become familiar to visitors and tourists who patronise its crypt café and shop, browse in its churchyard market, make their own personalised souvenirs at the London Brass Rubbing Centre or attend the concerts of the famed classical ensemble, the **Academy of St Martin-in-the-Fields**.

Charles II was baptised at St Martin-in-the-Fields and **Benjamin West** married. Burials include those of the miniaturist Nicholas Hilliard, **Nell Gwyn**, **Hogarth, Reynolds**, **Roubiliac**, **James 'Athenian' Stuart** and **Thomas Chippendale**.

(www.stmartin-in-the-fields.org)

St Martin's Hall

St Martin's Hall at the junction of **Long Acre** and **Endell Street** was built in 1850 to the designs of Richard Westmacott for the conductor and singing teacher John Hullah (1812-84), who intended to use it for concerts and classes. Capable of seating 3,000

St Martin-in-the-Fields. Pedestrianisation of the north end of the Square has radically improved the view of the church.

people, the venue soon found other uses. In 1854 T H Huxley gave a course of lectures on *The Educational Value of the Natural History Sciences*. **Charles Dickens**, an old friend who had provided the libretto for Hullah's opera *The Village Coquettes* in 1836, gave his first public readings there in 1857. In 1859 the hall accommodated the meeting which launched the volunteer rifle movement. Burned down in 1860, the Hall was rebuilt in 1862. In 1864 the Italian patriot Giuseppe Garibaldi was feted there by a packed audience of his admirers. In 1865 a public meeting at the hall established the Reform League to agitate for universal suffrage and the secret ballot. The League's activities helped to bring about the Second Reform Act of 1867 although this encompassed neither of the League's primary objectives. In 1867 St Martin's Hall was converted to become the **Queen's Theatre**.

St Martin's Lane

Originally a medieval track connecting the St Giles area to Charing Cross, St Martin's Lane began to be built up from ca. 1600. No. 31 dates from the late seventeenth century. As home to the **St Martin's Lane Academy** and **Old Slaughter's** coffee house, it particularly attracted artists as residents, including Mytens, **Thornhill**, **Roubiliac**, **Reynolds**, Henry Fuseli and portraitist Francis Hayman. John Middleton, a 'colourman' who sold artists' materials ran a highly profitable business here between 1785 and 1818. Other residents have included **Sir Kenelm Digby**, **Thomas Chippendale** and **Ellen Terry**, who lived in Burleigh Mansions. St Martin's Lane is home to a notably florid Victorian public house, **The Salisbury**, and three theatres, the **Duke of York's,** the **Noel Coward** and the **London Coliseum**.

St Martin's Lane Academy

Established in 1720 by the austere seventy-year-old Louis Cheron and the spendthrift twenty-six year-old John Vanderbank, London's first major art school charged two guineas per season for membership, the main attraction being a life class with a nude model. **Hogarth** and his bête-noire William Kent (1685-1748) were both among the first intake. Later students included the decorative painters Laguerre and Cipriani and the society portraitists Gainsborough and **Reynolds**. The St Martin's Lane Academy merged with the newly-established Royal Academy in 1768.

St Martin's School of Art, Charing Cross Road

St Martin's School of Art was founded in 1854 at the initiative of the parish of St Martin-in-the-Fields to provide instruction in useful crafts. It became independent in 1859. The main building on **Charing Cross Road** was built (1937-9) on the site of the former **Greek church**. St Martin's developed particular strengths in fine art, commercial art and fashion. Alumni have included not only distinguished painters such as Lucian Freud and Frank Auerbach and designers like Bruce Oldfield, Bill Gibb, Stella McCartney and John Galliano but also such diverse talents as the cartoonist Mel Calman, author Len Deighton and composer Lionel Bart. The teaching staff has included the eminent sculptors Dame Elisabeth Frink, Sir Anthony Caro and Sir Eduardo Paolozzi. In 1989 St Martin's merged with the Central School of Arts and Crafts to become Central St Martin's. In 2004 this became part of the University of the Arts, London. At the time of writing the institution is planning a major relocation to purpose-built premises at King's Cross.

(www.csm.arts.ac.uk)

St Martin's Theatre

Built (1914-16) in West Street to the designs of W G R Sprague, the St Martin's had a success in 1921 with *A Bill of Divorcement* by **Clemence Dane**, followed by another with Galsworthy's *Loyalties*, which ran for 407 performances. Since 1974 the theatre has been the home of ***The Mousetrap***. (www.stmartinsheatre.co.uk)

St Patrick's, Soho Square

In 1791 Parliament lifted longstanding limitations on Catholic worship and proposals were made to establish a chapel near **St Giles**, which was "inhabited principally by the poorest and least informed of the Irish who resort to this Country". The promoters, led by Fr Arthur O'Leary (died 1802), a Franciscan, bought and in 1792 converted the plain but spacious extension which **Mrs Cornelys** had erected in 1761 at the back of **Carlisle House** to serve as a ballroom and banqueting house. In 1860 'Father O'Leary's Chapel' was taken over by the energetic Fr Thomas Barge, who worked devotedly in the slums of St Giles and **Seven Dials**. Successfully establishing a temperance society and a Penny Savings Bank, he died before he could celebrate the reopening of his reconstructed church on St Patrick's Day 1893. The architect was John Kelly. (www.stpatricksoho.org)

St Patrick's church in Soho Square, c. 1926.

St Paul's, Covent Garden

Built in 1631-33, St Paul's was the first new church to be built in London for almost a century. According to Horace Walpole the economically-minded fourth Earl of Bedford charged **Inigo Jones** to avoid extravagance and design something "not much better than a barn", to which the architect replied "You shall have the handsomest barn in England". The result, in an unadorned Tuscan style, is both plain and majestic. The original design placed the entrance at the east by the piazza, which would have meant placing the altar at the west end. This was far too unorthodox for Archbishop Laud who required a complete reorientation which means that the 'front' doors on the Piazza are redundant and the church is entered from the 'rear' by the churchyard. The undivided interior is a double square, 100 feet by 50 feet.

In 1784 John Wesley recorded in his *Journal* that St Paul's was "the largest and best-constructed parish church that I have preached in for several years, yet some hundreds were obliged to go away, not being able to get in."

A major restoration was undertaken by Thomas Hardwick in 1788, when the exterior stucco was replaced by Portland stone. The church then had to be substantially rebuilt again after a fire in 1795, although it proved to be uninsured.

Long famed as the 'Actors' church', St Paul's was **Garrick**'s regular place of worship and is the burial place of William Wycherley and **Charles Macklin**. **Ellen Terry's** ashes are deposited here and there are memorial plaques to **Noel Coward**, Vivien Leigh, Boris Karloff, Marie Lloyd and dozens of other stars of stage and screen. Other burials include highwayman **Claude Duval** (possibly), **Samuel Butler, Grinling Gibbons, Sir Peter Lely, Thomas Arne** and the caricaturist Thomas Rowlandson. Baptisms at St Paul's include those of **J M W Turner** and W S Gilbert.

In 1664 **Samuel Pepys** saw Punch and Judy being played under the church portico which also provides the setting for the opening scene of ***My Fair Lady***. (www.actorschurch.org)

The portico of the east front of St Paul's Covent Garden, now the backdrop to many street performers.

The Salisbury, St Martin's Lane

"Real West End glitter, with all the stops out ... just about the perfect theatre bar"

Ian Nairn *Nairn's London* 1966

The Salisbury occupies the site of the former Coach and Horses at No. 90 St Martin's Lane. In 1843 it was taken over by prizefighter Ben Caunt (1815-61), who had beaten the famed Bendigo in 1838 but lost to him after 93 rounds on a doubtful decision in 1845. In 1851 the Coach and Horses burned down and two of Caunt's children died in the blaze. Caunt's last fight, in 1857, ended with an agreed draw after sixty rounds.

The present building, with its famously ornate windows and interior glass, as well as the flamboyant heraldic feature above the entrance, dates from the 1890s. During the 1950s it was a favoured haunt of the actors Michael Caine and Terence Stamp.

Savile House, Leicester Square

Savile House stood next to **Leicester House** on the north side of the Square. It was looted during the anti-Catholic Gordon Riots of 1780 because Sir George Savile the Younger had sponsored a Catholic Relief Act in Parliament. On the night of 5th June "a large mob of riotous persons ... gutted it of the best part of the furniture, which they piled up in the street and set fire to." They returned two days later and attacked "the shell". From 1786 until 1805 the plundered residence was a carpet factory. In 1806 the house was remodelled to accommodate both the factory and a gallery in which Mrs Mary Linwood (1755-1845) exhibited her celebrated collection of embroidery copies of famous paintings. Mrs Linwood's gallery later became a theatre, the Walhalla, and then a dance-hall, Salle Valentino. By 1852 the building housed displays of fencing, wrestling, ventriloquism, conjuring and fortune-telling, plus a wine-vault, coffee-house, billiard room, gunsmith's and a maker of invalid chairs. In 1865 a workman searched through the basement, looking for a gaslight with a naked candle-flame. The resulting inferno was watched with intense interest by the future Edward VII in a borrowed fireman's helmet.

Saville Theatre, Shaftesbury Avenue

One of three theatres opened in 1931, the Art Deco Saville Theatre at the upper end of **Shaftesbury Avenue** was initially dedicated to musical comedy and revue but from 1938 presented straight plays by Shaw and Priestley. Its architect was Sir Thomas Bennett (1887-1980). Damaged in 1940, but hastily repaired, in 1951 the house presented **Ivor Novello's** last work, *Gay's the Word*. In 1958 Michael Redgrave appeared with daughter Vanessa in *A Touch of the Sun* and in the same year Paul Scofield starred in *Expresso Bongo*, an early theatrical exploration of the emerging rock 'n' roll scene. In 1963 Harry Secombe took the lead in a musical version of *Pickwick Papers,* which ran for 694 performances. The last notable performance, by Leonard Rossiter in *The Resistible Rise of Arturo Ui*, was in 1969. In 1970 the Saville became a cinema. The frieze on the façade, by the versatile Gilbert Bayes, depicts an eccentrically episodic history of public entertainment, from Roman gladiators to the Charleston.

Jacob Schweppe

A jeweller by trade and self-taught scientist by choice, Jacob Schweppe (1740-1821) invented the first method of manufacturing artificial mineral waters on a commercial scale. Arriving in London in 1792, he established his first factory in **Drury Lane** and prospered sufficiently to retire to Geneva in 1802.

Ronnie Scott

The Cockney son of a saxophonist, Ronnie Scott (1927-96) was playing professionally in Soho at sixteen and by twenty was with the prestigious Ted Heath orchestra. In 1949-50 Scott ran his first jazz establishment, Club Eleven, in a rehearsal room on **Great Windmill Street**. In 1959 he opened 'Ronnie Scott's' at 39 **Gerrard Street**, which rapidly became London's most celebrated jazz venue, attracting such guest performers as Dizzy Gillespie, Coleman Hawkins and Stan Getz. In 1965 the club, by now with an international reputation, moved to larger premises in **Frith Street** *(see p. 103)*. In 1979 Ronnie Scott published *Some of my Best Friends are Blues* and in 1981was appointed OBE for his services to music. The removal of all his teeth failed to resolve a chronic dental problem which prevented him from performing in the last year of his life and was followed by his death from an overdose.

(J Fordham *Jazzman: the amazing story of Ronnie Scott and his club* (rev. ed. 1995); RScott and M Scott *A fine kind of madness: Ronnie Scott remembered* 1999; www.ronniescotts.co.uk)

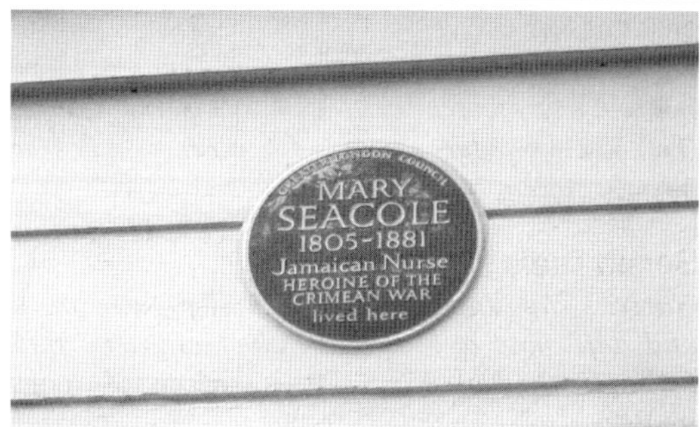

Mary Seacole's former home at 14 Soho Square.

Mary Seacole

Voted the 'Greatest Black Briton', Mary Seacole (née Grant) (1805-81) was born in Jamaica of a Scottish soldier father and a Jamaican mother, who ran a boarding-house and practised as a 'doctoress', tending particularly to British troops suffering from yellow fever, which was endemic to the island. Mary was, therefore, from youth accustomed to both nursing and the military. In 1836 she married Edward Seacole, who died soon afterwards, leaving her a widow. On the outbreak of the Crimean War (1854-6) Mary Seacole travelled at her own expense to Britain to volunteer her services as a nurse. Rejected but undeterred, she made her own way to the Crimea and opened a boarding-house which doubled as an informal soldiers' store and convalescent home. Florence Nightingale would have nothing to do with her, less because she was of mixed race than because she tolerated soldiers' habitual weaknesses for drink, tobacco, gambling and women. Unlike Miss Nightingale, however, 'Mother Seacole', risked her own life to collect casualties from the battlefield itself. When hostilities ended Mary found herself suddenly abandoned and bankrupt. Returning to London penniless she recouped her fortunes with a memoir *The Wonderful Adventures of Mrs Seacole in Many Lands* (1857). Soldiers grateful for her ministrations also rallied round with a benefit, enabling her to live out her later years in comfort. An English Heritage blue plaque records Mary Seacole's former residence at No. 14 **Soho Square**. (Jane Robinson *Mary Seacole: The Black Woman Who Invented Modern Nursing* Carrol and Graf 2004)

Seven Dials

"dirty, straggling houses ... as ill-proportioned and deformed as the half-naked children that wallow in the kennels" **Charles Dickens** *Sketches by Boz*

Seven Dials is now a popular and attractive shopping area, but its reputation for much of its existence has been one of poverty and crime.

Built up (1693-1710) by **Thomas Neale**, Seven Dials took its name from a marker column, supporting multiple sundials, which stood at the meeting point of seven streets, of which only six now exist. Diarist and aesthete John Evelyn inspected the area in 1694 and admired the ingenious and unusual radial plan which maximised the number of profitable frontages. Although intended as a fashionable residential area, Seven Dials became notorious for criminals, street-sellers and beggars, its most respectable trade being the printing of the cheapest sort of ballads and pamphlets. **Hogarth** used the area as the setting for his most famous print, *Gin Lane*. The French radical Flora Tristan noted in her *London Journal* in 1840 that "the cellars are nothing but kennels where the hapless people of Israel are crowded pell-mell". **Dickens** depicted it in *Bleak House* as the terrifying rookery known as Tom All Alone's. Much of the area was demolished to make way for **Charing Cross Road** and **Shaftesbury Avenue** but what remained was still very run down as late as the 1970s.

The replica Seven Dials column, today at the junction of six *roads. It was unveiled in 1989.*

The hurdy-gurdy man – music in a slum court in Seven Dials in the 19th century.

Since then a remarkable resurrection has taken place, exemplified by the Comyn Ching Triangle between Mercer Street, Monmouth Street and Shelton Street. Taking its sinister-sounding name from a former ironmonger's shop, this courtyard-centred complex of houses and shops represents a small miracle in the architecturally tactful reversal of dereliction. The Seven Dials column, removed in 1773, was replaced by a replica in 1989, unveiled by Queen Beatrix of the Netherlands to mark the three hundredth anniversary of the accession of William and Mary in succession to **James II**, an event in which Thomas Neale had played a significant part.

Shaftesbury Avenue

Created by widening Richmond, King and Dudley Streets, this thoroughfare was cut through the heart of Soho in 1884-6 and named in honour of Anthony Ashley Cooper, 7th Earl of Shaftesbury (1801-85) to acknowledge his efforts to control working hours and conditions in factories and mines, provide lodging-houses and 'ragged schools' and protect children and the mentally ill from abuse.

The Shaftesbury Estate

One of the largest land owners in the locality is the investment company called Shaftesbury which holds large chunks of property in Seven Dials and Covent Garden, and in Soho including the Carnaby Street area. They have recently announced plans to redevelop an area of Berwick Street.

Shaftesbury Theatre, Shaftesbury Avenue

Opened in 1888, the first Shaftesbury Avenue Theatre was built *south* of Cambridge Circus. This was financed by "a shrewd Manchester merchant", John Lancaster, to please his wife, the Shakespearean actress Ellen Wallis. Given his motives and her ambitions, *As You Like It* made an appropriate opening production. In 1891 *Cavalliera Rusticana* was given its London debut. The first major success came a decade later with *The Belle of New York*, which ran for 697 performances. Five years later came the milestone production of *In Dahomey*, featuring an all-black cast over a hundred strong, which was praised for "its wonderful vitality." A command performance was given for a Buckingham Palace garden party to mark the ninth birthday of the future Edward VIII. Although the production was a sell-out, running for 251 performances, its exuberant novelty dance – "the cakewalk" – was blasted by one critic as a "grotesque, savage and lustful heathen dance, quite proper in Ashanti, but shocking on the boards of a London hall." In 1909 the Shaftesbury enjoyed another hit with *The Arcadians* in which Cicely Courtneidge made her London debut.

Fred Astaire made his London debut at the Shaftesbury in 1923 in a musical farce *Stop Flirting*. Farce became the Shaftesbury's staple fare until it was bombed out on the night of 16/17 April 1941. The theatre was not rebuilt but its name was appropriated by the Prince's Theatre at the upper end of Shaftesbury Avenue.

(www.shaftesbury-theatre.co.uk)

Percy Bysshe Shelley

A blue plaque at No. 15 Poland Street commemorates the brief residence in 1811 of the poet Shelley (1792-1822) after his expulsion from University College, Oxford for circulating a pamphlet on *The Necessity of Atheism*. Having quarrelled violently with his father, Shelley eloped to Scotland with Harriet Westbrook, the sixteen-year-old daughter of a coffee-house proprietor, scarcely what his parents would have thought a suitable match. Ironically, matrimony, like meat-eating, royalty and religion, was contrary to Shelley's avant-garde principles. Two children issued of the marriage, which collapsed in 1814. Shelley then fled abroad to live in a ménage-a-trois with Mary Godwin, daughter of the radical philosopher and publisher William Godwin, and her fifteen-year-old stepsister.

Dick Sheppard

Hugh Richard Laurie – 'Dick' – Sheppard (1880-1937), son a clerical family and a protégé of Cosmo Gordon Lang, a future Archbishop of Canterbury, might be described as an absolute Christian who, through persistent overwork, drove himself to repeated breakdowns, undermining his health and his marriage and bringing him to an early death. As vicar of **St Martin-in-the-Fields** (1914-26) Sheppard drew on his brief but traumatic experience as an army chaplain on the Western Front to make his church a welcoming refuge for servicemen, open all through the night. It further served as an air raid shelter for local civilians. Sheppard also pioneered religious broadcasting and outreach work with the destitute. His critique of institutionalised religion, *The Impatience of a Parson* (1927), sold 100,000 copies. In 1927 he was made a Companion of Honour. Sheppard's last decade was devoted to the pacifist movement he founded, the Peace Pledge Union, in whose cause he travelled tirelessly.

He died leaving the not inconsiderable sum of £80,000.

Richard Brinsley Sheridan

"*Every man has his element: Sheridan's is hot water.*" Lord Eldon

Born in Dublin but brought up in fashionable Bath, Sheridan (1751-1816) lived a life as colourful as any he portrayed on the stage. Eloping with superstar soprano Elizabeth Linley, he fought not one but three duels to beat off a rival for her affections. In dire need of cash as a newly-wed, he dashed off

Richard Brinsley Sheridan.

his first hit play, *The Rivals*, in a matter of weeks, and, by inventing the absurdly pretentious, Mrs Malaprop, added 'malapropism' to the language she so perpetually mangled. Produced at **Covent Garden** in 1775, *The Rivals* enabled him to penetrate the social circles to which he had long aspired. Soon he was proposed for membership of **The Club** by **Johnson** himself. Showing an equal facility to turn out a farce and a comic opera at short notice, Sheridan readily found partners to finance a buy-out of **Garrick**'s share in the management of the **Theatre Royal Drury Lane**. In May 1777 he presented his best play, *The School for Scandal*, and by 1779 had assumed sole management of the theatre. Friendship with the future **George IV** enabled Sheridan to join the aristocratically exclusive Brooks's club. Elected to Parliament in 1780, Sheridan proved an indifferent minister but a sparkling speaker. Personal extravagance and the necessity of rebuilding Drury Lane after it was declared unsafe in 1792 drove him ever deeper into debt. His literary gifts, however, remained and when **Nelson** died it was Sheridan who was called upon to compose the epitaph on his monument in Guildhall. In 1809 Drury Lane was once again destroyed in a blaze. Sheridan was brought the news while speaking in the Commons but stayed on to finish his remarks. He then repaired to the Piazza coffee-house, drinking steadily as he calmly contemplated his ruination. Challenged for his *sang-froid*, Sheridan remarked memorably "*may not a man take a glass or two by his own fireside*?" Ousted from both the theatre and the Commons, Sheridan died deeply in debt but, characteristically, was buried with splendour in Westminster Abbey's Poets' Corner, where he lies near Garrick.

(Fintan O'Toole *A Traitor's Kiss: Life of Richard Brinsley Sheridan* Granta Books 1998)

Sarah Siddons

Mrs Sarah Siddons (1755-1831), the greatest *tragedienne* of her age, lived at No. 54 **Great Marlborough Street** from 1790 until 1804, when at the height of her powers and fame. An awe-struck **Hazlitt** declared that "in herself she is as great as any being she ever represented". The personification of dignity in looks, voice and manner, Mrs. Siddons was all stage-presence – and a corresponding disappointment to her admirers when off-stage, devoid of small talk and tarnished with a reputation for aloofness and avarice. Nevertheless she was appointed elocution tutor to the royal children, was painted by **Reynolds** (as 'The Tragic Muse', Dulwich Picture Gallery), by Romney, Gainsborough (**National Portrait Gallery**)

Sarah Siddons by George Romney.

and **Lawrence** and honoured after her death with both an imposing monument in Westminster Abbey and a statue on Paddington Green.

Augustus Siebe

Jeweller, silversmith and maker of clocks and scientific instruments, German-born Augustus Siebe (1788-1872) had a house and workshop at No. 5 **Denmark Street** from 1829 until his death. Here he invented a highly profitable rotary pump and the world's first dial weighing-machine and developed what became for over a century the standard diving suit.

Silversmithing

Soho's earliest recorded silversmith was Ellis Gamble of 'Cranbourn Alley, Lester Fields' who entered his mark at Goldsmiths' Hall in 1696 and marked his premises with the sign of the Golden Angel. In 1712 he took on fifteen year old **William Hogarth** as his apprentice; Hogarth later designed Gamble's bilingual trade card. The Goldsmiths' registers from 1698-1739 record twenty-eight names for the Soho area; by the end of the century some seventy-five Soho silversmiths had been recorded. Pre-eminent among them were the names of Harache, **de Lamerie** and Garrard. Paul de Lamerie (1688-1751) became silversmith to Sir Robert Walpole, **George II** and the Russian court and lived (1738-51) in **Gerrard Street,** where a plaque marks his former home. Examples of Lamerie's flamboyant work can be seen in the Victoria and Albert Museum. Garrard's, now the royal jewellers and previously on the Soho side of Regent Street, have now relocated to Albemarle Street. Soho silversmithing went into decline from the 1820s in the face of low-cost competition from Birmingham and Sheffield, although there were still eight firms still in business in the 1890s and another three specialising in electro-plating and gilding. Fine examples of English silver can be seen – and bought – at the fabulous Silver Vaults in Chancery Lane. (www.thesilvervaults.com)

Jeremiah Sisson

A scientific instrument-maker of European reputation, Jeremiah Sisson (1720-84) was no businessman. Sisson's instruments were used from Latvia to Italy and by **George III** himself. He was given responsibility for maintaining the equipment at Greenwich Observatory and advising the Board of Ordnance. But, despite inheriting a thriving business at Beaufort Buildings, **Strand**, Sisson was twice bankrupted, eventually losing his premises and his home in Southwark and leaving his widow in poverty.

Sir Robert Smirke RA FRS FSA

Smirke (1781-1867) was the son of a painter and Academician and travelled extensively in Italy and Greece and actually witnessed the removal of the Parthenon marbles by Lord Elgin. Twenty years later Smirke would design the British Museum, where they are still on display. In 1809 Smirke, the leading exponent of the 'Greek Revival' in architecture, rebuilt the **Covent Garden Theatre** in a severe Doric style.

Smirke was also responsible for designing the western block overlooking **Trafalgar Square**. Now the Canadian High Commission, it was originally two buildings made to look like one – the Royal Collage of Physicians, entered from Pall Mall East and the Union Club, entered from **Cockspur Street**. The Union Club had been established to mark the Union of Britain and Ireland. Smirke was himself a member, as was **R B Sheridan**.

J C Smith

John Christopher Smith (1712-95) was the son of Handel's treasurer, J C Schmidt. Educated at the **Soho Academy**, Smith became Handel's only personal pupil and, after the composer's sight failed in 1751, his accompanist and amanuensis. In 1754 **Garrick** mounted a triumphant production of *The Fairies*, Smith's operatic version of *A Midsummer Night's Dream.* In the same year Smith became the organist of the Foundling Hospital. His adaptation of *The Tempest* was less successful but his song *Full Fathom Five* proved to have enduring appeal. On Handel's death Smith inherited his manuscripts, his harpsichord and the bust of him by **Roubiliac.** Smith bequeathed them to **George III**. A plaque marks Smith's home at No. 6 **Carlisle Street** but gives the date of his death incorrectly. The harpsichord is now on display at Fenton House, Hampstead.

Dr John Snow

The son of a Yorkshire farmer, as a teenage apprentice apothecary John Snow (1813-58) treated Northumbrian miners during Britain's first cholera outbreak in 1831-2. Enrolled at the **Great Windmill Street** school of medicine in 1836, Snow lodged at 11 Bateman's Buildings in Soho and qualified as

A strict teetotaller, Snow would not have approved of having a pub named in his honour.

A replica marks the site in Broadwick Street of the fatal pump identified by Snow.

both a surgeon and an apothecary in 1838 when he set up his practice on **Frith Street**. Snow became one of Britain's first specialist anaesthetists, attending Queen Victoria during the births of Prince Leopold (1853) and Princess Beatrice (1857). During Britain's second cholera outbreak in 1848-9 Snow became convinced that the terrifying mystery disease was a waterborne infection but his theory commanded little support. The third outbreak in 1854, claiming five hundred lives in ten days, enabled Snow to make a detailed map of its incidence in the Soho area, thus identifying the polluted pump in Broad (now Broadwick) Street as the source of the epidemic, but his groundbreaking discovery was only generally accepted by the medical profession years after his premature death from kidney disease. The John Snow pub in **Broadwick Street** perpetuates his memory while a red granite kerbstone marks the former site of the lethal pump. A plaque marks the site of Snow's Frith Street residence. His grave in Brompton Cemetery bears a memorial "in remembrance of his great labours in science and of the excellence of his private life and character". In testimony of the enduring respect for Snow it has been restored three times. (www.ph.ucla.edu/epi/snow)

Steven Johnson *The Ghost Map: The Story of London's Most Terrifying Epidemic – and How It changed Science, Cities and the Modern World* (2006)

Soho Academy

A school was established at No. 1 Soho Square in 1717. From 1725 to 1805 it was located at No. 8 where the **French Protestant Church** now stands. The founding schoolmaster, Martin Clare (d.1751), was the author of *Youth's Introduction to Trade and Business*, which implies a narrowly vocational curriculum but in fact 'practical' subjects like mathematics, French and geography were complemented by instruction in drawing, dancing, fencing and science. Clare's successor, Dr Cuthbert Barwis (d. 1782) introduced theatrical performances of Shakespeare plays, produced to a high standard. Pupils of the school included the sons of **James Boswell**, Domenico Angelo and **Edmund Burke**, the artists Thomas Rowlandson and **J M W Turner** and the architect Philip Hardwick. In 1801, on the virtual eve of its closure the school was still being described as "the *first* academy in London."

Soho Square

In 1720 Soho Square was described as "a very large and open place, enclosed with a high Pallisado Pale, the Square within neatly kept, with Walks and Grass-plots, and in the midst is the Effigy of King **Charles the Second**, neatly cut in Stone to the Life, standing on a Pedestal … very good Buildings on all Sides, especially the East and South, which are well

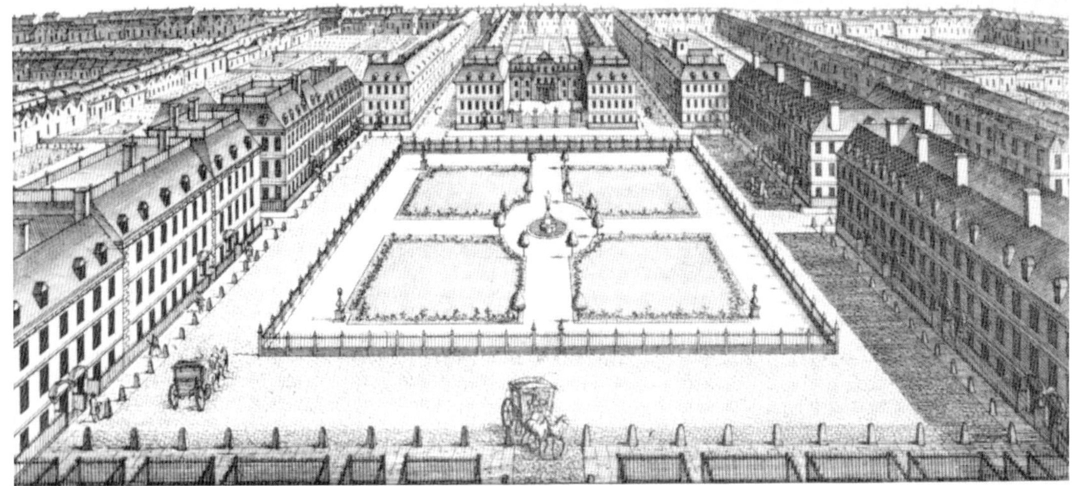

Soho Square. An 18th-century view looking south to a prospect of improbably uniform streets.

inhabited by Nobility and Gentry". By 1748 a new wall and railings had been erected around the square.

The residential character of the square was progressively eroded by the advent of **Mrs Cornelys**' assembly rooms at **Carlisle House**, **Trotter's Bazaar**, the **Crosse & Blackwell** factory and the **Hospital for Women**. Messrs Routledge, publisher of *Uncle Tom's Cabin,* occupied No. 36 from 1843 to 1848 and their Scottish rivals A & C Black, publishers of *Who's Who,* took over Nos. 4-6 in 1885. **St Patrick's** RC church came to dominate the east side of the square and the **French Protestant Church** the north side. Nevertheless the square still attracted residents of standing such as **Samuel Beazley** and **Mary Seacole**.

During the twentieth century Soho Square attracted a corporate presence in the form of the British Board of Film Censors, Twentieth Century Fox, the Football Association and McCartney Productions Limited. The publishing tradition is maintained at Nos. 36-7 by Bloomsbury, publishers of the *Harry Potter* stories. Surviving properties from the early square include No. 10, an adaptation of two previously separate houses, and No. 15.Soho Square

Originally developed by Richard Frith and provisionally known as Fryth's Square, then King's Square, by 1691 the square had forty-one houses, including the prestigious but ill-fated **Monmouth House**. Other important residences would include **Fauconberg House, Carlisle House** and the home of Alderman **William Beckford**. Its early reputation as a highly desirable residential address was confirmed in literature when the *belle-lettrist* Sir Richard Steele made it the London abode of his creation, Sir Roger de Coverley, a Worcestershire gentleman and archetype of the amiable but feckless Tory squire that smart metropolitans were wont to dismiss as a rude rural relic. Real residents, however, did actually include Sir Thomas Littleton, Speaker of the House of Commons (1698-1700), **Sir Arthur Onslow** also Speaker and **Sir Joseph Banks**. In the course of the eighteenth century it would also become home to the diplomatic missions of Venice, France, Spain, Russia and Sweden and to London's most prestigious private school, the **Soho Academy**.

South Africa House

Built on the site of **Morley's Hotel** in Trafalgar Square, South Africa House was designed by Sir Herbert Baker (1862-1946), architect of New Delhi. Its external statuary includes a gilded bronze Springbok, a statue of the Portuguese explorer Bartolomeo Diaz, who first rounded the Cape of Good Hope and, in the portico, the Goede Hoop (Good Hope) one of the five ships which brought the first white settlers to South Africa in 1650.

Southampton Street. David Garrick's house, No. 27, is to the right.

Above, Camisa's delicatessen in Old Compton Street. Below the Sitch lighting shop in Berwick Street.

Southampton Street

Rising from the **Strand**, this street was laid out in 1706-10 on the site of **Bedford House**. Nos. 26-27 are of 1707-8. **David Garrick** lived at No. 27 from 1749 until his death. **Colley Cibber** also lived here (1714-20) and Congreve was another resident. The librettist W S Gilbert (1836-1911) was born at No. 17. Architect **A H Mackmurdo** began his practice here. The ***Strand Magazine*** had its offices at Nos. 7-12, the headquarters of **Newnes'** printing empire. Founded in 1891 out of the profits from ***Tit-Bits***, the ***Strand*** achieved sales of half a million within five years thanks to the public mania for Conan Doyle's Sherlock Holmes stories. A youthful P G Wodehouse was a prolific contributor. **Boulestin's** restaurant stood at No. 25.

Specialist Shops

One of Soho's most famous delicatessens, **Fratelli Camisa** has been established at 61 (originally 66) **Old Compton Street** since 1929 and remains a family business. Readers can now order its famed imported Italian pasta, cheeses, charcuterie etc. on-line. (www.camisa.co.uk)

W. Sitch at 48 Berwick Street specialise in the restoration and reproduction of metal light fittings and their crowded workshop is full of them. The company, still a family-run concern, has been at this 5-storey house since 1903. Every space is filled with ornate and desirable light fittings – a treasure trove if you want to get away from contemporary minimalism.

Soul Jazz Records at 7 Broadwick Street is an independent record shop specialising in rare vintage recordings, and now new recordings or re-issues of classics, particularly Reggae. Its founders began in Camden Market in the late 1980s, going frequently to America to buy stock. They moved to Soho in 1991 and bought the former pub

Soul Jazz Records at 7 Broadwick Street.

called The Crown in 2002. Since the pub had closed it had been used as a violin workshop by J & A Beare. Legend also has it that the Rolling Stones had their first rehearsal on the first floor of the building.

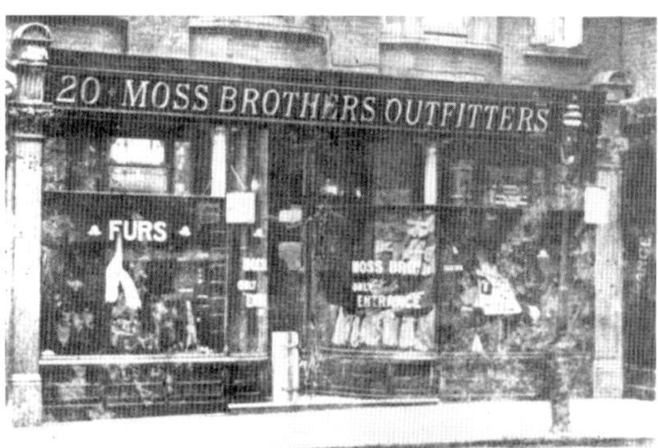

The first Moss Bros shop.

Moss Bros (Bros *always* pronounced by customers as in Moss!) is synonymous with Covent Garden. The present company, the result of a number of mergers or purchases of other tailoring businesses, such as Cecil Gee, Dormie, Beale & Inman, is best known for its hire business which, despite the fine tailoring in the rest of the shop, was what made the business famous.

The firm, begun by Moses Moses in 1851 in Covent Garden, moved to the corner of King Street and Bedford Street in 1881. The origin of the hire business is told in an anecdote. In 1897 Alfred Moss, one of the two brothers who inherited the firm, had a friend called Charles Pond, a stockbroker and amateur actor. Pond was much in demand at weekend house parties and when, despite hard times, he was still invited, it was made clear to him that he was still expected to entertain people. He told Moss one day that he had been obliged to pawn his dress clothes and asked if Moss could lend him a tail suit for the next party. Moss helped him out on a number of occasions thereafter and then decided to make a business out of hiring.

Stanford's bookshop, Long Acre

Stanford's famous map shop on **Long Acre** traces its origins to a shop selling books, stationery and maps, established at No. 6 Charing Cross by Trelawney William Saunders (1821-1910). In 1852 Saunders entered into a short-lived partnership with Edward Stanford (1827-1904). Within a year Stanford took over the enterprise as Saunders left it to become Librarian and Map Curator at the Royal Geographical Society, of which, with Saunders' support, Stanford soon became a Fellow.

Stanford, born in Holborn to a commercial family, evidently impressed Saunders, even though his education at the City of London School had stopped at fourteen and he had failed to complete

A map for every journey – Stanford's bookshop in Long Acre.

an apprenticeship as a printer. Stanford, however, was well aware of his own limitations and developed a real talent for spotting talent in others, as cartographers, authors or advisers. He also had an eye for an opportunity and realised that printing his own maps might offer better margins than selling those of others. Buying plates originated for the Society for the Diffusion of Useful Knowledge, which had closed down in 1846, he not only used them to reissue updated versions but recycled a selection to create *The Harrow Atlas of Modern Geography*, thereby linking the name of his business with that of an ancient and prestigious public school. At the same time he developed a close association with the Ordnance Survey which was to generate a growing cash-flow for him as the approved distributor of the Survey's ever-expanding range of definitive maps.

Stanford's entry into the map business occurred at a favourable time. The British empire was growing and new maps were needed for new purposes, not only by soldiers and sailors and merchants and missionaries but by new purchasers – pilgrims and prospectors, teachers and tourists. There was, moreover, a constant need for updating thanks to the discoveries of explorers, the development of new mines and plantations, the extension of railway lines and shipping routes, the proliferation of international agreements over borders and fishing rights and, not least, the rapid emergence of geography as a recognised academic discipline.

Stanford's first major original publishing achievement was a series of 'Library Maps' of the continents, each twenty-five feet square, published between 1858 and 1866. These were matched by his ground-breaking *Library Map of London* (1862) which was the first to incorporate the detailed information recently compiled by the Ordnance Survey. Stanford meanwhile complemented his cartographic output with a publishing programme which embraced volumes on descriptive geography and in cognate fields, like geology and astronomy, as well as on colonial affairs and history and travel tips. The firm also provided cartographic services to mainstream publishers, notably John Murray. Whether a publisher required a geography of the Homeric world or a representation of the African odyssey of the intrepid journalist H M Stanley, Stanford's could oblige. Stanley was himself a customer of Stanford's, as were Florence Nightingale, General Gordon and John Ruskin. In *The Hound of the Baskervilles* Sherlock Holmes begins his investigations by sending to Stanford's for large-scale maps of Dartmoor.

In 1874 the business moved its sales operations to 55 Charing Cross while the printing and cartographic departments were relocated to 13-14 **Long Acre**. In 1882 Edward Stanford handed over control to his son, a second Edward (1856-1917). Aristocratic in looks, autocratic in style, the second Edward had completed a public school education and studied abroad, becoming fluent in both French and German. Under his direction the company enjoyed its 'golden age', extending its publication programme to embrace school textbooks, popular science and county and regional guides and a multi-volume, encyclopaedic *Compendium of Geography and Travel*. The advent of cycling and later motoring opened up more new markets for the map side of the business. Edward Stanford enjoyed the fruits of his success, drawing a colossal salary, taking frequent holidays, lunching at **Kettner's** and styling himself 'Geographer to the King'.

Sales were moved once again in 1888 to 26-7 Cockspur Street before in 1901 the whole business was consolidated at what had become 12-14 Long Acre, where the architect Herbert Read, a friend of the Stanfords, devised a handsome new gabled façade. The business then entered the twentieth century equipped for the first time with the novel conveniences of typewriters and telephones.

After more than half a century of expansion and success the Great War proved a disaster for Stanford's. The 1914 profits of £1,322 became a loss of £2,276 in 1915. The tourism and travel markets collapsed. The demands of recruitment decimated the staff and Stanford's own three sons went off to fight, leaving him to soldier on alone to an early death.

After the war the firm lost direction and impetus. Although it did develop new specialist lines catering for the yachtsman, the aviator and the fisherman it really failed to take advantage of the opportunities offered by an age of increased personal mobility created by ever cheaper bicycles and motor vehicles and improved public transport. Even the Long Acre showroom was leased off. The fact that the third Edward Stanford (1885-1944) was devoted to the army and that his brother, J K Stanford (1892-1971) was always known as 'the Colonel' showed precisely where the family's interests now lay. In 1946 Stanford's was finally sold to its old rival George Philip and absorbed into an empire dominated by atlases and school textbooks. The single surviving strand of individual endeavour was the establishment of 'Stanford Maritime', which specialised in navigation, leisure yachting and boat-building. Finally 'demerged' from George Philip in 1951, Stanford's at last reverted to its original distinctive mission to become once more *the* specialist retailer of international maps. Boosted by the age of mass-travel and the upgrading of Covent Garden as a *chic* shopping district, it has renewed its links with the Royal Geographical Society, upgraded its premises and established branches in Bristol and Manchester. Having celebrated its 150th anniversary in 2003 Stanford's has re-established itself as a distinct metropolitan institution with a reputation to match its renewed sense of purpose.

(Peter Whitfield *The Mapmakers: A History of Stanford's* Compendium 2003).

Maude Stanley

Born into an aristocratic, political family Maude Stanley (1833-1915) in her capacity as a Poor Law Guardian of **St Anne's, Soho** in 1880 founded the first Club for Working Girls at No. 59 **Greek Street**. Members, recruited from domestic servants, shopgirls, dressmakers and factory hands, could take classes in singing, art, cooking, needlework and 'musical drill'. On Bank Holidays there were excursions to the countryside. This imaginative initiative was so swiftly and widely copied that within three years there was a London-wide federation of working girls' clubs.

Bram Stoker

Irish-born Abraham Stoker (1847-1912) worked for **Henry Irving** at the **Lyceum** as theatre manager and specialist lighting director and pioneered the numbering of seats to simplify reservations. In 1897 Stoker published *Dracula* and, as Irving's fortunes faded, turned to writing for a living, enjoying great success with *The Lady of the Shroud*, which ran to twenty editions. Ironically *Dracula*, the inspiration for some four hundred films, proved to be a posthumous triumph.

(Barbara Belford – *Bram Stoker: A Biography of the Author of 'Dracula'* Phoenix 1997)

Bram Stoker – creator of Dracula.

The Strand

The Strand takes its name from the Anglo-Saxon word for edge or beach, as this major thoroughfare once bordered the much wider (and shallower) River Thames itself. By the sixteenth century it was lined with aristocratic residences, like **Bedford House**. By the eighteenth century the Strand was renowned for lodgings, **coffee-houses** and the premises of specialised producers of maps, like **Rocque**, and scientific instruments, like **Sisson**. **Garrick** lived on one of the side-streets and **Sarah Siddons** and **Mrs Inchbald** had lodgings on the Strand itself. As the major thoroughfare linking the two nuclei of the metropolis – the financial City of London and royal Westminster – the Strand was so much 'improved' by **Nash** that Prime Minister Benjamin Disraeli considered it "the finest street in Europe". Thronged with pedestrian traffic, to writers like **Charles Lamb** it epitomized London itself. In its 1890s heyday the Strand had more theatres and music halls than any other street in London. **Romano's** famous restaurant closed in 1948.

The Strand Magazine

Founded in 1891 by **George Newnes**, *The Strand Magazine*, an illustrated monthly, had its editorial offices in **Southampton Street** and prospered mightily as the major vehicle for publishing the exploits of Sherlock Holmes. H G Wells and P G

Wodehouse were also major contributors. Newnes recognized the marketing value of the Strand name – "this celebrated street – perhaps the most widely known of any in the world – is permanently associated with this pioneer magazine." Publication finally ceased in 1950.

Strand Theatre, Aldwych

Built (1905) as a twin to the **Aldwych Theatre** and opened as the Waldorf (then the Strand, then the Witney, then the Strand again), this theatre staged outstanding Christmas productions of *Treasure Island* in the 1920s and during the **Blitz** presented lunchtime performances of Shakespeare by (Sir) Donald Wolfit. It has been remarkable for a succession of long runs – *Arsenic and Old Lace* (1942, 1,337 performances), *Sailor Beware* (1955, 1,082) and *No Sex Please, We're British* (1971, 1,338) which then transferred to the **Garrick Theatre** for four more years, clocking up over 5,000 performances and claiming a record as the world's longest-running comedy. Tom Stoppard's *The Real Thing* ran for over two years and *Buddy*, a musical version of the life of Buddy Holly for seven. **Ivor Novello** lived in a flat above the theatre until his death.

James 'Athenian' Stuart

"... his face declared him to be fond of what is called friendly society." J T Smith

James Stuart (1713-88) began his career as a humble fan-painter in the **Strand** before walking most of the way to Rome, where he studied the art and architecture and taught himself Latin and Greek. The years 1751 to 1753 were spent in Athens with Nicholas Revett (1720-1804), recording and measuring the antiquities. As a project this was a European first and conducted under conditions of considerable difficulty and danger. Greece was still very much bandit country, with a high risk of being not just robbed, but murdered. The result of their labours was a handsomely illustrated volume on *The Antiquities of Athens*, published by the Society of Dilettanti in 1762. This not only secured Stuart's place among their ranks but also secured his election as a Fellow of the Royal Society and of the Society of Antiquaries. Henceforth he would be regarded as *the* expert on classical antiquity, whose opinion and advice was to be sought on the designs of monuments, medallions, coins and décor. Following the death of **Hogarth** in 1764 he succeeded him as Serjeant-Painter. Stuart took to architecture, securing prestigious projects but failing to prosecute his career with vigour, often preferring to spend his time socializing at the Feathers in **Leicester Place** or the Blue Posts in **Dean Street**. London examples of his work include a house for Admiral Lord Anson at 15 St James's Square, rooms at Spencer House in St James's and the rather feminine chapel at Greenwich Hospital which was to figure in *Four Weddings and a Funeral*. Stuart died at his house at 15 **Leicester Square** and was buried in **St Martin-in-the-Fields.**

(David Watkin *Athenian Stuart:Pioneer of the Greek Revival* George Allen & Unwin 1982)

The Swiss in Soho

A French-speaking community of Swiss Protestants was established in Soho by the mid-eighteenth century. As they came mostly from Geneva, Vaud and Neuchatel, which were not then part of the Swiss Confederation they were, strictly speaking, Swiss by culture rather than nationality. The most prominent family were the Vulliamys who, over succeeding centuries, would achieve eminence as clock-makers and architects. Soho-born Francis Hobler (1765-1844) became Principal Clerk (i.e. chief legal officer) to the Lord Mayors of London. An *Eglise Helvetique* was moved to purpose-built premises in Moor Street, and then to **Endell Street**. The church, designed by George Vulliamy, was opened in 1853.

What is now Compton's gay bar at 53 **Old Compton Street** was two centuries ago a Swiss hotel. As late as the 1890s Soho had a Swiss population of more than two hundred and fifty. Its existence is recalled in the name of the Sun and Thirteen Cantons public house on the corner of Beak Street. One of London's few Swiss restaurants is the St Moritz, a self-proclaimed 'fondue heaven' on **Wardour Street**. New Coventry Street was renamed Swiss Court in 1991 in recognition of the seven hundredth anniversary of the formation of the Swiss Confederation in 1291. The Swiss Centre, an unlovely 1960s complex of shops, cinema, offices and restaurants at the north-west corner of Leicester Square, was sold for £47 million. At the time of writing it is being demolished and rebuilt as a major hotel and shopping amenity.

Tapestry

Following the closure of the Mortlake workshops in 1703 Soho became the main centre for tapestry production in London although the industry failed to outlast the century. Leading Soho craftsmen included Joshua Morris of **Frith Street**, whose designs characteristically included arabesques, scrollwork, vases, exotic birds etc. and Paul Sanders, who used 'Oriental' motifs and called his **Soho Square** premises 'The Royal Tapestry Manufactory'. *The Oxford Companion to the Decorative Arts* summarises Soho output as "hardly comparable with the best French tapestries of the period" but "of good quality and excellent decorative effect."

Tavistock Street

The section of Tavistock Street between **Wellington Street** and **Catherine Street** was laid out ca. 1631 and originally known as York Street, then extended westward in 1706-14 and completed eastwards to **Drury Lane** in 1899-1900. The three sections were renamed Tavistock Street in 1937. Thomas **de Quincey** lived here in 1821. No. 6 – "an early example of Hampton Court Wrenaissance" (Pevsner) – was built by Sir Edwin Lutyens for his patron, Edwin Hudson, proprietor of ***Country Life***. The former St Michael's Vicarage was built (1860) by William Butterfield. Investigative journalist Henry Mayhew (1812-87) died at No. 8. The offices of *Vanity Fair* magazine were here 1868-1881, by when the street housed *The Insurance Record* (No.15), *Bicycling News* (No.17), *The Stage* (Nos.19/21), *The Whitehall Review* (No.34), *The Statist* (38), *The British Journal of Photography* (No.40) and *The World* (No.42).

William Terriss

William - 'Breezy Bill' – Terriss (1847-97) made a disastrous provincial acting debut and then tried his hand as a merchant seaman, tea-planter and sheep farmer. Returning to the stage in 1873,Terriss, after a spell with **Irving**, went to the **Adelphi** where his muscularity in swashbuckling hero parts won him the punning sobriquet 'No. 1 Adelphi Terriss'. Terriss was sensationally murdered at his own stage-door in **Maiden Lane** when an actor he had sacked literally stabbed him in the back. The murderer, Richard Prince, served life in Broadmoor prison for the criminally insane. Terriss's funeral at Brompton cemetery drew a mass of admirers. An apparition of a tall man in a grey suit and homburg hat is said to have appeared repeatedly at Covent Garden Tube station in the 1950s. Terriss was a regular customer at a baker's which once stood there.

William Terriss with trademark Homburg hat.

Ellen Terry

Born into a theatrical family, (Alice) Ellen Terry (1847-1928) made her debut at nine. A brief, disastrous marriage to painter G F Watts was followed by a successful liaison with architect E W Godwin but she found her soulmate in **Henry Irving**. After his death she married again, lectured on Shakespeare, corresponded with George Bernard Shaw and wrote an autobiography. She was created a Dame of the British Empire in 1925. Watts' portrait of the teenage Ellen, an ambiguous compound of innocence and eroticism, is in the **National Portrait Gallery**. An ultra-dramatic depiction of her as *Lady Macbeth*, by John Singer Sargent, is in Tate Britain.

(Moira Shearer *Ellen Terry* Sutton Publishing 1998; Michael Holroyd *A Strange Eventful History:The Dramatic Lives of Ellen Terry, Henry Irving and their Remarkable Families* Chatto and Windus 2008)

The young Ellen Terry.

Theodore, King of Corsica

Soldier of fortune Theodor von Neuhoff fell in with Corsican exiles who agreed to make him king if he could rid them of Genoese rule. After a successful landing he ruled as Theodore I from March to November 1736. Expelled by combined Franco-Genoese forces, he tried three more times to reclaim 'his' throne before coming to England in 1749 to raise funds. All he found was a debtors' prison until a new Act of Parliament enabled him to get free by declaring himself bankrupt and pledging 'his' kingdom to his creditors. Penniless, he "took a chair and went to the Portuguese minister but did not find him at home; not having sixpence to pay, he persuaded the chairman to carry him to a tailor he knew in Soho, whom he prevailed upon to harbour him, but he fell sick the next day, and died in three more." A Compton Street oilman paid for Theodore's burial at **St Anne's**. Horace Walpole paid for a tombstone and composed a fitting epitaph:

> "*The grave, great teacher, to a level brings*
> *Heroes and beggars, galley-slaves and kings.*
> *But Theodore this moral learn'd e'er dead;*
> *Fate pour'd its lesson on his living head,*
> *Bestow'd a kingdom and denied him bread.*"

Despite being reduced to beggary Theodore did leave a legacy, being responsible for adding the distinctive moor's head motif to the Corsican flag. The luckless 'monarch' is commemorated by the King of Corsica pub at 90 **Berwick Street**.

Francis Thompson

A devout Irish Catholic, Francis Thompson (1849-1907) disappointed his parents by becoming neither a priest nor a doctor. Fleeing to London in 1885, he gravitated to Soho as a devotee of both **Blake** and, disastrously, **de Quincey**, whose opium addiction he soon acquired. He also acquired another, less corrosive, addiction in watching cricket. After living semi-destitute for three years – giving Charing Cross Post Office as his address – Thompson finally attracted literary attention with his densely-wrought poems. A fellow Catholic, Wilfrid Meynell, publisher of *Merry England*, to which Thompson later contributed prolifically, found Thompson dead drunk outside the **Pillars of Hercules** and took over organising the writer's life and lodging. Thompson was also a successful literary critic, particularly expert on **Shelley**.

Sir James Thornhill

Thornhill (1675-1734) is commended by the *Oxford Companion to Art* as "the only English painter who could challenge on their own ground the many foreign decorative painters then at work in England." He is chiefly remembered for the dome of St Paul's Cathedral (1715-19), depicting eight passages from St.Paul's life, and the ceiling of the Painted Hall at Greenwich (1708-27), which celebrates the triumph of Protestant constitutional monarchy. He also designed the rose window in the north transept of Westminster Abbey. Thornhill's portraits include one of **Newton**. Initially a director of the painting academy of which **Kneller** was governor, Thornhill tried to set up a rival institution in **James Street**. This failed twice but gained him a son-in-law – initially unwanted – in William **Hogarth**. Thornhill lived at 75 **Dean Street** and then, from 1722, at No. 12 the **Piazza**.

Mrs Hester Thrale

In 1763 Hester Lynch Salusbury (1741-1821) was married, much against her wishes, to brewer Henry Thrale at **St Anne's, Soho**. Mrs Thrale, constantly moving between her home by the brewery in Southwark and the family's rural retreat at Streatham, nevertheless became a supportive wife and endlessly accommodating hostess to her husband's friend, irascible **Samuel Johnson**. When Mr Thrale, to whom she had borne twelve children, died, she remarried – to Johnson's outrage – taking as her spouse a personable Italian musician named Piozzi. Originally from **Dean Street** Mrs. Piozzi returned to Soho to live for a while in **Great Marlborough Street** and later in the **Leicester Square** hotel which had once been **Hogarth**'s home. Beryl Bainbridge's novel, *According to Queenie* (Fourth Estate 2001) tells the story of Mrs Thrale's relationship with Dr Johnson through the eyes of Mrs Thrale's daughter, Queenie.

Thurston's

John Thurston of **Catherine Street** revolutionised the game of billiards by replacing the wooden bed of the table with a slate one (1826) and changing the usually cotton or horse hair cushions with rubber ones (1834-5). Thurston's billiard hall at No. 45 **Leicester Square** (1901-40) became a mecca for devotees of the game.

Tit-Bits *(from all the Interesting Books, Periodicals and Newspapers of the World)*

Established by **George Newnes** in Manchester in 1881, *Tit-Bits* gave its readers a weekly miscellany of undemanding 'human interest' trivia, aimed at the newly-literate products of the 'Board Schools' established by W E Forster's Education Act of 1870. The first edition of the magazine sold 5,000 copies in two hours. Newnes later moved into London offices in Burleigh Street and at 8-14 **Southampton Street**. Newnes' genius for marketing enabled him to build circulation through competitions with prizes ranging from a house in Dulwich to a job on the magazine, won by the future press tycoon, Alfred Harmsworth, Lord Northcliffe (1865-1922). Future publisher Cyril Arthur **Pearson** (1866-1921) was another staff member. *Tit-Bits'* competitions eventually raised the magazine's circulation to more than 500,000 copies a week. By then the content included short stories and longer factual articles. Winning a *Tit-Bits* competition encouraged novelist Arnold Bennett (1867-1931) to embark on a literary career. *Tit-Bits* also published the first humorous piece by P G Wodehouse (1881-1975). Other contributors ranged from Rider Haggard to Isaac Asimov and Ken Livingstone. Literary references to *Tit-Bits* can be found in James Joyce's *Ulysses* and George Orwell's *Animal Farm*.

Burleigh Street in 1890 showing the offices of Tit-Bits *magazine.*

Mary Tofts

Around 1725 No. 27 **Leicester Square** was converted into a **bagnio**. Shortly afterwards anatomist Nathaniel St André used it to accommodate illiterate Mary Tofts, a Surrey mother of three, who claimed to have given birth to rabbits. Mary's fraud deceived St André but not Sir Richard Manningham, the leading *accoucheur* of the day, who, after examining her, denounced her as a charlatan. Mary provided damning confirmation of his verdict when she was caught trying to procure rabbits rather than produce them. **Hogarth**, never one to miss a chance, produced a satirical print, *Cunicularii*, whose title was an obscure and obscene Latin pun. (His father had been a failed Classics master). The episode put many people off eating rabbits for months.

Tom's Coffee House, Russell Street

Tom's was established in 1700 by Captain Thomas West on the first floor of 17 Russell Street above a bookseller's. West, a martyr to gout, committed suicide in 1722 by jumping from the second floor.

Tom's Coffee House was above No. 17 Russell Street.

The establishment nevertheless prospered, attracting an eminent and diverse clientele. Government spy John Macky thought Tom's a model of egalitarian *politesse*, with nobles, gentry and bourgeois "talking with the same freedom as if they had left their Quality and Degrees of Distance at Home" and where "the stranger tastes with Pleasure the universal Liberty of Speech of the English Nation". Celebrated physician Dr Richard Mead (1673-1754) used Tom's as his consulting room, receiving apothecaries, who described the symptoms of their patients, rather than the patients themselves. Regular patrons of Tom's included **Garrick**, **Dr Johnson**, **Sir Joshua Reynolds** and **Sir John Fielding**. In 1768 Tom's became a guinea a year subscription club.

Tom King's Coffee House, Piazza

Named for its Etonian landlord, this Covent Garden 'coffee house' was a ramshackle affair, patronised by drunks and whores in the early hours, as supposedly depicted by **Hogarth** in *The Four Times of Day: Morning* (1738). In fact it stood, not in the shadow of **St Paul's** church, as shown, but on the south, rather than the west, side of the **Piazza** and consisted of three structures little better than sheds. After King's death in 1739 his widow, Moll, was frequently charged with keeping a disorderly house. She died in 1747 and the establishment probably expired with her.

Toole's

What began (1840) at No. 24 William IV Street as the Lowther concert rooms, became the Polygraphic Hall in 1855 and in 1869 the Royal Charing Cross Theatre, which flourished as Toole's, a home of comedy and farce under the management (1879-95) of comic actor John Toole (1830-1906), a lifelong friend of **Dickens** and **Irving**, until gout forced his retirement. Toole's was demolished (1896) to make way for the outpatients' department of **Charing Cross Hospital**.

Trafalgar Square

Edward I (reigned 1272-1307) established a royal mews here to accommodate his falcons and their handlers. Rebuilt as stables in the sixteenth century, the building was used during the civil wars of the 17th century as a barracks and to hold royalist prisoners of war. In 1732 William Kent rebuilt the stables on what is now the site of the **National Gallery**. The notion of turning the entire area into a major public square was first broached by **John Nash** but not effected until 1840, under the direction of Charles Barry.

The square is named, of course, from the pivotal Battle of Trafalgar on 21 October 1805, which saw the Franco-Spanish fleet scuppered off Cape Trafalgar on the Spanish coast. The British triumph made impossible a threatened French invasion, but in its hour of glory the British fleet lost its inspired admiral, **Lord Nelson**, shot by a French sniper.

Nelson, aboard *HMS Victory*, rejected the orthodox tactic of sailing parallel to the enemy fleet exchanging broadsides. Instead, he divided his fleet into two columns and attacked the opposition at right angles. It was a risky innovation which could have been disastrous.

The fighting was savage but over by four in the afternoon. The *Redoubtable*, the flagship of the French, suffered 88% casualties. In the rout the British captured eighteen enemy ships and set another ablaze. Not one British ship was lost. The French and the Spanish lost over two thousand men, the British five hundred.

In front of the National Gallery are statues of

The statue of Henry Havelock in Trafalgar Square. The inscription promises lasting fame for his soldiers.

Master of the Mediterranean, Admiral Cunningham, commemorated in Trafalgar Square.

James II and **George Washington**. Other major features of the square include **Nelson's Column**, statues of **George IV** and generals Napier and Havelock, busts of Admirals Beatty, Jellicoe and Cunningham and the **Fourth Plinth**.

A direct descendant of **Charles II**, Charles Napier (1782-1853) was five times wounded between 1808-12. As 'uncrowned king' of British-occupied Kephalonia, he modernised the island's infrastructure and was nominated by the dying Byron as a possible commander of the Greek army of independence. In 1842-3 Napier rapidly conquered the Indian province of Sind, quickly bringing good order, symbolized by the scroll clutched in the hand of his statue. Popular myth attributed him with a witty Latin telegram – *Peccavi* (= I have sinned). The statue, by G G Adams, was paid for by small subsciptions from admirers and unveiled (1855) without ceremony. A masterpiece of artistic licence, it moderates his beaky nose, banishes his thick-lensed spectacles and tucks his leonine mane of beard neatly into his collar. Napier in New Zealand is named for him.

Henry Havelock (1795-1857) was unknown to the public at sixty but died a national hero. An ardent promoter of Bible study and temperance, Havelock had fought Burmese, Afghans and Sikhs before commanding the relief force for the besieged cities of Cawnpore (Kanpur) and Lucknow during the Indian army uprising of 1857.

Havelock, imitating a brilliant ruse of Frederick the Great, sent a crack unit of just eighteen cavalrymen against 5,000 mutineers, provoking them into a deadly ambush which gave him Cawnpore. At Lucknow he personally led the charge which brought the relief force right through the enemy lines – only to be besieged in turn. Havelock, exhausted, died before Lucknow was relieved. The mourning in England rivalled that for Nelson. Havelock's statue, sculpted by Behnes, was raised by public subscription and unveiled (1861) without ceremony. The first statue in London to be modelled from a photograph, it shows the general holding a curved India-pattern sword.

Dashing David Beatty (1871-1936) at 39 was the youngest admiral since Nelson. During World War One he commanded the Battlecruiser Squadron which was to find and engage the enemy until the Grand Fleet arrived. When he did just this at the Battle of Jutland (1916) he failed to keep his superior, Jellicoe, adequately informed so the Grand Fleet came too late to complete victory. Beatty's own force, meanwhile, was severely mauled, eliciting Beatty's laconic observation that "there seems to

The Charles Napier statue in Trafalgar Square.

be something wrong with our bloody ships today". But the German High Seas Fleet never ventured out of Kiel again. Beatty's bust (1948) is by William Macmillan.

As commander of the Grand Fleet during World War One John Jellicoe (1859-1935) was, in Churchill's words, the man who could lose the war in an afternoon and he was fully aware of his awesome responsibilities. The public looked for a second Battle of Trafalgar but Jellicoe knew that to risk losing the fleet was to risk losing the empire which it alone protected. Blamed for failing to support Beatty's aggressive action at Jutland, Jellicoe knew it was more important to make a German victory impossible rather than a British one certain. Jellicoe's bust (1948) is by Sir Charles Wheeler.

Andrew Cunningham (1883-1963) was Britain's star admiral of World War Two. Britain's Mediterranean fleet was outmatched by Italy's larger and more modern navy but Cunningham capitalised on two key strengths the Italians lacked – an aircraft carrier and experience of night fighting. On 11 November 1940 he ordered the world's first ever carrier-based aerial attack, targeting the main Italian base at Taranto. Twenty-one obsolescent Fairey Swordfish biplanes flew 150 miles from *HMS*

One of the magnificent lions by Sir Edwin Landseer, added to the Column in 1867.

Illustrious to disable three of four Italian battleships at anchor. Two aircraft were lost. Japanese observers were quick to note British success with aerial torpedoes in shallow waters and planned their Pearl Harbor assault accordingly. Cunningham's other major victory was a night action off Cape Matapan on 16 March 1941. Decoded intelligence intercepts enabled him to surprise an Italian strike force, sinking three cruisers and two destroyers for the loss of one plane. Cunningham subsequently covered the Anglo-American landings in North Africa and planned the amphibious invasions of Sicily and Italy. His bust (1967) is by Franta Belsky.

To the east stand **South Africa House** and **St Martin-in-the-Fields**, to the south the statue of **Charles I.** A statue of Sherlock Holmes' personal hero, the charismatic General Gordon (1833-85) also once stood on Trafalgar Square but has been demoted to the Embankment, outside the Ministry of Defence.

Trafalgar Square, a traditional gathering-place on New Year's Eve and on celebratory occasions such as VE Day in May 1945, has also served as a focal point for confrontations as on 'Bloody Sunday' 1887, when police and soldiers fought radical demonstrators, leaving two dead and 200 injured, or in 1990 when a protest against Mrs Thatcher's poll tax proposals led to unexpected violence. More peaceful occasions have included the conclusion of the 1936 march of the unemployed known as the 'Jarrow Crusade' and, from 1959, the

On 13 November 1887 a large demonstration was suppressed by police and soldiers. Two demonstrators died. This illustration is of a later commemoration of that day.

fifty-mile march from Aldermaston of supporters of the Campaign for Nuclear Disarmament, an annual event for some three decades. Every December the city of Oslo sends a large Christmas tree for the square, remembering Britain's role as a refuge for the Norwegian royal family and base of resistance during World War Two. The north side of Trafalgar Square was pedestrianised in 2003 to improve public access and end its use as a traffic roundabout.

(Jean Hood *Trafalgar Square: A Visual History of London's Landmark Through Time* Batsford 2005)

The Trocadero

In 1744 covered tennis-courts (for 'Real' – i.e. *royal* – not lawn, tennis) were erected on land adjacent to what had been Shaver's Hall, a gaming house. By the 1820s the tennis-courts were used for circus performances, rope-dancing, conjuring and ventriloquism. Over the following half century the premises housed a billiard-room, a wax-works and a theatre for farces, pantomimes and melodramas. As the Argyll Rooms, it became a notorious pick-up place for **prostitutes**. In 1882 it became a music hall, the Trocadero Palace, where, in 1886, Charles Coborn scored a huge hit with *Two Lovely Black Eyes*, a parody of a Christy Minstrel ballad. In 1895-6 the recently-established catering firm of **J Lyons & Co.** converted the building into an opulent restaurant which finally closed in 1965. Part of its original façade still overlooks **Shaftesbury Avenue**.

The name Trocadero recalls a French victory of 1823 over liberal rebels in southern Spain. This was commemorated in the name of an imposing 'Place' in Paris, from which the name of the London restaurant was taken, inspiring in turn the naming of many lesser restaurants and cinemas throughout the English-speaking world.

The building now contains a multi-entertainment complex. The illustration on page 115 shows the Trocadero roughly at the time it became a Lyons restaurant.

Trotter's Bazaar

By the age of fifty army contractor John Trotter (1757-1833) was controlling over a hundred depots containing army supplies insured for £600,000. When the Napoleonic wars ended Trotter founded a 'Bazaar' at 4, 5 and 6 **Soho Square** to promote 'female and domestic industry' by providing an outlet for the home-produced preserves, millinery, lace, embroidery and pot-plants on which the distressed widows and dependants of army officers relied to supplement their meagre incomes. Vendors could rent counter space, change clothes in the privacy of a dressing-room, prepare a meal and, rather than expose themselves to the vulgarities of a common street-market, deal with customers who shared their social background. Although it was intended as a philanthropic venture, Trotter's Bazaar proved a profitable enterprise and carried on until 1889.

Turk's Head Tavern

A plaque at 9 **Gerrard Street** marks it as the former Turk's Head Tavern, the meeting place of **'The Club'** founded by **Sir Joshua Reynolds** and **Dr. Johnson.** During the anti-Catholic **Gordon Riots** of 1780 it served as a headquarters for the local magistrates. In 1825 it became the **Westminster General Dispensary**. It is now a Chinese provision store.

J M W Turner

"He seems to paint with tinted steam...." John Constable 1826

Arguably England's greatest landscape painter, Joseph Mallord William Turner (1775-1851), was born at No. 21 **Maiden Lane**. His barber father later moved to No. 26, where they lived (1790-99) in cramped apartments. Turner entered the Royal Academy schools at fourteen. Topographical artist Thomas Malton took him on as an assistant but soon dismissed him as insufficiently talented. Turner's breakthrough came with his painting of *Norham Castle* (1799), now in Tate Britain. In the same year he was elected an Associate of the Royal Academy. By 1801 **Benjamin West** was remarking of one of Turner's pictures that it was "what Rembrandt thought of but could not do." **Hazlitt** was not an admirer; conceding that Turner's "powers of eye, hand and memory are equal to anything", he declared that the artist's pictures "give pleasure only by the excess of power triumphing over the barrenness of the subject." But, then, Turner never set out to do pretty. A plaque marks his birthplace and there is a statue in the south transept of St. Paul's Cathedral, where he is buried.

Turner's boyhood home above a barber shop in Maiden Lane.

Vaudeville Theatre, Strand

Still surviving on the **Strand** and first opened in 1870, the Vaudeville staged **Irving**'s West End debut in 1871. In 1891 came the first English productions of Ibsen's *Rosmersholm* and *Hedda Gabler*. In 1901 Seymour Hicks was acclaimed in the title role of *Scrooge*, adapted from **Dickens**' *A Christmas Carol*. The musical *Salad Days* ran from 1954 to 1960. (www.vaudeville-theatre.co.uk)

Voltaire

Having offended an aristocrat and been beaten up for it, François Marie Arouet de Voltaire (1694-1778) was packed off into English exile for two years (1727-8), much of which he passed in lodgings at No. 10 **Maiden Lane**. Here he mastered English so well that he kept his own notes in the language and remained a fluent speaker for the rest of his life. The free discussion of politics and religion which he experienced in the **coffee-houses** of Covent Garden deeply impressed him as a manifestation of the English liberty which he believed to be the key to the nation's economic and military prowess. The coffee-houses also gave him the opportunity to meet Pope, Swift and Congreve. Exposed to the plays of Shakespeare for the first time, he was appalled by the 'barbarism' of the productions but enthralled by their depth of characterisation and the power of their plots. Voltaire summarised his sojourn in his *Philosophical Letters on the English* (1733) and also became the self-appointed promoter of **Newton**'s work on the Continent by producing popularised explanations of his ideas in French.

(Roger Pearson *Voltaire Almighty: a life in pursuit of freedom* Bloomsbury 2005; www.voltaire.ox.ac.uk)

Wardour Street

Long the home of the film industry, this lengthy thoroughfare features on a map of 1585 as Commonhedge – later Colman Hedge – Lane. In 1631 the area was acquired by an Exchequer official, Sir Edward Wardour. Built up, at first rather poorly, with "Shedds or meane habitacons", it was developed by Wardour's grandson, another Edward in collaboration with paviour Thomas Green, plasterer Richard Hopkins and brickmaker Richard Tyler – hence Green's Court, Hopkins Street and Tyler's Court. The street was much rebuilt between 1720 and 1740 (e.g. Nos. 7-11, 27-31, 157-65). The Intrepid Fox pub at No. 99 was so named at the general election of 1784 when the publican was a rabid partisan of the maverick politician, gambler, drunk and womaniser, Charles James Fox. In the nineteenth century Wardour Street was associated with the sale of (often faked) antiques and **musical instruments**. The **furniture** workshop of Thomas Sheraton was at No. 103 (then 106) in 1793-5 and then (1798-1800) at No. 147 (then 98). **Flaxman** the sculptor was another resident. Mitchell & Hughes, specialised in printing pedigrees, family histories and the works of the Swedish mystic Swedenborg. Kimpton's was one of London's three specialist medical booksellers. A large tinplate works, belong to R & W Wilson, was behind nos. 84-92, covering a two-acre site between Wardour Street and Dean Street. The firm of **Novello** had its head office at Nos.152-60. Wigmaker **Willy Clarkson** was at Nos. 41-3. In 1995 Sir Terence Conran opened Mezzo, with seven hundred covers London's largest postwar restaurant.

George Washington statue

The statue of George Washington (1732-99) which stands in front of the **National Gallery** was the gift in 1921 of the Commonwealth of Virginia and is a bronze copy of the marble original by Jean-Antoine Houdon (1741-1828) which stands in the Capitol at Richmond, Virginia. Houdon and three assistants travelled all the way to Washington's home at Mount Vernon and spent seventeen days making sketches and measurements and a plaster cast of the subject's face to ensure a completely lifelike and accurate representation. Washington, standing to his true height of six feet two inches, is shown wearing the epaulettes of a general, rather than in the civilian dress of a president. The adjacent pillar consists of thirteen staves, representing the thirteen colonies, bound together in unity, like the *fasces* which were the symbol of the ancient Roman republic. The arrows are a nod to the existence of Native Americans.

(Joseph J Ellis *His Excellency: George Washington* Faber & Faber 2005)

*George Washington, commemorated in a statue in front of the **National Gallery**.*

Josiah Wedgwood

The main London showroom of the celebrated potter Josiah Wedgwood (1730-95) was at the corner of Great Newport Street and **St Martin's Lane** from 1768 to 1774 and at 12 **Greek Street** from 1774 to 1797, an indication of the still fashionable standing of these thoroughfares at that time. The extensive Greek Street premises included "Painting Shops, Stable, damaged ware room, Scowering room, retort room, Pearl ware room, Laboratory, Printing and Pattern rooms." Wedgwood opened with a characteristically bravura stunt, displaying, in five rooms over two floors, the huge 'Frog' dinner service he had just made to order for the Empress Catherine the Great of Russia. Consisting of 952 pieces decorated with 1,244 views of British mansions and gardens, Wedgwood assured his partner that it would "bring an immense number of People of Fashion into our Rooms". It did. Visitors included Queen Charlotte and the King and Queen of Sweden. Hundreds of landowners, whose country seats were represented on the service, trekked up from the shires to inspect the prestigious commission before its despatch to Russia. Another Royal visit to Greek Street followed in 1779. Items from the Frog service can be seen in the Victoria and Albert Museum, although most are in Russia. Designs for Wedgwood were supplied by a youthful **John Flaxman**.

(Brian Dolan *Josiah Wedgwood: Entrepreneur to the Enlightenment* Harper Perennial 2005; www.wegdwood.co.uk; www.wedgwoodmuseum.org.uk)

Wellington Street

The north part, originally Charles Street, was built up between 1631 and 1635. Residents have included actors **Colley Cibber** and Barton Booth (1721-33). In 1792 the first meeting of the proto-revolutionary London Corresponding Society was held at the Old Bell Tavern. The street was extended to the Strand in 1833-5 to improve access to Waterloo Bridge but by then it had become notorious for brothels. Renaming it after the national hero was doubtless intended to provide a veneer of respectability. No. 15 was from 1839 to 1863 a factory for making pâpier-maché, then rebuilt as the Victoria Sporting Club for London's bookies. The editorial offices of **Dickens'** publications *Household Words* and *All the Year Round* were at No. 26. The Co-operative Movement's *Reynolds' News* occupied Nos. 25-31. Café Rouge was once the Dome restaurant where Andie MacDowell catalogues her sexual track record for the enlightenment of Hugh Grant in *Four Weddings and a Funeral* (1994).

Benjamin West

Self-taught Benjamin West (1738-1820), the first American artist to visit Italy, arrived in London in 1764 and married his American sweetheart in **St Martin-in-the-Fields** that same year. While living in **Panton Square** (1768-75) West came to the notice of **George III**, supported **Reynolds** in establishing the Royal Academy and established his reputation and a new genre of 'history painting' in contemporary costume with *The Death of General Wolfe* (1770). Inarticulate but well-mannered, well-built, handsome, generous and blessed by good fortune, West later became Surveyor of the King's Pictures, succeeded Reynolds to become second President of the Royal Academy for almost thirty years and was buried in St. Paul's Cathedral.

West Street

West Street was developed in 1684 by **Barbon** out of the site of Newport House. The West Street Episcopal Chapel at No. 24 was established in 1700. Initially used by **Huguenots**, it was remodelled in 1840 and used as a mission house for the parish of **St Giles**. A plaque proclaims that John Wesley preached there. Other notable features include The **Ivy restaurant** and two theatres, the **New Ambassador's** and the **St Martin's**.

Westminster General Dispensary

The Westminster General Dispensary, established in 1774 under the patronage of **George III**, was initially located at 33 **Gerrard Street** but from 1825 re-established at No. 9, the former **Turks' Head Tavern**. Supported by voluntary contributions, the dispensary was intended to provide "Advice and Medicine to such useful persons as support themselves by their industry when in Health, but are utterly unable to struggle with the Expenses of Sickness; and cannot, without injury to their private affairs, leave their Habitations to receive the benefit of other Institutions."

Sir Mortimer Wheeler *A Life in Ruins*

Brigadier Sir Robert Eric Mortimer Wheeler CH (1890-1976) was for some forty years the public face of British archaeology. Director of the National Museum of Wales at just thirty-four, Director of the Archaeological Survey of India, de facto founder of the National Museum of Pakistan, he also revitalised the London Museum and the British Academy, established the University of London's Institute of Archaeology and served with distinction in the artillery in two World Wars, fighting at both Passchendale and El Alamein. Wheeler's archaeological achievements included excavations of the Iron Age fort of Maiden Castle in Dorset, the Roman settlement of Verulamium (St Albans) and the city of Mohenjo Daro in the Indus Valley. A charismatic personality with the spectacular moustaches and curly locks of a latter-day cavalier, Wheeler proved to be a brilliantly persuasive advocate for his discipline, becoming one of the earliest of media 'celebrities' and BBC Television Personality of the Year at the age of sixty-four. As an archaeologist he pioneered the widely imitated 'box-grid' system of excavation which combined systematic coverage of an area with the preservation of intact strata for dating purposes. He also did much to involve women in archaeological work and promoted the large-scale use of volunteer labour, which greatly cheapened the costs of excavation while freeing the archaeological professionals to focus on identifying and classifying its results. Wheeler's magnetic personal charm involved him in serial womanising but, allied with his flair for popularisation, also made him a hugely effective fund-raiser and enabled him to use the media to immense advantage, if not always to the taste of the more staid members of the archaeological establishment. Wheeler's modest London pied-a-terre, marked by an English Heritage blue plaque, was above a shop at No. 27 Whitcomb Street, tucked away beside the **National Gallery.**

Oscar Wilde

Oscar Fingal O'Flahertie Wilde (1854-1900) frequently lunched at the **Café Royal**, often dined at **Kettner's**, occasionally entertained rent boys at a less glamorous establishment in **Rupert Street** and kept an account at **Liberty's**. Wilde is commemorated by a plaque at the rear of the **Haymarket Theatre** and by Maggi Hambling's 1998 monument in **Adelaide Street.** Pointedly titled *A Conversation with Oscar Wilde*, this shows him rising from his coffin – and originally holding a cigarette. The onlooker is encouraged to sit awhile and banter with the wit who once observed, as the inscription notes, "*we are all living in the gutter but some of us are looking at the stars.*" (See illustration on page 9.)

(Richard Ellmann *Oscar Wilde* Penguin 1988)

Epitome of elegance – Oscar Wilde, caricature in Vanity Fair, 1884.

Will's coffee house

"*To Will's I went, where Beau and Wit*
In mutual Contemplation sit;
But which were Wits and which were Beaus,
The Devil sure's in him who Knows.
For either may be which you please,
These look'd like those, who talk'd like these...".
John Dennis *A Day's Ramble in Covent Garden*

William Urwin's coffee-house at No. 1 Bow Street/ 21 Russell Street was above a haberdasher's shop. The poet **John Dryden** became its resident muse. **Pepys** in 1664 found "all the wits of the town there" and "very witty and pleasant discourse". **Samuel Butler,** Jonathan Swift and the dramatists **Killigrew** and Wycherley were also patrons. The establishment of **Button's** led to Will's eclipse as a literary gathering-place. By 1710 the *Tatler* was deploring its decline – "Where you used to see songs, epigrams and satires in the hands of every man you met, you have now only a pack of cards." Will's had become Chapman's by 1743 and the name transferred to another coffee house on the **Piazza**. **Boswell** was consequently confused when he came to seek it out as a literary shrine. The historian T B Macaulay a century later still regarded the original Will's as "sacred to polite letters". Cunningham in 1849 devoted almost two pages of his *Handbook of London* to quotations about Will's.

Between 1817 and 1823 **Charles Lamb** lived with his sister Mary at this address. They held 'literary evenings' each Wednesday.

Windmill Theatre, Great Windmill Street

The theatre was built in 1897 and converted to a cinema ca. 1909. The turrets were added in 1931 and it became a theatre again, reversing the apparently ordained order of things. Seating just 326, it found a foolproof formula by presenting non-stop (2.30 – 11.00) variety, featuring nude tableaux, punctuated by stand-up comedians. Famously the Windmill was one of only two London theatres to stay open right through the **Blitz** ("We never clothed").

A rarely noticed decorative plaque on the side of Leicester Square Underground station in Cranbourn Street, denoting the former premises of John Wisden.

John Wisden *'The Little Wonder'*

Cricketer John Wisden (1826-84) once took all ten wickets, all clean bowled, in a single innings and, on another occasion, six wickets in six successive balls, both feats that have never been equalled before or since in the history of the first class game. Whereas most professional sportsmen of the day gave little thought to how they would support themselves after their playing days were at an end, Wisden had cannily long before established a cigar and cricketing business at No. 2 New **Coventry Street** by the time he gave up the professional game in 1863. A year later he branched out into a new venture, publishing the first *Wisden* cricketing almanac from this address. Editorially speaking it was rather a mess, including not only cricketing data but also the results of 'classic' races, 'useful' facts about canals and coinage, the rules of quoits and, just for good measure, a short history of China. The 1865 edition included, for the first time, all the scores from the previous season's first class matches. From 1867 the deaths of cricketers were included and, from 1870, descriptions of matches. In 1872 the business transferred to 21 Cranbourn Street where Wisden lived and died. An unregarded plaque marks his occupancy to this day. His almanac has become the cricket-lovers' bible worldwide. (www.wisden.com)

Peg Woffington

As a child Margaret 'Peg' Woffington (?1714-60) graduated to the stage from selling fruit on the streets of her native Dublin. Her voice too harsh for tragedy, she excelled in 'breeches parts', most notably Sir Harry Wildair in Farquhar's *The Constant Couple*, which she played at **Covent Garden** in 1740 to immediate and tremendous success. After what the *Dictionary of National Biography* delicately calls "a tripartite domestic arrangement" at 6 **Bow Street,** involving **David Garrick** and **Charles Macklin**, Peg decamped to **Southampton Street** with Garrick, who wrote the charming song '*My Lovely Peggy'* in her praise. He got as far as buying a ring but they quarrelled and she established herself separately at **Dean Street**. The most beautiful, and least vain, actress of her day Peg Woffington was painted by **Hogarth**, **Reynolds** and **Zoffany**. Witty and fascinating to men, she was the sole female member of the **Beefsteak Society** and had many lovers. When she remarked to fellow actor James Quin that half the male population of London believed her to be a man he instantly replied that the other half *knew* she was a woman. In 1757 she was stricken by illness on stage but lingered for three years, devoting herself to good works, including the foundation of almshouses at Teddington where she died and was buried.

Wyndham's Theatre

This theatre on **Charing Cross Road** was built (1899) for actor-manager Sir Charles Wyndham (1837-1919). Wyndham was already a qualified

Peg Woffington, painting by ***William Hogarth****.*

doctor when he made his stage debut at twenty-five. Medicine soon reclaimed him, however, as he emigrated to the USA and served as a surgeon in the Union army during the American civil war. Returning to London and the stage he played in society farces, though his own favourite role was the name part in ***David Garrick***, which he staged for the opening of the theatre he had named for himself. In 1903 Wyndham's staged the first English performance of Rostand's *Cyrano de Bergerac*. *An Englishman's Home* (1909) filled the house for six months and was alleged to have substantially boosted recruitment to the newly-reorganized Territorial Army. Suave matinee idol Gerald Du Maurier (1873-1934) became manager in 1910. Sandy Wilson's *The Boy Friend* (1954) ran for 2,078 performances and Yasmina Reza's *Art* from 1996 to 2001. Madonna made her West End stage debut at Wyndham's in 2002. Several productions have transferred to the theatre from the bijou **Donmar Warehouse**. Handsome into old age, Wyndham finally married his long-term mistress and leading lady, Mary Moore, when he was just short of eighty. The ghost of a "distinguished-looking gentleman with a mass of wavy grey hair" is said to wander the backstage area.

(www.wyndhams-theatre.com)

Zimbabwe House

"*A building of more virile character than almost anything of that date in London*". Pevsner

What is now Zimbabwe House, at the corner of Agar Street and the **Strand,** was built in 1907-8 as a new headquarters for the British Medical Association to the designs of a youthful Charles Holden (1876-1960). The ground floor and first two storeys are of grey Cornish granite, the rest of Portland stone. The second floor windows are framed by the celebrated eighteen nude figures carved *in situ* by Jacob Epstein (1880-1959), his first major work in England. They variously represent the goddess of healing, *Hygeia* and such abstractions as *Primal Energy, Youth, Man, Matter, Mentality* and *Maternity*. Epstein charged £100 per figure, less than half the going rate and committed himself to a punishing schedule of fourteen months, ending up not a penny in profit. The finished sculptures provoked a furious public reaction, led by **Pearson**'s *Evening Standard*, which astonished both their creator and the doctors who had approved the design.

Some of the surviving figures on Zimbabwe House.

In 1935 the building was sold to the government of Southern Rhodesia, which deemed the statuary inappropriate and sought to remove it. Epstein sprang once more to the defence of his work, successfully enlisting the support of the painter Walter Sickert, gallery director Kenneth Clark, architectural historian H S Goodhart-Rendel and the Royal Fine Art Commission itself. The new proprietors were about to back down when a small piece of one of the carvings broke off and fell to the pavement beneath, a victim of chemical erosion from exposed metalwork, the result of a defect in Holden's design for the roof parapet. The supposed hazard to passers-by proved sufficient to justify wholesale mutilation. Pevsner explains "erosion, not Puritanism, lay behind the decision to hack parts off" but this is disingenuous and small comfort is to be derived from the lame conclusion that " ... what remains is very eloquent."

(Stephen Gardiner *Epstein: Artist Against the Establishment* Michael Joseph 1992)

Johann Zoffany

Having studied in Italy for twelve years, German-born Johann Zoffany (1733-1810) arrived in England in 1758 to starve in a garret in **Drury Lane** until he found salvation painting clock-faces in **Seven Dials**. Enrolling in the **St Martin's Lane Academy** enabled him to launch his artistic career with the first of many studies of **Garrick**, who became a steady patron of his work. At this time Zoffany was living at No. 9 **Denmark Street**. The theatre proved a profitable genre enabling the artist to move his studio to an auction room on the **Piazza**. Elected to the Royal Academy in 1769, the following year, in **Frith Street**, Zoffany exhibited a group portrait of the royal family. He also painted a portrait of **Macklin** and another of **William Hunter** Zoffany's picture of *The Clandestine Marriage* is in the **Garrick Club** collection; self-portraits and portraits of Garrick and **J C Smith** are in the **National Portrait Gallery**.

Around Covent Garden

This walk takes in most of Covent Garden's main thoroughfares and highlights, but the area is compact enough for the visitor to make easy diversions using the map on the front flap of this book

Exit Tottenham Court Road Underground station and pass the tall 1960s tower, Centre Point, to enter Charing Cross Road. Turn left along Denmark Street into St Giles High Street to reach the church of St Giles-in-the-Fields (1731-3). It was here that many prisoners, on their way from Newgate Prison to be hanged at Tyburn (today's Marble Arch), stopped for a last drink.

Continue east to the traffic lights and turn right into Shaftesbury Avenue, then fork left into Monmouth Street and turn left through the picturesque Neal's Yard to reach Short's Gardens. Turn right to cross Seven Dials – note the modern column – and pass along Earlham Street to re-enter Shaftesbury Avenue. Turn left past the Marquis of Granby PH and then left down West Street passing the Ivy restaurant; at no 24, the Episcopal chapel bears a plaque commemorating John Wesley. Go past the St Martin's theatre to reach Upper St Martin's Lane. Turn right and right again via Great Newport Street – see the former Photographer's Gallery and a plaque to Joshua Reynolds on nos. 10-11. Turn left down Charing Cross Road, past Wyndham's Theatre, then left through the pedestrianised Cecil Court and its fascinating collectors' shops. Cross St Martin's Lane at the end and go through the narrow entrance opposite into Dickensian Goodwin's Court. Exit on to Bedfordbury.

Turn left into New Row, then right onto Garrick Street, passing the Garrick Club; turn right at the cross roads into Long Acre – Stanford's bookshop on the right. Cut right via Rose Street for the Lamb and Flag PH to emerge back onto Garrick Street and then turn left into King Street. Turn right through an arched passageway before you reach the Piazza into the delightfully secluded churchyard of St Paul's church. Exit by using the central path back into Bedfordbury, turn left and left again into Maiden Lane where there are plaques for Turner and Voltaire. At the end turn right down Southampton Street where there is a plaque on No. 27 to David Garrick. Turn left at the end and walk along the Strand, past the Lyceum Theatre in Wellington Street, and then left up Catherine Street for the Theatre Royal and the Nell Gwyn PH. At the top turn right into Russell Street, past the Fortune theatre and enter Drury Lane. Turn left to reach Great Queen Street, overhadowed by the bulk of the Freemasons' Hall. Turn left into Long Acre and then left again down Bow Street to pass the Royal Opera House and the old Floral Hall adjacent. Turn right into Russell Street and left to the Piazza. The London Transport Museum is in the south-east corner to the left. Fowler's splendid market buildings are straight ahead. Exit on the north side via James Street to Covent Garden Underground station on the Piccadilly line, or else it is a short walk along Long Acre to Leicester Square station which is also on the Northern line.

PH – Public House

A Soho Saunter

This walk takes in most of Soho's main thoroughfares but the area is compact enough for the visitor to make easy diversions using the map on the back flap of this book.

Start from Soho Square which contains the French Protestant church, St Patrick's RC church, the Charles II statue, and a plaque to Mary Seacole at No. 14. Exit into Greek Street and pass the House of St Barnabas, the Gay Hussar restaurant, Manette Street, the Pillars of Hercules PH, L'Escargot restaurant, and a plaque to Wedgwood on 12-13. Cross Old Compton Street and pass the Coach and Horses PH and Kettner's restaurant, to turn right into Romilly Street, then left again into Dean Street for the French House PH, to pass briefly along Shaftesbury Avenue and then right back up Wardour Street to see the remaining part of of St Anne's Soho. Go back into Old Compton Street and see a plaque for the legendary coffee house the 2i's at 59. Also note the Italian delicatessen, Camisa's at 61, the Admiral Duncan PH and the Algerian Coffee Shop. Turn left up Frith Street where there are plaques to Mozart and John Logie Baird, pass back into Soho Square and exit left via Carlisle Street to turn left along Dean Street for Quo Vadis restaurant and a plaque to Karl Marx, the Crown and Two Chairmen PH and the Groucho Club. Half way down, turn right through pretty Meard Street, then right up Wardour Street and left across lively Berwick Street market to enter Broadwick Street which contains the John Snow PH, named after the local doctor who discovered the connection between tainted water supplies and a cholera epidemic.

Exit Broadwick Street and turn left into Carnaby Street, renowned for its role in the 1960s fashion upheaval, and then into Beak Street, turn right and left through Upper John Street to reach Golden Square for the George II statue. Exit via Lower John Street and turn left along Brewer Street to turn right down Great Windmill Street which contains the old Windmill theatre.

Turn left along Shaftesbury Avenue, cross and turn right down Rupert Street, left into Coventry Street and left again up Wardour Street and then right into Gerrard Street,the heart of Chinatown, which also contains plaques to Burke and Dryden, de Lamerie and the Turk's Head Tavern. At the eastern end turn right through Newport Market and right into Lisle Street, then left through pedestrianised Leicester Place for Notre Dame de France, and into Leicester Square. Here there is the black granite Odeon cinema on the east, the Half Price Ticket Booth, statues of Shakespeare and Charlie Chaplin and busts of Reynolds, Hunter, Hogarth and Newton.

Exit via Irving Street at the south-east corner, past the statue of Henry Irving, turn right past the National Portrait Gallery, the statue of Nurse Cavell and the church of St Martin-in-the Fields, to reach Trafalgar Square for Nelson's Column, the Fourth Plinth, South Africa House, the National Gallery and numerous statues.

PH – Public House

Index of Themes and Topics

Charles Dickens
Adelphi Theatre, Aldwych Theatre, Beak Street, Bedford Coffee House, Burying Grounds, Charles Dickens, Drury Lane, Garrick Club, George II, Golden Square, Henrietta Street, House of St Barnabas, Henry Irving, Manette Street, National Portrait Gallery, Royalty Theatre, St Martin's Hall, Seven Dials, Wellington Street.

Education
Adelaide Street, Bedford Street, Charing Cross Hospital, Greek Street, Huguenots, Sir Francis Kynaston, Karl Marx, Meard Street, Soho Academy

Entertainment, *see also* Theatre
Bagnios, Burford's Panorama, Café de Paris, Carlisle House, Cider Cellars, Peter Cook, Mrs Cornelys, Gargoyle Club, The Great Globe, Homosexuality, Hotels, Leicester House, London Pavilion, London Transport Museum, The Pantheon, Prostitution, The Trocadero, Windmill Theatre

Food, Restaurants (*see also* Cafés, Coffee Houses)
Friedrich Accum, Beefsteak Society, Berwick Street, Blanchard's Restaurant, Peter Boizot, Boulestin's, Café Royal, Chinatown, Crosse & Blackwell, L'Escargot, Gay Hussar, Huguenots, The Ivy, Kettner's, Restaurants, Rule's, Jacob Schweppe

France, French
Alhambra, Argyll Street, Book Trade, Boulestin's, Fanny Burney, Caves de France, John Singleton Copley, Claude Duval, Chevalier D'Eon, L'Escargot, 'The French' House, French Hospital and Dispensary, French Protestant Church, George II, Marquis of Granby, Great Newport Street, Greek Street, Joseph Haines, Augustus Harris, William Hogarth, Hotels, Huguenots, Kettner's, Paul de Lamerie, Lisle Street, Notre Dame de France, Old Compton Street, Palace Theatre, Restaurants, John Rocque, Louis-Francois Roubiliac, Royalty Theatre, Trafalgar Square, The Trocadero, Voltaire

Gay
Admiral Duncan, Francis Bacon, Muriel Belcher, Bow Street Magistrates Court, Noel Coward, Homosexuality, Neal Street, Ivor Novello, Old Compton Street, Oscar Wilde

Germany, Germans
Friedrich Accum, Adelaide Street, J C Bach, Nurse Cavell, William Heinemann, Hotels, Sir Godfrey Kneller, Karl Marx, Johann Zoffany

India, Indians
Henry Havelock, Charles Napier, Henrietta Moraes, Johann Zoffany

Ireland, Irish
Alhambra, Francis Bacon, Burford's Panorama, Edmund Burke, Charles Macklin, St Giles, St Patrick's, R B Sheridan, Bram Stoker, Francis Thompson, Peg Woffington

Italy, Italians
Beefsteak Society, Canaletto, Carlisle House, Covent Garden Theatre, Ugo Foscolo, James Gibbs, Baron Grant, William Hogarth, Italians, Inigo Jones, Restaurants

Journalism
Jeffrey Bernard, *Country Life*, Charles Dickens, Daniel Farson, Henry Fielding, *Morning Chronicle, Morning Post*, George Newnes, Odham's, Sir Cyril Pearson, *Private Eye*, Strand Magazine, Tavistock Street, *Tit-Bits*

Literature
Adelaide Street, Argyll Street, Jane Austen, William Blake, James Boswell, Fanny Burney, Samuel Butler, Button's, Café Royal, The Club, Joseph Conrad, Edmund Curll, Clemence Dane, Thomas De Quincey, Detection Club, Charles Dickens, John Dryden, Henry Fielding, Gerrard Street, Benjamin Haydon, William Hazlitt, Elizabeth Inchbald, Dr Samuel Johnson, Charles Lamb, Andrew Marvell, Lady Mary Wortley Montagu, Frank Norman, Samuel Pepys, Dr Polidori, Restaurants, R B Sheridan, Bram Stoker, Francis Thompson, Hester Thrale, Oscar Wilde, Will's

Markets and Shops (*see also* Bookshops)
Berwick Street, Civil Service Stores, Covent Garden Market, Liberty's, Neal Street, Newport Market, Specialist Shops, Stanford's, Trotter's Bazaar

Medicine
Dr George Armstrong, Sir Charles Bell, Book Trade, Andrew Boorde, British Lying-In Hospital for Married Women, Nurse Cavell, Charing Cross Hospital, John Harrison Curtis, Dean Street, French Hospital and Dispensary, Golden Square, Great Marlborough Street, Henrietta Street, Hospital for Women, John Hunter, Lady Mary Wortley Montagu, Elizabeth Nihell, Dr Polidori, John Radcliffe, St Giles Leper Hospital, Mary Seacole, Dr John Snow, Mary Tofts, Tom's Coffee House, Westminster General Dispensary, Zimbabwe House